HTML / XHTML

HTML / XHTML

Preeti Jain

CENTRUM PRESS
NEW DELHI-110002 (INDIA)

CENTRUM PRESS

H.O.: 4360/4, Ansari Road, Daryaganj,
New Delhi-110002 (India)
Tel: 23278000, 23261597, 23255577, 23286875

B.O.: No. 1015, Ist Main Road, BSK IIIrd Stage,
IIIrd Phase, IIIrd Block, Bangalore-560085 (INDIA)
Tel: 080-41723429

Email: centrumpress@gmail.com
Visit us at: www.centrumpress.com

HTML / XHTML

First Edition, 2011

PRINTED IN INDIA

Printed at Tarun Offset Printers, Delhi-110053

Contents

	Preface	*vii*
1.	History	1
2.	HTML Tags	9
3.	Character Style Tags	19
4.	Special Character	34
5.	HTML Lists	38
6.	HTML Links	43
7.	Images within HTML	49
8.	Tables within HTML	56
9.	Forms within HTML	81
10.	XML	93
11.	XML Base	153
12.	DTD and DSD	204
	Bibliography	285
	Index	287

Preface

HTML, or HyperText Markup Language is designed to specify the logical organisation of a document, with important hypertext extensions. It is not designed to be the language of a WYSIWYG word processor such as Word or WordPerfect. HTML instructions divide the text of a document into blocks called elements. These can be divided into two broad categories to those that define how the BODY of the document is to be displayed by the browser, and those that define information `about' the document, such as the title or relationships to other documents. The rules for HTML/XHTML are defined using another language known as the standard generalized markup language, or SGML. SGML is wickedly difficult, and was designed for massive document collections, such as repair manuals for F-16 fighters, or maintenance plans for nuclear submarines. Fortunately, HTML is much simpler!

Author

Preface

[illegible]

1

History

INTRODUCTION

H-T-M-L are initials that stand for HyperText Markup Language (computer people love initials and acronyms – you'll be talking acronyms ASAP).

Let me break it down for you:

- Hyper is the opposite of linear. It used to be that computer programs had to move in a linear fashion. This before this, this before this, and so on. HTML does not hold to that pattern and allows the person viewing the World Wide Web page to go anywhere, any time they want.
- Text is what you will use. Real, honest to goodness English letters.
- Mark up is what you will do. You will write in plain English and then mark up what you wrote. More to come on that in the next Primer.
- Language because they needed something that started with "L" to finish HTML and Hypertext Markup Louie didn't flow correctly. Because it's a language, really – but the language is plain English.

HTML is a subset of SGML, the most frequently used document type in the Web. It defines a single, fixed type of document with markup that lets you describe a common class of simple office style report, with headings, paragraphs, lists, illustrations, etc., and some provision for hypertext and multimedia. HTML was defined to allow the transfer, display and linking of documents over the internet and is the key enabling technology for the WWW. Prior to the emerging of the internet, it was unusual in the word of computing to hear the word "page" used to describe elements of data. But HTML web pages have amazing similarities with paper in their role of information publishing.

Both HTML and paper pages:

- Are optimized for visual clarity,
- Focus on ultimate usability (but not on reusability),
- Contain no contextual information, and
- Have no document structure to enable automation.

Today's web is created by Hand for Eyes only. HTML has too low an "Information IQ" to enable many desirable applications. HTML was designed as a markup language an with simple structures, strong emphasis on formatting and was weak for encoding content. It was not designed to encode structure and semantics needed for complex applications.

UNDERSTANDING HTML

Web pages are written in HyperText Mark-up Language (HTML). HTML contains special markers, or tags, which define the style and structure of the page.

To understand HTML let's start by taking a look at an example of some basic HTML source code:

```
<HTML>
<HEAD>
<TITLE>My Home Page</TITLE>
</HEAD>
<!– Written by me –>
<!– Created: yesterday –>
<!– Last modified: today –>
<BODY>
This is where the text goes.
</BODY>
</HTML>
```

HTML look a little confusing at first, but it is easy to learn.To publish information for global distribution, one needs a universally understood language, a kind of publishing mother tongue that all computers may potentially understand.

HTML gives authors the means to:

- Publish online documents with headings, text, tables, lists, photos, etc.
- Retrieve online information via hypertext links, at the click of a button.
- Design forms for conducting transactions with remote services, for use in searching for information, making reservations, ordering products, etc.
- Include spread-sheets, video clips, sound clips, and other applications directly in their documents.

HISTORY

HTML was originally developed by Tim Berners-Lee while at CERN, and popularized by the Mosaic browser developed at NCSA. During the course of the 1990s it has blossomed with the explosive growth of the Web. During this time, HTML has been extended in a number of ways. The Web depends on Web page authors and vendors sharing the same conventions for HTML. This has motivated joint work on specifications for HTML.HTML 2.0 was developed under the aegis of the Internet Engineering Task Force (IETF) to codify common practice in late 1994.

HTML and HTML 3.0 proposed much richer versions of HTML. Despite never receiving consensus in standards discussions, these drafts led to the adoption of a range of new features. The efforts of the World Wide Web Consortium's HTML Working Group to codify common practice in 1996 resulted in HTML 3.2Most people agree that HTML documents should work well across different browsers and platforms. Achieving interoperability lowers costs to content providers since they must develop only one version of a document.

If the effort is not made, there is much greater risk that the Web will devolve into a proprietary world of incompatible formats, ultimately reducing the Web's commercial potential for all participants.Each version of HTML has attempted to reflect greater consensus among industry players so that the investment made by content providers will not be wasted and that their documents will not become unreadable in a short period of time.HTML has been developed with the vision that all manner of devices should be able to use information on the Web: PCs with graphics displays of varying resolution and colour depths, cellular telephones, hand held devices, devices for speech for output and input, computers with high or low bandwidth, and so on.

Internationalization

This version of HTML has been designed with the help of experts in the field of internationalization, so that documents may be written in every language and be transported easily around the world. This has been accomplished by incorporating [RFC2070], which deals with the internationalization of HTML.One important step has been the adoption of the ISO/IEC:10646 standard ([ISO10646]) as the document character set for HTML.

This is the world's most inclusive standard dealing with issues of the representation of international characters, text direction, punctuation, and other world language issues.HTML now offers greater support for diverse human languages within a document. This allows for more effective indexing of documents for search engines, higher-quality typography, better text-to-speech conversion, better hyphenation, etc.

Accessibility

As the Web community grows and its members diversify in their abilities and skills, it is crucial that the underlying technologies be appropriate to their specific needs. HTML has been designed to make Web pages more accessible to those with physical limitations.

HTML 4.0 developments inspired by concerns for accessibility include:

- Better distinction between document structure and presentation, thus encouraging the use of style sheets instead of HTML presentation elements and attributes.
- Better forms, including the addition of access keys,

the ability to group form controls semantically, the ability to group SELECT options semantically, and active labels.

- The ability to markup a text description of an included object (with the OBJECT element).

  A new client-side image map mechanism (the MAP element) that allows authors to integrate image and text links.
- The requirement that alternate text accompany images included with the IMG element and image maps included with the AREA element.

  Support for the title and lang attributes on all elements.
- Support for the ABBR and ACRONYM elements.

  A wider range of target media (tty, braille, etc.) for use with style sheets.
- Better tables, including captions, column groups, and mechanisms to facilitate non-visual rendering.

  Long descriptions of tables, images, frames, etc.

Authors who design pages with accessibility issues in mind will not only receive the blessings of the accessibility community, but will benefit in other ways as well: well-designed HTML documents that distinguish structure and presentation will adapt more easily to new technologies.

Tables

The new table model in HTML is based on RFC1942. Authors now have greater control over structure and layout. The ability of designers to recommend column widths allows user agents to display table data incrementally rather than waiting for the entire table before rendering.

Compound Documents

HTML now offers a standard mechanism for embedding generic media objects and applications in HTML documents. The OBJECT element (together with its more specific ancestor elements IMG and APPLET) provides a mechanism for including images, video, sound, mathematics, specialized applications, and other objects in a document. It also allows authors to specify a hierarchy of alternate renderings for user agents that don't support a specific rendering.

Style Sheets

Style sheets simplify HTML markup and largely relieve HTML of the responsibilities of presentation. They give both authors and users control over the presentation of documents – font information, alignment, colours, etc.Style information can be specified for individual elements or groups of elements. Style information may be specified in an HTML document or in external style sheets.The mechanisms for associating a style sheet with a document is independent of the style sheet language.Before the advent of style sheets, authors had limited control over rendering.

HTML 3.2 included a number of attributes and elements offering control over alignment, font size, and text colour. Authors also exploited tables and images as a means for laying out pages. The relatively long time it takes for users to upgrade their browsers means that these features will continue to be used for some time. However, since style sheets offer more powerful presentation mechanisms, the World Wide Web Consortium will eventually phase out many of HTML's presentation elements and attributes. Throughout the specification elements and attributes at risk are marked as "deprecated". They are accompanied by examples of how to achieve the same effects with other elements or style sheets.

Scripting

Through scripts, authors may create dynamic Web pages (*e.g.*, "smart forms" that react as users fill them out) and use HTML as a means to build networked applications.The mechanisms provided to include scripts in an HTML document are independent of the scripting language.

Printing

Sometimes, authors will want to make it easy for users to print more than just the current document. When documents form part of a larger work, the relationships between them can be described using the HTML LINK element or using W3C's Resource Description Language (RDF).

WORLD WIDE WEB

The *World Wide Web (Web)* is a network of information resources. The Web relies on three mechanisms to make these resources readily available to the widest possible audience:A uniform naming scheme for locating resources on the Web (*e.g.*, URIs).Protocols, for access to named resources over the Web (*e.g.*, HTTP).Hypertext, for easy navigation among resources (*e.g.*, HTML).The ties between the three mechanisms are apparent throughout this specification.

INTRODUCTION TO URIS

Every resource available on the Web — HTML document, image, video clip, programme, etc. — has an address that may be encoded by a *Universal Resource Identifier*, or "URI".

URIs typically consist of three pieces:

1. The naming scheme of the mechanism used to access the resource.
2. The name of the machine hosting the resource.
3. The name of the resource itself, given as a path.

Consider the URI that designates the current HTML specification: This URI may be read as follows: There is a document available via the HTTP protocol (see [RFC2068]), residing on the machine www.w3.org, accessible via the path "/TR/REC-html4/". Other schemes you may see in HTML documents include "mailto" for e-mail and "ftp" for FTP.

Here is another example of a URI. This one refers to a user's mailbox:

...this is text...

For all comments, please send e-mail to

```
<A href="mailto:joe@someplace.com">Joe Cool</A>.
```

FRAGMENT IDENTIFIERS

Some URIs refer to a location within a resource. This kind

of URI ends with "#" followed by an anchor identifier (called the *fragment identifier*). *For instance, here is a URI pointing to an anchor named section_2:*

http://somesite.com/html/top.html#section_2

RELATIVE URIS

A *relative URI* doesn't contain any naming scheme information. Its path generally refers to a resource on the same machine as the current document. Relative URIs may contain relative path components (*e.g.*, ".." means one level up in the hierarchy defined by the path), and may contain fragment identifiers.Relative URIs are resolved to full URIs using a base URI. As an example of relative URI resolution, assume we have the base URI "http://www.acme.com/support/intro.html".

The relative URI in the following markup for a hypertext link:

```
<A href="suppliers.html">Suppliers</A>
```

Would expand to the full URI "http://www.acme.com/support/suppliers.html", while the relative URI in the following markup for an image

```
<IMG src="../icons/logo.gif" alt="logo">
```

In HTML, URIs are used to:

- Link to another document or resource, (the A and LINK elements).
- Link to an external style sheet or script (see the LINK and SCRIPT elements).
- Include an image, object, or applets in a page, (see the IMG, OBJECT, APPLET and INPUT elements).Create an image map (the MAP and AREA elements).
- Submit a form (FORM).
- Create a frame document (the FRAME and IFRAME elements).
- Cite an external reference The Q, BLOCKQUOTE, INS and DEL elements).
- Refer to metadata conventions describing a document (see the HEAD element).

2

HTML Tags

DESCRIPTION

The simplest HTML tags arrange text into blocks, designate the font or letter-style, and size of the type. Bold, italic and underline are each identified within an HTML tag that precedes the letter or word(s) to be effected. The tag appears again at the end of the chosen text with a slash to indicate the effect ends there. For example, see how the following sentence appears in HTML:HTML tags are the core of Hypertext Markup Language. <b>HTML tags</b> are the core of Hypertext Markup Language.

The "b" stands for bold and HTML tags are always enclosed in angled brackets, with the closing tag starting with a forward slash. If the forward slash is forgotten, the remainder of the page will assume the effect.In addition to changing fonts, HTML tags also create hyperlinks, or clickable text. The hyperlink tag includes an embedded website address (URL or Uniform Resource Locator). By placing a hyperlink tag around a phrase or name, clicking on it will take the surfer to the desired address.

This can be a remote website or another page within the same website.HTML tags can also be used to take a surfer to another spot within the same page. This is handy for Frequently Asked Questions (FAQs) or indexes that reside on a single page. By clicking on a question or an indexed subject, the visitor can jet to the exact information he or she needs without paging down through the entire document.Other HTML tags imbed graphics, movies, sound effects, animation or Flash scripts in webpages. Frames, borders, background and page layouts are also designated by HTML tags.On websites with multiple pages there are often characteristics the webmaster wants to repeat on each page.

These might include the font type, website colours, background and text blocking or layout. Rather than repeat these HTML tags on every page, HTML allows for a bit of code at the top of each page that points the browser to a master style sheet which contains the HTML tags that apply. A master style sheet is known as *Cascading Style Sheet (CSS)* because its effects can "cascade" across several pages.A tag is a reference in an HTML document which describes the style and structure of the document. All tags start with < and end with >. Tags which mark a beginning have no/. Tags which mark an ending have a/ immediately after <, as in </.

```
<HTML>
<HEAD>
<TITLE>My Home Page</TITLE>
</HEAD>
<!- Written by me ->
<!- Created: yesterday ->
<!- Last modified: today ->
<BODY>
This is where the text goes.
</BODY>
</HTML>
```

HEAD AND BODY OF TAG

HTML documents are separated into two sections, the head and the body. The beginning of the head section is marked by the <HEAD> tag, and the end of the head section with the </HEAD> tag. Likewise, the beginning of the body section is marked by the <BODY> tag, and the end of the body section with the </BODY> tag. The example below highlights these tags.

```
<HTML>
<HEAD>
<TITLE>My Home Page</TITLE>
```

```
</HEAD>
<!- Written by me ->
<!- Created: yesterday ->
<!- Last modified: today ->
<BODY>
This is where the text goes.
</BODY>
</HTML>
```

TITLE TAG

The title of the page must be placed within the head section. The beginning of the title is marked by the <TITLE> tag, and the end with the </TITLE> tag. Most browsers display the title on the top portion of the frame of the page. Some browsers give the user the option to hide the display of the title. Many browsers also display the title of the document in the document title field, and use the title as the bookmark listing.Titles should be short, but descriptive, and limited to one line, so they can fit within the frame of the page. You should avoid accentuation within the title because it is the window manager, and not the browser, that interprets the title. Some window managers do not support accents.

```
<HTML>
<HEAD>
<TITLE>My Home Page</TITLE>
</HEAD>
<!- Written by me ->
<!- Created: yesterday ->
<!- Last modified: today ->
<BODY>
This is where the text goes.
</BODY>
</HTML>
```

COMMENT TAG

The comment tag is different from the other tags for the following reasons. It can be placed anywhere in the HTML file; inside the head section, inside the body section, or in between the head and the body. It does not end with a/. It starts with an <!— and ends with an →.It is always a good idea to put comments into your source code. In this simple example the comments state who is the author, the creation date of the document and the date of most recent update.

```
<HTML>
<HEAD>
<TITLE>My Home Page</TITLE>
</HEAD>
<!- Written by me ->
<!- Created: yesterday ->
<!- Last modified: today ->
<BODY>
This is where the text goes.
</BODY>
</HTML>
```

TYPES OF TAGS

There are two kinds of tags. Those tags which require an ending, are called range tags. They are called "range tags" because they cover a range of text.

Examples of range tags are <HTML>, <HEAD>, <BODY>, <TITLE>. Range tags require ending tags (</HTML>, </HEAD>, </BODY>, </TITLE>)

```
<HTML>
<HEAD>
<TITLE>My Home Page</TITLE>
</HEAD>
<!- Written by me ->
<!- Created: yesterday ->
<!- Last modified: today ->
<BODY>
This is where the text goes.
</BODY></HTML>
```

Those tags which do not require an ending, are called point tags. They are called "point tags" because they mark up the page only at a specific point on the page. A tag is also sometimes called an element. You may think of HTML elements as nouns or verbs within a language. Nouns have adjectives and verbs have adverbs.

- I have a cat.
- What kind of a cat?
- A big cat.
- What colour is your big cat?
- I have a big black cat.

In this example the noun is "cat" and it has two adjectives, "black" and "big". In HTML these adjectives are called attributes.

EXAMPLE: CREATE AN HTML FILE

It is time for an exercise. Create an HTML file similar to the example shown below:

```
<HTML>
<HEAD>
<TITLE>My Home Page</TITLE>
</HEAD>
<!- Written by me ->
<!- Created: yesterday ->
<!- Last modified: today ->
<BODY>
This is where the text goes.
</BODY>
</HTML>
```

Once you have created your HTML file, run it to see if you get the same results I obtained. You should get a page which has a title of "My Home Page" and text within the page that says "This is where the text goes."

LIST OF HTML TAGS

Tags	Short description
<!— —>	Inserts hidden comments
<!DOCTYPE>	Sets the document type
<a>	Inserts links or bookmarks
<abbr>	Explains abbreviations
<acronym>	Explains acronyms
<address>	Provides contact information

Tags	Short description
<applet>	Inserts an applet (scripts)
<area>	Defines sectors for image maps
<b>	Text in bold style
<base>	Sets the base URI to solve relative URIs
<basefont>	Sets the default font size
<bdo>	Overrides the bidirectional algorithm
<big>	Text in "large" font
<blockquote>	Paragraph quotation
<body>	Contains the renderable elements
 	Forces a line break
<button>	Creates a button
<caption>	Set a table's caption
<center>	centers it's content
<cite>	Inserts a citation or reference
<code>	Represents computer code
<col>	Sets attributes for table's columns
<colgroup>	Groups columns in a table
<dd>	Defines descriptions in a list
<del>	Indicates deleted text
<dfn>	Assings a definition to a term
<dir>	Inserts a directory list (tree)
<div>	Defines a block of content
<dl>	Defines a list<dt>Inserts a term in a list
<em>	Indicates emphasis
<fieldset>	Groups controls in a form
<font>	Sets the font style
<form>	Inserts a form
<frame>	Inserts a single frame
<frameset>	Inserts a set of frames
<h1>	Heading level 1
<h2>	Heading level 2
<h3>	Heading level 3
<h4>	Heading level 4
<h5>	Heading level 5
<h6>	Heading level 6
<head>	Defines the document's header block
<hr>	Draws an horizontal line or rule

<html>	Contains the document
<i>	Renders italic text
<iframe>	Inserts a frame inside a document
<img>	Inserts an image
<input>	Display input controls
<ins>	Indicates inserted text
<isindex>	Single line prompt
<kbd>	Represents text to be entered by users
<label>	Sets a label for a control
<legend>	Assigns a caption for a fieldset
<li>	Defines a list item
<link>	Gives relational info about documents
<map>	Defines a client-side image map
<menu>	Menu list
<meta>	Provides info about the document
<noframes>	Alternative content for frames
<noscript>	Alternate content for scripts
<object>	Runs external applications
<ol>	Inserts an ordered list
<optgroup>	Groups options in a select control
<option>	Defines an option in a select control
<p>	Defines a paragraph
<param>	Sets a parameter for an object
<pre>	Defines a block of preformatted text
<q>	Inserts a inline quotation
<s>	Renders strike-through text
<samp>	Represents sample output for programs
<script>	Contains scripts
<select>	Creates a select control
<small>	Renders text in "small" font
<span>	Assings attributes to text (inline)
<strike>	Renders strike-through text
<strong>	Indicates strong emphasis
<style>	Defines visual attributes (style sheets)
<sub>	Defines subscript text
<sup>	Defines superscript text
<table>	Inserts a table
<tbody>	Defines a body in a table

<td>	Regular cell of a table
<textarea>	Creates a multiline text input
<tfoot>	Defines a footer in a table
<th>	Header cell of a table
<thead>	Defines a header in a table
<title>	Defines the document's title
<tr>	Inserts a row in a table
<tt>	Renders teletype text
<u>	Renders underlined text
<ul>	Inserts an unordered list
<var>	Indicates an instance of a variable

HTML SEPARATORS

LINE SEPARATORS

Now that we have learned a bit about tags, let us take a closer look at a body tags, starting with those which are used to separate lines of text.

In this chapter we will learn about:

- The <P> tag, or paragraph tag.
- The <BR> tag, or line break tag.
- The <HR> tag, or horizontal line tag.

PARAGRAPH TAG

To separate your text into paragraphs use the <P> tag. For example, the following HTML source code:

```
This is should be the end of my first paragraph in HTML.This should be the start of my second paragraph in HTML.<P>And this is should be my third paragraph in HTML.<P>
```

Would display this on the user's screen:This is should be the end of my first paragraph in HTML. This should be the start of my second paragraph in HTML. And this is should be my third paragraph in HTML.Normally all text in an HTML document is treated like one long paragraph.

Indented or blank lines which normally indicate start of paragraphs in text are ignored. The <P> tag is used to separate paragraphs of text within an HTML document. The <P> tag forces an end of line and forces a blank line before the next paragraph.The <P> tag is only required to separate paragraphs in a document. It is not required after other tags which imply a line break.

BR TAG

Normally different browsers decide where is the best place to line breaks in your HTML document. However, there may be times when you want to control where one line ends and the next begins.

Use the <BR> tag to do this.The <BR> tag is very similar to the <P> tag in that both separate text, but the <BR> tag does not include a blank line before starting the next line of text. In other words, the lines are single spaced, not double spaced. For example, the following HTML source code:

```
This is should be the end of my first paragraph in HTML.
This should be the start of my second paragraph in HTML.<BR>
And this is should be my third paragraph in HTML.<BR>
```

Would display this on the user's screen: This is should be the end of my first paragraph in HTML. This should be the start of my second paragraph in HTML. And this is should be my third paragraph in HTML.The <BR> tag is only required when you want to control where the line breaks. It is not required after other tags which imply a line break, such as the horizontal rule tag.

HORIZONTAL RULE TAG

The <HR> tag draws a horizontal line across the page, like the line above this paragraph. It also acts as a paragraph break. There is no need to use the <BR> before or after the <HR> tag. *For example, the following HTML source code:*

```
A paragraph of text. <HR> Another paragraph of text.
```

Would display this on the user's screen: A paragraph of text. Another paragraph of text.

EXAMPLE

To the HTML file you created in the previous chapter, add some text with line breaks similar to the example shown below.

```
<HTML>
<HEAD>
<TITLE>My Home Page</TITLE>
</HEAD>
<!– Written by me –>
<!– Created: yesterday –>
<!– Last modified: today –>
<BODY>
This is where the text goes. <HR>
My favourite cities are: Rio de Janeiro, Paris,
and Venice. <P>Some of my favourite foods are:
Lasagna, Pizza, Prosciutto, Ravioli,
Spaghetti, <BR>Apples, Bananas, Cherries,
Figs, Grapes, Melon, Nectarines, Oranges,
Papaya, etc.
</BODY>
```

SOLUTION

My favourite cities are: Rio de Janeiro, Paris, and Venice.Some of my favourite foods are: Lasagna, Pizza, Prosciutto, Ravioli, Spaghetti, Apples, Bananas, Cherries, Figs, Grapes, Melon, Nectarines, Oranges, Papaya, etc.

3

Character Style Tags

THE PRE TAG

The <PRE> tag is used to include preformatted text into your HTML document. Text will be displayed with spaces just like you type it, in a fixed pitch font.

For example, the following HTML source code:

```
<PRE>
This is should be the end of my first paragraph
in HTML.This should be the start of my second
paragraph in HTML.And this is should be my
third paragraph in HTML.
</PRE>
```

Would display this on the user's screen:

This is should be the end of my first paragraph in HTML.This should be the start of my second paragraph in HTML.And this is should be my third paragraph in HTML.

EXAMPLE

```
<html>
<body>
<pre>
Text in a pre element is displayed in a fixed-
width font, and it preserves both spaces
and line breaks
</pre>
<p> The pre element is often used to display
computer code: </p> <pre> for i = 1 to 10
    print i
```

```
next i
</pre>
</body>
</html>
```

Solution: Text in a pre element is displayed in a fixed-width font, and it preserves both spaces and line breaks

The pre element is often used to display computer code:

```
for i = 1 to 10
    print i
next i
```

STANDARD ATTRIBUTES

The <pre> tag supports the following standard attributes:

Attribute	Value	Description	DTD
Class	*classname*	Specifies a classname for an element	STF
Dir	rtl ltr	Specifies the text direction for the content in an element	STF
Id	*id*	Specifies a unique id for an element	STF
Lang	*language_code*	Specifies a language code for the content in an element	STF
Style	*style_definition*	Specifies an inline style for an element.	STF
Title	*text*	Specifies extra information about an element.	STF
xml:lang	*language_code*	Specifies a language code for the content in an element, in XHTML documents.	STF

EVENT ATTRIBUTES

The <pre> tag supports the following event attributes:

Attribute	Value	Description	DTD
Onclick	*script*	Script to be run on a mouse click	STF
Ondblclick	*script*	Script to be run on a mouse double-click	STF

Onmouse-down	*script*	Script to be run when mouse button is pressed	STF
Onmouse-move	*script*	Script to be run when mouse pointer moves	STF
Onmouse-out	*script*	Script to be run when mouse pointer moves out of an element	STF
Onmouse-over	*script*	Script to be run when mouse pointer moves over an element	STF
Onmouseup	*script*	Script to be run when mouse button is released	STF
Onkeydown	*script*	Script to be run when a key is pressed	STF
Onkeypress	*script*	Script to be run when a key is pressed and released	STF
Onkeyup	*script*	Script to be run when a key is released	STF

THE BLOCKQUOTE TAG

The <BLOCKQUOTE> tag is used to include indented text in a document. If, for example, you wanted to quote a piece of text from another source, such as Shakespeare:

```
The last words of Julius Caesar were:
<BLOCKQUOTE> "Et tu? Brute." </BLOCKQUOTE>
```

Would display this on the user's screen:

The last words of Julius Caesar were:

"Et tu? Brute."

The <BLOCKQUOTE> tag displays an indented block of text. Both the left and right margin are indented. Thus the <BLOCKQUOTE> tag may be used just for indenting text.

DEFINITION

The HTML blockquote tag defines a quotation. It's commonly used to define long quotations like paragraphs (instead of HTML q tag used for in-line content).

ATTRIBUTES

Id (Name)

The "id" attribute assigns an identifier to the associated element. This identifier must be unique in the document and can be used to refer to that element.

Example:

<p id="paragraph1"> This is the first paragraph named as paragraph1. To dynamically change its properties use this identifier.</p>

Class (Cdata)

The "class" attribute assigns a class name (or a list of class names separated by spaces) to the container element. It's used with style sheets and tells the browser the class to which the element is associated with. A class gives visual attributes to elements.

Example:

<p class="references">This article is based on the book "Wind in the trees" by Jhon L. Brooks</p>

```
<p class="references important">
```

This article is based on the book "Wind in the trees" by Jhon L. Brooks... and is more important than the one before.</p>

Style (Style)

Defines a visual style of this element. Is a better practice to define styles attributes in external style sheets grouping them in classes.

Ttributes in the "style" parameter must preserve this order "name: value" and be separated by a semi-colon.If you're writing XHTML code it's recommended not to use this attribute and try style sheet classes (with the "class" attribute).

Example:

```
<p style="colour: #0000FF; font-size:
12pt">This is a paragraph with a defined
style</p>
<p>And this is another text without style.</
p>
```

Title (text)

Indicates a title for the element. Used to give a short description about the element that is usually shown as a "tool tip" when the user put the mouse pointer over the element.

Example:

Code
<atitle="HTMLQuick.com"href="http://www.htmlquick.com">HTML code</a>

Lang (Langcode)

Specifies the language of an element's content. The default value in "unknown".When writing XHTML code the syntax "xml:lang" represents a preferred alternative in XHTML 1.0 and a replacement in XHTML 1.1 (*e.g.*, xml:lang="en").

Example:

```
<p lang="en">This is a paragraph in english.</
p>
<p lang="es">Este es un p&aacute;rrafo en
espa&ntilde;ol.</p>
```

Dir

Specifies the text direction of the element's contents and attribute values, as well as tables directionality.

It has two possible values that are case insensitive:

1. STF: Right to left.
2. LTR: Left to right.

Example:

```
<q lang="he" dir="rtl">...a Hebrew
quotation...</q>
```

Cite (Uri)

The value of this attribute is a **URI** that designates a source document or message. This attribute is intended to point to information about the element's purpose.

Example:

```
<blockquote cite="http://www.bookstore.com/
bfd.html">
...paragraph...
</blockquote>
```

THE ADDRESS TAG

The <ADDRESS> tag defines text that gives an address or other contact information. It is typically displayed in *italics,* and is usually placed at the bottom of HTML documents to indicate the electronic mail address of the author of the document.

For example:

```
<HTML>
<HEAD>
<TITLE>My Home Page</TITLE>
</HEAD>
<!– Written by me –>
<!– Created: yesterday –>
<!– Last modified: today –>
<BODY>
This is where the text goes.
<ADDRESS>
Written by me@mycompany.com
</ADDRESS>
</BODY>
</HTML>
```

The HTML address tag is used for indicating an address, usually related to authorship of the current document.

EXAMPLE

```
<address>
W3C Indian Office<br>
CSIRO ICT<br>
Building 108, North Road, Indian University
Campus<br>
Acton, New Delhi<br>
ACT 2601, New Delhi<br>
</address>
```

ATTRIBUTES

Id (Name)

The "id" attribute assigns an identifier to the associated element. This identifier must be unique in the document and can be used to refer to that element.

Example:

<p id="paragraph1">This is the first paragraph named as paragraph1. To dynamically change its properties use this identifier.</p>

Class (Cdata)

The "class" attribute assigns a class name (or a list of class names separated by spaces) to the container element. It's used with style sheets and tells the browser the class to which the element is associated with. A class gives visual attributes to elements.

Example:

```
<p class="references">This article is based on
the book "Wind in the trees" by Jhon L. Brooks</
p>
<p class="references important">This article is
based on the book "Wind in the trees" by Jhon L.
Brooks... and is more important than the one
before.</p>
```

Style (Style)

Defines a visual style of this element. Is a better practice to define styles attributes in external style sheets grouping them in classes. Attributes in the "style" parameter must preserve this order "name: value" and be separated by a semi-colon.If you're writing XHTML code it's recommended not to use this attribute and try style sheet classes (with the "class" attribute).

Example:

```
<p style="colour: #0000FF; font-size:
12pt">This is a paragraph with a defined
style</p>
<p>And this is another text without style.</
p>
```

Title (Text)

Indicates a title for the element. Used to give a short description about the element that is usually shown as a "tool tip" when the user put the mouse pointer over the element.

Example:

Code
`<a title="HTMLQuick.com" href="http://www.htmlquick.com">HTML code</a>`

Lang (Langcode)

Specifies the language of an element's content. The default

value in "unknown".When writing XHTML code the syntax "xml:lang" represents a preferred alternative in XHTML 1.0 and a replacement in XHTML 1.1 (*e.g.*, xml:lang="en").

Example:

```
<p lang="en">This is a paragraph in english.</
p>
<p lang="es">Este es un p&aacute;rrafo en espa
&ntilde;ol.</p>
```

Dir

Specifies the text direction of the element's contents and attribute values, as well as tables directionality.

It has two possible values that are case insensitive:

1. *RTL*: Right to left.
2. *LTR*: Left to right.

Example:

```
<q lang="he"dir="rtl">...a Hebrew
quotation...</q>
```

THE HEADINGS TAGS

Topic headings are used as titles for sections in HTML documents. A *heading* is different than a *header*. Only one *header* (<HEAD>) appears in an HTML document, but you can have as many *headings* as you like. *Headings* come in six different sizes, and are displayed differently from regular text, usually in bold and left justified. The format of the *heading* tag is:

```
<Hn>Text</Hn>
```

Where *n* is a number from 1 to 6. It is recommended that you use <H1> to represent main headings, <H2> tags to represent subheadings, etc. On adding some more text to the body of document will show the different headings.

```
<HTML>
<HEAD>
<TITLE>My Home Page</TITLE>
</HEAD>
<!– Written by me –>
<!– Created: yesterday –>
<!– Last modified: today –>
<BODY>
```

```
<H1>This is heading H1.</H1>
<H2>This is heading H2.</H2>
<H3>This is heading H3.</H3>
<H4>This is heading H4.</H4>
<H5>This is heading H5.</H5>
<H6>This is heading H6.</H6>
This is where the text goes.
<ADDRESS>
Written by me@mycompany.com
</ADDRESS>
</BODY>
</HTML>
```

HTML uses six levels of "heading level" tag pairs; the smaller the heading level number, the larger is the print size:

- **<H1>heading</H1>**: creates heading level #1 (24 point type—largest)
- **<H2>heading</H2>**: creates heading level #2 (18 point type)
- **<H3>heading</H3>**: creates heading level #3 (14 point type)
- **<H4>heading</H4>**: creates heading level #4 (12 point type)
- **<H5>heading</H5>**: creates heading level #5 (10 point type)
- **<H6>heading</H6>**: creates heading level #6 (8 point type—smallest)

A *line space* automatically is inserted before and after a heading (that is, an entire line is skipped between a heading and any text before and after it).

The <H#> tag may contain within it an *alignment* parameter (recognized by most browsers) as part of the command:

`ALIGN="LEFT"|"CENTER"|"RIGHT":` positions the heading at a specific location on the page.

- "LEFT" (the *default*) aligns the heading with the left margin of the page.
- "CENTER" centers the heading horizontally on the page.

- "RIGHT" aligns the heading with the right margin of the page.

In most cases, it is preferable for a heading to be centered horizontally on the page. However, since some browsers so not recognize the ALIGN parameter for headings, it is a good idea to center a heading by using <CENTER> & </CENTER> tags. Below are 2 groups of headings (along with a horizontal rule, or <HR>, in each group), followed by what the marked up versions look like as displayed on a web browser. The first group employs the ALIGN parameter in the <H#> tags. The second group is centered using <CENTER> & </CENTER> tags.

If the ALIGN parameter is recognized by a browser, this group of headings:

```
<H1 ALIGN="CENTER">Heading Alignment</H1>
<HR WIDTH="36%" SIZE="5" NOSHADE="NOSHADE">
<H1 ALIGN="LEFT">Heading Level #1</H1>
<H2 ALIGN="CENTER">Heading Level #2</H2>
<H3 ALIGN="RIGHT">Heading Level #3</H3>
<H4 ALIGN="LEFT">Heading Level #4</H4>
<H5 ALIGN="CENTER">Heading Level #5</H5>
<H6 ALIGN="RIGHT">Heading Level #6</H6>
```

Would appear properly centered, left justified, and right justified on a browser like this:

HEADING ALIGNMENT

Heading Level #1
Heading Level #2
Heading Level #3
Heading Level #4
Heading Level #5
Heading Level #6

These same headings centered with <CENTER> & </CENTER> tags:

```
<CENTER>
<H1>Heading Centering</H1>
<HR WIDTH="35%" SIZE="5" NOSHADE="NOSHADE">
<H1>Heading Level #1</H1>
<H2>Heading Level #2</H2>
```

```
<H3>Heading Level #3</H3>
<H4>Heading Level #4</H4>
<H5>Heading Level #5</H5>
<H6>Heading Level #6</H6>
</CENTER>
```

Would look like this:

HEADING CENTERING

Heading Level #1
Heading Level #2
Heading Level #3
Heading Level #4
Heading Level #5
Heading Level #6

The appearance of any heading may be matched with bold print of the appropriate font size.

These two groups of HTML commands:

`<H1>Heading Level #1</H1>`	`<FONT SIZE="6"><B>Heading1 Level#1</B></FONT>`
`<H2>Heading Level #2</H2>`	`<FONT SIZE="5"><B>Heading Level #2</B></FONT>`
`<H3>Heading Level #3</H3>`	`<FONT SIZE="4"><B>Heading Level#3</B></FONT>`
`<H4>Heading Level #4</H4>`	`<FONT SIZE="3"><B>Heading Level#4</B></FONT>`
`<H5>Heading Level #5</H5>`	`<FONT SIZE="2"><B>Heading Level #5</B></FONT>`
`<H6>Heading Level #6</H6>`	`<FONT SIZE="1"><B>Heading Level #6</B></FONT>`

Will produce identical markups on a browser:

Heading Level #1	Heading Level #1
Heading Level #2	Heading Level #2
Heading Level #3	Heading Level #3
Heading Level #4	Heading Level #4
Heading Level #5	Heading Level #5
Heading Level #6	Heading Level #6

In some cases, one may not wish for the headings on a web page to be limited to six (6) standard fontsizes. There is a way to make every heading level, throughout the entire page, be any size and colour one wishes it to be, using "style" tags:

```
<STYLE>H_ {FONT-SIZE: ___pt; COLOUR: ___}</
STYLE>:
```

Specifies the *exact* font size and colour of a particular heading.

Normally, heading levels 2 (<H2> & </H2>) and 3 (<H3> & </H3>) are sizes 18-point and 14-point, respectively. As typically written here, these headings:

```
<CENTER>
<H2>Heading #2</H2>
<H3>Heading #3</H3>
</CENTER>
```

Would appear this way:

Heading #2

Heading #3

However, one might wish for the respective size of each of these heading levels to be somewhat larger, as well as the same respective colour to be uniform, throughout a page. In such a case, the following size and colour specifications:

```
<STYLE>H2 {FONT-SIZE: 21pt; COLOUR: #000080};
H3 {FONT-SIZE: 17pt; COLOUR: #008000}</STYLE>
<CENTER>
<H2>Heading #2</H2>
<H3>Heading #3</H3>
</CENTER>
```

Now would cause the headings to appear like this:

Heading#2

Heading#3

CHARACTER HIGHLIGHTING

Character style tags are used to give text a different look when displayed by a browser. HTML has both physical, or typogaphical, styles and logical, or idiomatic, styles.

It is highly recommended to use logical styles instead of physical styles because the browser handles the display of logical styles and not all browsers support physical styles.Character styles are displayed differently by different browsers.

For example, LYNX (a text-based browser), displays text marked with B, EM, I, and STRONG tags as underlined text, and text marked with SAMP and TT tags as normal text.

LOGICAL STYLE TAGS

Logical, or idiomatic style tags can be used to give your text a different look when displayed by browsers. Logical style tags are preferred because they let the browser handle the look and feel of the logical tag.

Here are the idiomatic style tags:

Citation: **<CITE>** Is used to indicate the title of a book or other citation. It is typically displayed in italics.

For example:

`My favourite Shakespeare play is <cite>Julius Caesar</cite>.`

***Code*: <CODE> Indicates an example of code, typically displayed in a uniform font. CODE is intended for short segments of computer code. The PRE tag is more appropriate for multiple lines of code. For example:`<code>A = A + 1</code>`**

Emphasis: **<EM>***Is for emphasizing phrases, and is typically displayed in italics. For example:*

`It is my <EM>favourite</EM> Shakespeare play.`

Keyboard: **<KBD>** Indicates text typed by a user. It is typically displayed in a font and is commonly used in instructional manuals.

For example:

`Enter <kbd>your password</kbd>.`

***Sample*: <SAMP> Indicates a sequence of literal characters. It is typically displayed in a uniform font. For example:**

`Use <samp>*.*</samp> to delete every file.`

Strong Emphasis: <STRONG> indicates strong emphasis, and typically appears in bold. This is preferred over <B> which is a physical tag.

For example:

```
Do <strong>NOT</strong>, be late again!
```

Variable: <VAR> *indicates a variable, typically displayed in italic. For example:*

```
The function returns a <VAR>filename</VAR>.
```

PHYSICAL STYLE TAGS

Physical, or typographical, style tags can be used to give your text a different, but exacting look. Not all browsers support physical styles, and that is why their use is discouraged.

However, since they are easy to learn, many people use them. To be complete, I have included the typographical style tags, and here they are:

Bold: <B> indicates bold text.

Italic: <I> *indicates italics.*

`Teletype: <TT> indicates teletype or typewriter text, which is a uniform font.`

ADDING CHARACTER STYLES

It is time for an exercise. To the HTML file you created in the previous chapter, add some character style tags to the text similar to the example shown below.

```
<HTML>
<HEAD>
<TITLE>My Home Page</TITLE>
</HEAD>

<!– Written by me –>
<!– Created: yesterday –>
<!– Last modified: today –>

<BODY>

<H1>This is where the text goes.</H1><HR>
My <EM>favourite</EM> cities are: Rio de
Janeiro, Paris,
and <STRONG>Venice.</STRONG> <P>
```

```
    Some of my <EM>favourite</EM> foods are:
Lasagna, Pizza,
    Prosciutto, Ravioli, Spaghetti, <BR>Apples,
    Bananas,Cherries,Figs, <EM>Grapes, Melon,
Nectarines,   Oranges, Papaya,</EM>
etc.

    </BODY>
    </HTML>
```

4

Special Character

INTRODUCTION

To make special characters and accented letters show up on your pages, use a special set of codes called character entities, which you insert into your HTML code and which your browser will display as the corresponding symbols or characters you want. The most common character entities have been collected by the International Organization for Standardization and compiled in the ISO Alphabet, which includes special characters, letters with diacritical marks (accents, umlauts, etc.), and scientific and currency symbols. So, have you been wondering how to add an extra space on your page, or how to get a copyright symbol to show up? Then let's see how right now!

Special characters are placed on your page by using a special reference to the character you want to use. The reference will begin with an ampersand (&), will be followed by some text or numbers, and end with a semicolon (;). So as an example, let's say you wanted to place an extra space between two words. To do this, you place the reference   where you would like to add the extra space. Here is what you would do:

```
Hello  there!
```

This gives us two spaces between "Hello" and "there!", like this:

```
Hello  there!
```

The first space is added just using the "space" bar on the keyboard. The Web browser will see the first space, but after that additional spaces will make no difference— you will only see one space in the browser. By adding the   reference, we forced the browser to add an extra space between the two words. You can add as many spaces as you would like by repeating the   reference, like this:

```
Hello     There!
```

This will create the first space, and 4 additional spaces between the two words, for a total of five spaces.

It will be displayed like this:

```
Hello There!
```

The other one we will discuss is the copyright symbol. You use it the same way as an extra space, by placing its reference where you would like to see the symbol on the page. The reference for a copyright symbol is ©. Here's an example:

```
This page Copyright &copy; 1999 by me!
This page Copyright © 1999 by me!
```

This will work the same way for any special character you want to use. Just place the reference where you want the character to be on your page.

ESCAPE SEQUENCE CHARACTERS

The characters listed below have special meanings in HTML documents. These codes are required so you can use them without confusing HTML, since all HTML markers, or tags start with an “<“ and end with an “>”.

There are the four escape sequences:

```
<    &lt; (Less than sign)
>    &gt; (Greater than sign)
&    &amp; (Ampersand sign)
"   &quot; (Double quote)
```

Each of these special characters has a logical name, for example “lt” for the less than sign. To use these characters, start with an ampersand, then the name (lt, gt, amp, or quot), and end it with a semicolon. An ampersand written in HTML would be &Be sure to end the sequence with a semicolon, because if you do not you will not get the desired result. An ampersand written in HTML without the semicolon will look like this &amp. An ampersand properly written in HTML with the semicolon at the end will look like this &

ISO LATIN-1 CHARACTERS

Languages based on Roman characters use accent marks, dieresis or other methods in the spelling of words so they may be pronounced properly. HTML uses an international standard [ISO-8859-1] which incorporates the ASCII character set to represent these special characters. This character set also includes characters not normally found on keyboards, but which are used everyday such as the divide sign, ÷. Like the escape sequence characters of the previous page, the majority of these Roman characters have a logical name

(< > & ").

All characters in the ISO Latin-1 character set have a numeric representation ranging from 0 to 255. To properly represent these characters in HTML use the following escape sequence. Start with an ampersand, &, immediately followed by a number sign, #, then a number from 0 to 255, and end with a semicolon. For example, small c with a cedilla can be written as ç or as ç. Note that the numeric representation has a # after the &.Be sure to end the sequence with a semicolon, because if you do not you will not get the desired result. An small c with a cedilla written in HTML without the semicolon will look like this &ccedil. An small c with a cedilla properly written in HTML with the semicolon at the end will look like this ç

EXAMPLE

To the HTML file you created in the previous chapter, add some ISO Latin-1 characters to the text similar to the example shown below.

```
<HTML>
<HEAD>
<TITLE>My Home Page</TITLE>
</HEAD>
<!— Written by me —>
<!— Created: yesterday —>
```

```
    <!- Last modified: today ->
    <BODY>
    <H1>&#161;Viva M&eacute;xico&#33;</H1> <HR>
    My <EM>favourite</EM> cities are: Rio de
Janeiro,Paris,and <STRONG>Venice.</STRONG> <P>
    Some of my <EM>favourite</EM> foods are:
Lasagna, Pizza,Prosciutto, Ravioli, Spaghetti,
<BR>Apples, Bananas,Cherries,Figs, <EM>Grapes,
Melon, Nectarines, Oranges,Papaya,</EM> etc.
    </BODY>
    </HTML>
```

RESULT

My *favourite* cities are: Rio de Janeiro, Paris, and Venice.Some of my *favourite* foods are: Lasagna, Pizza, Prosciutto, Ravioli, Spaghetti, Apples, Bananas, Cherries, Figs, *Grapes, Melon, Nectarines, Oranges, Papaya,* etc.

5

HTML Lists

UNORDERED LISTS

Use the <UL> tag to start an unordered list of items, and use the </UL> to end the unordered list.Each item in an unordered list is indented. Start each item of the list with the <LI>, or list item, tag. The item will be preceded by a "bullet".

For example, the following HTML source code:

Here is a list of Mexican cities.

```
<UL>
<LI>Mexico City
<LI>Guadalajara
<LI>Monterrey
<LI>Acapulco
<LI>Tasco
</UL>
```

Would display this unordered list on the user's screen:

Here is a list of Mexican cities.

- Mexico City
- Guadalajara
- Monterrey
- Acapulco
- Tasco

Items in the list can contain more than one paragraph. For that use the <P> tag.

ORDERED LISTS

Use the <OL> tag to start an ordered list of items, and use the </OL> to end the ordered list.Each item in an ordered list is indented, just as they are with unordered lists. Also, each list item in an ordered list is preceded with a number, in order, instead of a "bullet".

For example, the following HTML source code:

```
Here is a list of Mexican cities.
<OL>
<LI>Mexico City
<LI>Guadalajara
<LI>Monterrey
<LI>Acapulco
<LI>Tasco
</OL>
```

Would display this ordered list on the user's screen:

Here is a list of Mexican cities.

- Mexico City
- Guadalajara
- Monterrey
- Acapulco
- Tasco

NESTED LISTS

You can create nested lists in HTML by simply including the list tags inside a list item tag.

For example, the following HTML source code:

```
Foods
<UL>
<LI>Fruits
 <UL>
     <LI>Peaches
     <LI>Pears
 </UL>
<LI>Vegetables
 <UL>
 <LI>Broccoli
     <LI>Cauliflower
 </UL>
</UL>
```

Would display this nested list on the user's screen:

```
Foods
  Fruits
 Peaches
Pears
 Vegetables
Broccoli
Cauliflower
```

DEFINITION LISTS

The definition list tag, or <DL>, can be used to define a definition. It is commonly used to describe items found in a glossary. The definition list is made up of a term,<DT>, and followed by one or more definition descriptions <DD> items. (It is preferable to use <BR> instead of multiple <DD> tags within a <DT>.) The </DT>and </DD> are optional, but recommended so when you look at the code you have an indication of the ending of the definition. Most browsers indent the definition under each t erm, with no blank lines around them.

For example, the following HTML source code:

```
<DL>
<DT><STRONG>TCP/IP</STRONG>
<DD>Stands for Transmission Control Protocol/
Internet Protocol.
The most prevalent communication protocol
found on the Internet. It is used to transfer
data and communicate between computers,
especially computers running on the UNIX
operating system.
</DL>
```

Would display this definition list on the user's screen:

TCP/IP

Stands for Transmission Control Protocol/Internet Protocol. The most prevalent communication protocol found on the Internet. It is used to transfer data and communicate between computers, especially computers running on the

UNIX operating system.Remember, a definition list starts with the <DL> tag and ends with the </DL> tag.

MAKING A LIST

It is time for an exercise. To the HTML file you created in the previous chapter, make an ordered lists out of the cities, an unordered nested list out of the Italian foods and fruits and a definition for "favourite", similar to the example shown below.

```
<HTML>
<HEAD>
<TITLE>My Home Page</TITLE>
</HEAD>
<!– Written by me –>
<!– Created: yesterday –>
<!– Last modified: today –>
<BODY>
<H1>&#161;Viva M&eacute;xico&#33;</H1><HR>
My <EM>favourite</EM> cities are:
<OL>
<LI>Rio de Janeiro
<LI>Paris
<LI>Venice
</OL>
<P>
Some of my <EM>favourite</EM> foods are:
<UL>
   <LI>Italian
   <UL>
    <LI>Lasagna          <LI>Pizza
    <LI>Prosciutto <LI>Ravioli
    <LI>Spaghetti
   </UL>
   <LI>Fruits
   <UL>
    <LI>Apples       <LI>Bananas
    <LI>Cherries         <LI>Figs
    <LI>Grapes       <LI>Melon
```

```
        <LI>Nectarines <LI>Oranges
          <LI>Papaya
        </UL>
    </UL>
    <DL>
    <DT><STRONG>favourite</STRONG>
    <DD>A person, or thing liked or prefered above
    all others; regarded with special favour;
special. Things I really like.
    </DL>
    </BODY>
    </HTML>
```

6

HTML Links

SERVICES

A browser lets you link to other resources on the Internet using different types of services.

The most common ones are:

- *Http*: Uses the Hyper Text Transfer Protocol to access a World Wide Web server. For example: http://www.nrie.org/ connects to the NRC home page.
- *Gopher*: Gopher is software which follows a simple protocol for tunneling through TCP/IP. It is a distributed document search and retrieval system based on a client/server model. It was invented at the University of Minnesota. For example: gopher://gopher.tc.umn.edu connects you to the Gopher at the University of Minnesota.
- *Ftp*: Uses the File Transfer Protocol to access an FTP Server. FTP is used to transfer files and it can be done anonymously. Versions of the File Transfer Protocol have been around since 1971. For example: ftp://ftp.fda.gov connects you to the FTP Server of the Food and Drug Administration.
- *Mailto*: This allows the reader to send electronic mail to the electronic mail address specified. It is often used with the <ADDRESS> tag to allow the reader to quickly send mail to the author of a document. For example: mailto:comments@www.hq.nasa.gov would send electronic mail to comments@www.hq.nasa.gov

- *News*: Uses the Network News Transport Protocol to access an NNTP (Usenet News) Server. It is the browser that determines which NNTP server to use. The format of the NEWS URL is different. For example: news:rec.humour allows the reader to access the newsgroup rec.humour.
- *Telnet*: The purpose of the Telnet protocol is to provide a fairly general, bi-directional, eight-bit byte oriented communications facility. Its primary goal is to allow a standard method of interfacing terminal devices and terminal-oriented processes to each other. It is mostly used to login to a host on the Internet. For example:telnet://cyber.gate.net will create a TELNET session for you to login on CyberGate, an Internet Service Provider.

THE A TAG

HTML has the ability to create links to other documents from within the current document. This is done using the <A> tag. The <A> tag is also known as an "Anchor". The <A> tag has two attributes, NAME and HREF. One is a source, and the other is a destination.

The <A> tag uses one of the following formats:

```
<A NAME="anchor name"></A>
<A HREF="#anchor name">text of link</A>
<A HREF="URL"></A>
<A HREF="URL#anchor name">text of link</A>
```

Where:

- NAME is the name of the anchor. When no name and no # is given, the link takes you to the top of the page.
- HREF is the reference which defines the relationship and service between this document and the link.
- The text of link is any text you wish to include which will become HyperText.
- URL is the Uniform Resource Locator of the document you to go to when the link has been selected.

URL

A Uniform Resource Locator is a reference that points to a resource, or file, on the Internet. This resource can be a text file, an image file, an HTML file, etc. The format of a URL is:

`service://hostname/filename`

Where: Service is the type of service requested. The name of the service for accessing Web pages is http.hostname is the name of the computer system. The name is usually made up of machine name followed by a dot (.) followed by the domain name.filename is the name of the file you are accessing. This could be a relative path name or an absolute path name.Absolute

ABSOLUTE URL

An absolute URL is one which has a full URL specification, meaning it has a fully qualified domain name. An absolute URL includes the service, the host name, and the full path name of the file. For example:

`http://www.nasa.gov/hqpao/library.html`

This absolute URL has specified the http service on the system www which resides in the nasa.gov domain, and is asking for file library.html which is in the/hqpaodirectory.It is better to use a relative URL instead of an absolute URL for two reasons.

It is easier to move a group of related HTML documents to a different directory or a different server, without modification, if you use relative URL specifications.The system does not have to go out and find the same IP address again, thus finding the requested document more efficiently.

RELATIVE URL

A relative URL is one which only has the relative (to the current directory) path name of the file. For example:

```
<A HREF="index.html">[index]</A>
```

This relative URL does not specify the service nor the machine name. The browser assumes the current server is the requested system.

NAME IN URL

An anchor can be named. To name an anchor use the following syntax.

```
<A NAME="name"></A>
```

To tell the browser to go to a specific anchor, use the following syntax.

```
<A HREF="#name">text</A>
```

If no name is specified for an anchor within the HREF specification, the link will go to the top of the page. Notice that the title of this page is linked. Click on the HyperText and see where it take you.

EXAMPLE

To the HTML file you have been working on, add an absolute URL link to the NASA home page and some links to points within your home page, similar to the example shown below.

```
<HTML>
<HEAD>
<TITLE>My Home Page</TITLE>
</HEAD>
<!- Written by me ->
<!- Created: yesterday ->
<!- Last modified: today ->
<BODY>
Go to my favourite:
<BR><BLOCKQUOTE>
<A HREF="http://www.nasa.gov">Web Site</A> |
<A HREF="#CITIES">Cities</A> |
<A HREF="#FOODS">Foods</A>
</BLOCKQUOTE><BR>
<H1>&#161;Viva M&eacute;xico&#33;</H1> <HR>
<A NAME="CITIES"></A>
My <EM>favourite</EM> cities are:
<OL>
<LI>Rio de Janeiro
```

```
<LI>Paris
<LI>Venice
</OL>
<P>
<A NAME="FOODS"></A>
Some of my <EM>favourite</EM> foods are:
<UL>
   <LI>Italian
   <UL>
    <LI>Lasagna          <LI>Pizza
    <LI>Prosciutto  <LI>Ravioli
 <LI>Spaghetti
   </UL>
   <LI>Fruits
   <UL>
    <LI>Apples      <LI>Bananas
    <LI>Cherries         <LI>Figs
    <LI>Grapes      <LI>Melon
    <LI>Nectarines  <LI>Oranges
    <LI>Papaya
   </UL>
</UL>
<DL>
<DT><STRONG>favourite</STRONG>
<DD>A person, or thing liked or prefered above
all others;regarded with special favour;
special. Things I really like.
</DL>
</BODY>
</HTML>
```

Result

My favourite cities are:

Rio de Janeiro

Paris

Venice

Some of my favourite foods are:

- Italian
  - Lasagna

  - Pizza
  - Prosciutto
  - Ravioli
  - Spaghetti
- Fruits
  - Apples
  - Bananas
  - Cherries
  - Figs
  - Grapes
  - Melon
  - Nectarines
  - Oranges
  - Papaya

FAVOURITE

A person, or thing liked or prefered above all others; regarded with special favour; special. Things I really like.

7

Images within HTML

One of the attractive features of the World Wide Web is that we can include graphical images.

In this chapter we will learn about:

- The <IMG> tag.
- How to add textual descriptions to your image for non-graphical browsers.
- How to align text with your image.
- How to make clickable images.

THE IMG TAG

The HTML <img> tag is used to put an image in an HTML document. In HTML the <img> tag has no end tag. In XHTML the <img> tag must be properly closed.The *align, border, hspace,* and *vspace* attributes of the image element are deprecated in HTML as well as in XHTML.

EXAMPLE

```
<img src="http://www.tutorialspoint.com/
images/html.gif" alt="HTML Tutorial"/>
```

The <IMG> tag in your HTML document to insert images. The basic syntax of this tag is:

```
<IMG SRC="URL">
```

Where IMG states this is an inline image, and SRC specifies the source of the image as a URL. The <IMG> tag does not use an ending tag (</IMG>). The <IMG> tag is a point tag. We learned in the previous chapter that an URL (Uniform Resource Locator) is a file which can reside locally on the server or on another server.

Here are some important things to remember about an image:

- The file specified should be an image in binary form, preferably in one of the following formats since most browsers support them.
  - Gif
  - Jpg
- The image file should not be too large because:
  - It will take a long time to load.
  - It may be too big for the display window.

ALIGN IMAGE

Now that you have placed the inline image into your HTML document, you probably want to align it just right. To align images use the ALIGN attribute within the <IMG> tag. Here is the syntax:

```
<IMG SRC="URL" ALIGN="alignment" ALT="alternate text information">
```

Where alignment can be one of the following options:

- Top
- Middle
- Bottom

Newer browser versions also support the following options:

- Left
- Right
- Texttop
- Absmiddle
- Absbottom
- Baseline

Aligning pictures can help you better space out your web site and make it easier for your visitors to read. In this section you will learn the tags that will help you align your pictures in different areas.

ALIGN LEFT

Here, you will learn how to align your picture to the left of the screen. The tag to align the picture left is ALIGN="LEFT". This adds onto the picture tag so the final result looks like:

```
<IMG SRC="url" ALIGN="LEFT">
```

ALIGN RIGHT

Here, you will learn how to align your picture to the right of the screen. The tag to align the picture right is ALIGN="RIGHT". This adds onto the picture tag so the final result looks like:

```
<IMG SRC="url" ALIGN="RIGHT">
```

ALIGN CENTER

Here, you will learn how to align your picture to the center of the screen. The starting tag is <CENTER> and the closing tag is </CENTER>. The picture(s) between these two tags is what is aligned to the center.

ALIGN TOP

This functions specifies where the text is placed in relation to the picture. Here, the text will be placed at the top of the picture. The tag to align the text to the top of the picture right is ALIGN="TOP".

This adds onto the picture tag so the final result looks like:

```
<IMG SRC="url" ALIGN="TOP">
```

ALIGN MIDDLE

This functions specifies where the text is placed in relation to the picture. Here, the text will be placed in the middle of the picture. The tag to align the text to the middle of the picture right is ALIGN="MIDDLE".

This adds onto the picture tag so the final result looks like:

```
<IMG SRC="url" ALIGN="MIDDLE">
```

ALIGN BOTTOM

This functions specifies where the text is placed in relation to the picture. Here, the text will be placed at the bottom of the picture. The tag to align the text at the bottom of the picture right is ALIGN="BOTTOM".

This adds onto the picture tag so the final result looks like:

```
<IMG SRC="url" ALIGN="BOTTOM">
```

CLICKABLE IMAGES

A clickable image is a combination of an image with an anchor. We have already seen the <A> tag and the <IMG> tag, so now let's combine them to make a clickable image.

The syntax is as follows:

```
<A HREF="URL of link"> <IMG ALT="alternate
text" SRC="URL of image"></A>
```

The syntax is similar to that of the <A> tag except that instead of the text of the link you have an image.

MAKING IMAGE

- Another cool trick you can do with images is to make them clickable. That is, you can put an anchor tag around them so that when the user moves their mouse over the image, they will be able to click on the image in order to go to some other page.
- The process is exactly the same as for making text-based links except that you place the image where the text was.
- In the following example, we make the icon clickable so that when the user clicks on it, they will be transported to the table of contents page for this tutorial. Remember that you can click on your browser's back button to return to this page.
- Below we have added the above code to this page and made the clickable image for you to try out.
- Notice that the image above is surrounded by a box. This box is like the underlining of link text. It lets the user know that the image is clickable.
- However, in many cases, you will not want the box around your image. If this is the case, you need only set the BORDER attribute of the IMG tag to "0". For example, we can turn the border in the above image off by using the following code:
- In this case, our clickable image would appear as below:

EXAMPLE

To the HTML file you have been working on, use the same button used to make a clickable image, similar to the example shown below.

```
<HTML>
<HEAD>
<TITLE>My Home Page</TITLE>
</HEAD>
<!– Written by me –>
<!– Created: yesterday –>
<!– Last modified: today –>

<BODY>

Go to my favourite:
<BR><BLOCKQUOTE>
<A HREF="http://www.nri.gov">
<IMG SRC="images/na_btn.gif" ALT="logo"
ALIGN=top></A> |
<A HREF="#CITIES">Cities</A> |
<A HREF="#FOODS">Foods</A>
</BLOCKQUOTE><BR>
<H1>&#161;Viva M&eacute;xico&#33;</H1> <HR>
<A NAME="CITIES">
</A> My <EM>favourite</EM>
<OL>
<LI>New delhi
<LI>Delhi
<LI>India
</OL>
<P>
<A NAME="FOODS"></A>
Some of my <EM>favourite</EM> foods are:
<UL>
    <LI>Italian
    <UL>
       <LI>Lasagna        <LI>Pizza
       <LI>Prosciutto<LI>Ravioli
```

```
        <LI>Spaghetti
    </UL>
    <LI>Fruits
    <UL>
        <LI>Apples          <LI>Bananas
        <LI>Cherries  <LI>Figs
        <LI>Grapes          <LI>Melon
        <LI>Nectarines<LI>Oranges
        <LI>Papaya
    </UL>
</UL>
<DL>
<DT><STRONG>favourite</STRONG>
<DD>A person, or thing liked or prefered above
all others;
regarded with special favour; special. Things
I really like.
</DL>
</BODY>
</HTML>
```

Result:

My *favourite*:

1. New delhi
2. Delhi
3. India

Some of my *favourite* foods are:

- Italian
  - Lasagna
  - Pizza
  - Prosciutto
  - Ravioli
  - Spaghetti
- Fruits
  - Apples
  - Bananas

- Cherries
- Figs
- Grapes
- Melon
- Nectarines
- Oranges
- Papaya

8

Tables within HTML

Tables allow us to organize and present our data in an orderly and concise manner.

In this chapter we will learn about:

- The <TABLE> tag
- The <CAPTION> tag
- Table data, table headers, and table rows
- Table size and shape
  - Alignment
  - Border
  - Cell spacing
  - Width
- Spanning multiple rows and columns

THE TABLE TAG

Unfortunately, not all browsers support tables. However, tables can contain a wide variety of information, such as headers, anchors, lists, paragraphs, forms, images, preformatted text and even nested tables. Tables have rows and columns. HTML specifies tables by rows moving from left to right and from top to bottom. HTML tables are composed of cells. Information is contained in each cell. You can have empty cells. Cells can span multiple rows and multiple columns.

This may sound complicated, but fortunately HTML makes it simple. Start out with the <TABLE> tag, which tells HTML you are starting a table. Always end your table with the </TABLE> tag. Information about the table must be placed between the two markers, <TABLE> and </TABLE>.Tables are defined with the <table> tag. A table is divided into rows (with the <tr> tag), and each row is divided into data cells (with the <td> tag). The letters td stands for "table data," which is the content of a data cell. A data cell can contain text, images, lists, paragraphs, forms, horizontal rules, tables, etc.

```
<table border="1">
<tr>
<td>row 1, cell 1</td>
<td>row 1, cell 2</td>
</tr>
<tr>
<td>row 2, cell 1</td>
<td>row 2, cell 2</td>
</tr>
</table>
```

How it looks in a browser:

row 1, cell 1	row 1, cell 2
row 2, cell 1	row 2, cell 2

TABLES AND BORDER ATTRIBUTE

If you do not specify a border attribute the table will be displayed without any borders. Sometimes this can be useful, but most of the time, you want the borders to show.

To display a table with borders, you will have to use the border attribute:

```
<table border="1">
<tr>
<td>Row 1, cell 1</td>
<td>Row 1, cell 2</td>
</tr>
</table>
```

HEADINGS IN A TABLE

Headings in a table are defined with the <th> tag.

```
<table border="1">
<tr>
```

```
<th>Heading</th>
<th>Another Heading</th>
</tr>
<tr>
<td>row 1, cell 1</td>
<td>row 1, cell 2</td>
</tr>
<tr>
<td>row 2, cell 1</td>
<td>row 2, cell 2</td>
</tr>
</table>
```

How it looks in a browser:

Heading	Another Heading
row 1, cell 1	row 1, cell 2
row 2, cell 1	row 2, cell 2

EMPTY CELLS IN A TABLE

Table cells with no content are not displayed very well in most browsers:

```
<table border="1">
<tr>
<td>row 1, cell 1</td>
<td>row 1, cell 2</td>
</tr>
<tr>
<td>row 2, cell 1</td>
<td></td>
</tr>
</table>
```

How it looks in a browser:

row 1, cell 1	row 1, cell 2
row 2, cell 1	

Note that the borders around the empty table cell are missing (NB! Mozilla Firefox displays the border).

To avoid this, add a non-breaking space ( ) to empty data cells, to make the borders visible:

```
<table border="1">
<tr>
<td>row 1, cell 1</td>
<td>row 1, cell 2</td>
</tr>
<tr>
<td>row 2, cell 1</td>
<td> </td>
</tr>
</table>
```

How it looks in a browser:

Row 1, cell 1	row 1, cell 2
Row 2, cell 1	

BORDERS

Border="1"

Example Code Code Result

Border="7"

Example Code	Code Result

CAPTION

Caption Align="Top" (default)

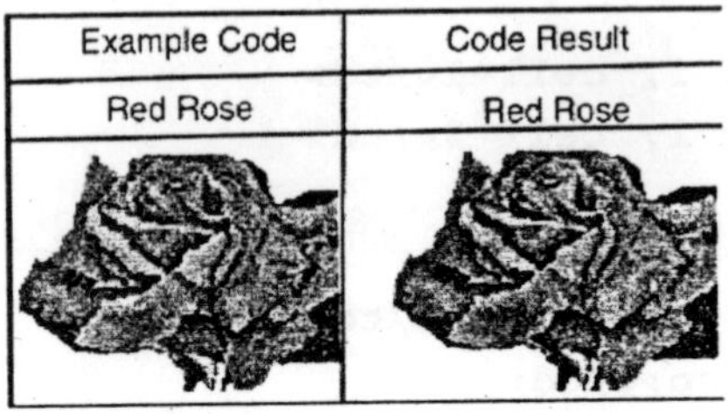

Caption="Bottom"

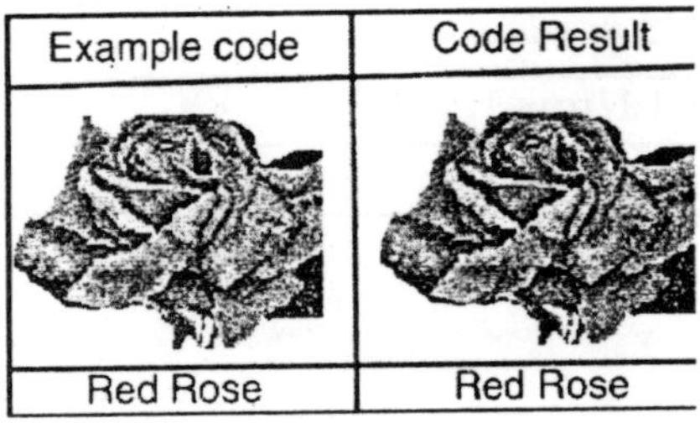

CELLPADDING

Cellpadding="5"

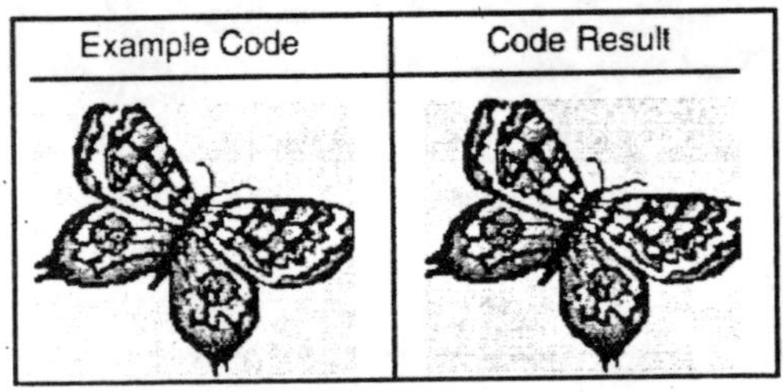

Cellpadding="10"

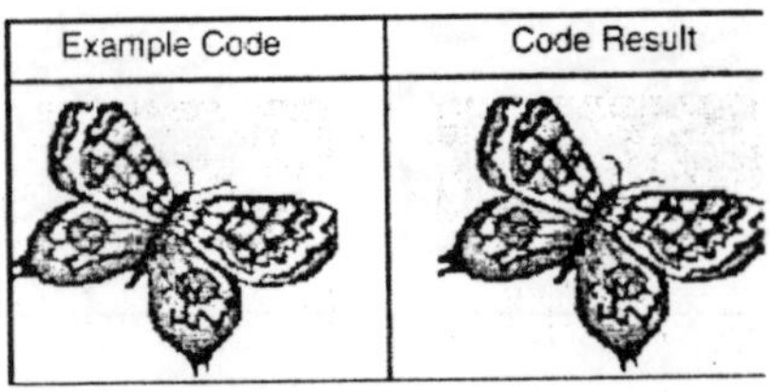

CELLSPACING

Cellspacing="5"

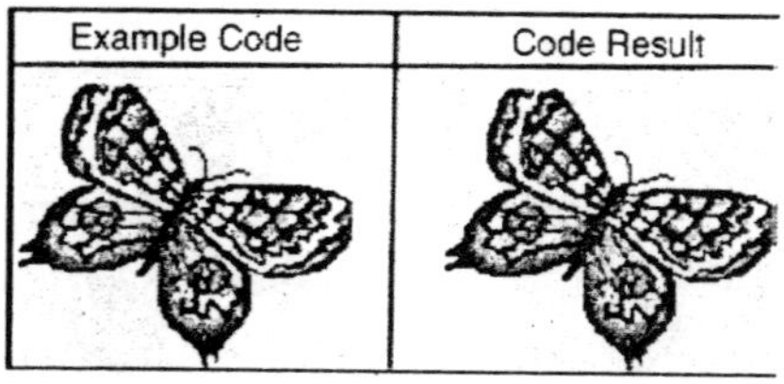

Cellspacing="10"

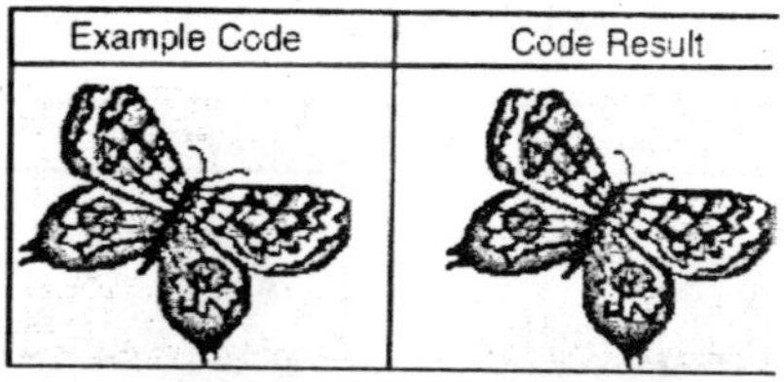

CELLPADDING AND CELLSPACING

Cellpadding="10" Cellspacing="10"

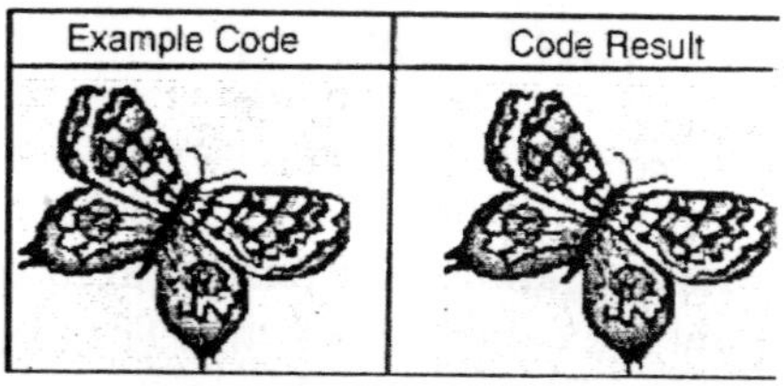

CELLPADDING, CELLSPACING AND IMG BORDER

Cellpadding="10", Cellspacing="10", Img Border="5"

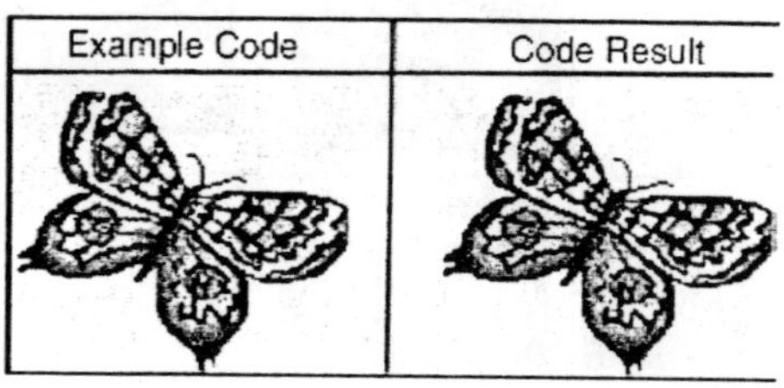

TABLE WITHIN TABLE

1x1 Table Within A 1x1 Table, Borders=1 & 3

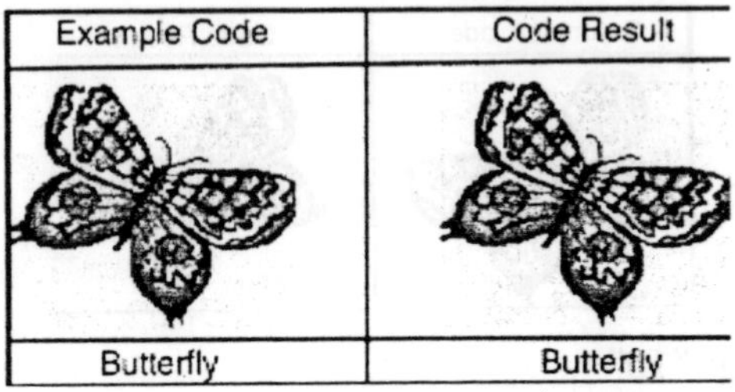

1x1 Table Within A 1x1 Table, Borders=7 & 7

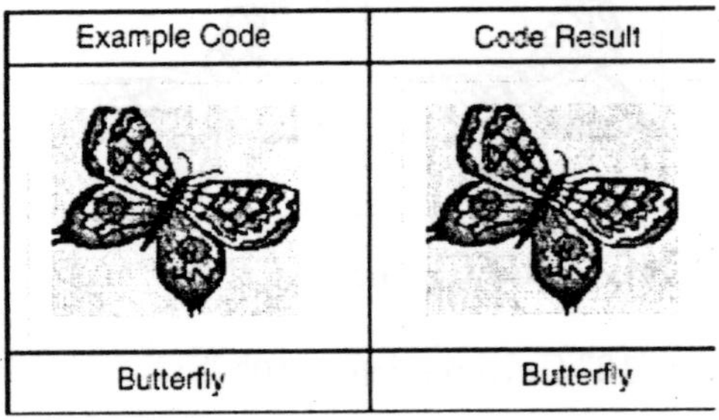

CENTERING IMAGES IN TABLES

In placing images in a table cell, any spaces between the tags in the coding may, depending upon the browser, get collapsed into space characters. These spaces can off center your image. Below are examples of this. For clarity, only the coding for the table cell with the image in it is shown. The table on the left has an image that is off-centered, the table on right has its image centered.

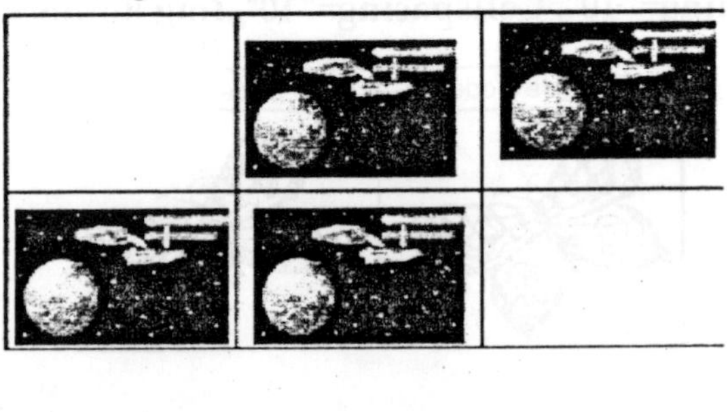

CELLPADDING

Cells within HTML tables can also have borders around them. One can specify the thickness of the border between cells. For example:

```
<TABLE BORDER="1" CELLPADDING="number"
CELLSPACING="number">
```

The CELLPADDING attribute separates text of the cell from the cell border with a padding with the specified number of pixels.

```
<TABLE BORDER="1" CELLPADDING="10"
CELLSPACING="0">
<CAPTION>Example 1: CELLPADDING</CAPTION>
<TR>
<TD>Apples</TD> <TD>Bananas</TD>
<TD>Cherries</TD>
</TR;
<TR>
<TD>Nectarines</TD> <TD>Oranges</TD>
<TD>Papaya</TD>
</TR>
</TABLE>
```

Example 1: CELLPADDING

Apples	Bananas	Cherries
Nectarines	Oranges	Papaya

CELLPADDING="10"

```
<TABLE BORDER="7"CELLPADDING="10">
<TR>
<TD>This is a TD cell</TD>
<TD><PRE> </PRE></TD>
<TH>This is a TH cell</TH>
</TR>
<TR>
<TH VALIGN="TOP">Text aligned top</TH>
<TH>Image in TH cell with default alignments
-></TH>
<TH><IMG SRC="blylplne.gif" ALT="airplane"></
```

```
TH>
</TR>
<TR>
<TH VALIGN="BOTTOM">Text aligned bottom</TH>
<TD><Image in TD cell with default alignments
-></TD>
<TD><IMG SRC="blylplne.gif" ALT="airplane"></
TD>
</TR>
</TABLE>
```

This is a TD cell		This a TH cell
Text aligned top	Image in TH cell with default alignments →	
Text aligned bottom	Image in TD cell with default alignments →	

CELLSPACING

The CELLSPACING attribute creates a space, or border, of the specified number of pixels, between each cell. The higher the number, the thicker the border.

```
    <TABLE BORDER="1" CELLPADDING="0"
CELLSPACING="10">
    <CAPTION>Example 2: CELLSPACING</CAPTION>
    <TR>
    <TD>Apples</TD> <TD>Bananas</TD>
    <TD>Cherries</TD></TR><TR><TD>Nectarines</TD>
    <TD>Oranges</TD> <TD>Papaya</TD>
    </TR>
    </TABLE>
```

Example: CELLSPACING

Apples	Bananas	Cherries

Nectarines	Oranges	Papaya

CELLSPACING="10"

```
<TABLE BORDER="7" CELLSPACING="10">
<TR>
<TD>This is a TD cell</TD>
<TD><PRE> </PRE></TD>
<TH>This is a TH cell</TH>
</TR>
<TR>
<TH VALIGN="TOP">Text aligned top</TH>
<TH>Image in TH cell with default alignments
-></TH>
<TH><IMG SRC="blylplne.gif" ALT="airplane"></
TH>
</TR>
<TR>
<TH VALIGN="BOTTOM">Text aligned bottom</TH>
<TD><Image in TD cell with default alignments
-></TD>
<TD><IMG SRC="blylplne.gif" ALT="airplane"></
TD>
</TR>
</TABLE>
```

This a TD cell		**This is a TH cell**
Text aligned top	Image in TH cell with default alignments →	
Text aligned bottom	Image in TD cell with default alignments →	

CELL WIDTH

Two Columns: First Cell Width="50%"

```
<TABLE BORDER="7">
```

```
<TR>
<TH WIDTH="50%">This cell will expand to 50%if
the contents of the other cell will allow.</
TH>
<TH>The first cell will expand to 50%if the
contents of this cell will allow.</TH>
</TR>
</TABLE>
```

This cell will expand to 50% if the contents of the other cell will allow.	The first cell will expand to 50% if the contents of this cell will allow.

Three Columns: First Cell Width="50%"

```
<TABLE BORDER="7">
<TR>
<TH WIDTH="50%">This cell will expand to 50%if
the contents of the other cells will allow.</
TH>
<TH>The first cell will expand to 50%if the
contents of the other cells will allow.</TH>
<TH>The first cell will expand to 50%if the
contents of the other cells will allow.</TH>
</TR>
</TABLE>
```

The first cell will expand to 50% if the contents of the other cells will allow.	The first cell will expand to 50% if the contents of the other cells will allow.	The first cell will expand to 50% if the contents of the other cells will allow.

COLSPAN

Colspan="2"

```
<TABLE BORDER="7">
<TR>
```

```
    <TD>This is a TD cell</TD>
    <TH COLSPAN="2">This TH cell spans two
columns</TH>
    </TR>
    <TR>
    <TD><PRE> </PRE></TD>
    <TD><PRE> </PRE></TD>
    <TH ALIGN="LEFT">Text aligned left</TH>
    </TR>
    <TR>
    <TD><PRE> </PRE></TD>
    <TH><IMG SRC="redball.gif" ALT="*"></TH>
    <TH ALIGN="RIGHT">Text aligned right</TH>
    </TR>
    </TABLE>
```

This a TD cell	This TH cell spans two columns
	Text aligned left
	Text aligned right

NULCELL

```
    <TABLE BORDER="7">
    <TD><PRE> </PRE></TD>
    <TH>Below is a null cell.</TH>
    <TD><PRE> </PRE></TD>
    </TR>
    <TR>
    <TD><PRE> </PRE></TD>
    <TD></TD>
    <TD><PRE> </PRE></TD>
    </TR>
    <TR>
    <TD><PRE> </PRE></TD>
    <TH>Above is a null cell.</TH>
    <TD><PRE> </PRE></TD>
    </TR>
    /TABLE>
```

Below is a null cell.
Above is a null cell

ROWSPAN

Rowspan="3"

```
<TABLE BORDER="7">
<TR>
<TD>This is a TD cell</TD>
<TH ROWSPAN="2"><This TH cell spans three
rows</TH>
<TH>This is a TH cell</TH>
</TR>
<TR>
<TD><PRE> </PRE></TD>
<TD><PRE> </PRE></TD>
</TR>
<TR>
TH ALIGN="LEFT">Text aligned left</TH>
<TH ALIGN="RIGHT">Text aligned right</TH>
</TR>
</TABLE>
```

This is a TD cell	This TH cell spans three rows	This is a TH cell
Text aligned left		Text aligned right

TABLE WITHIN A 3X3 TABLE

```
<TABLE BORDER="7" CELLSPACING="10">
<TR>
<TH><IMG SRC="redball.gif" ALT="*"></TH>
<TD><PRE> </PRE></TD>
<TH><IMG SRC="redball.gif" ALT="*"></TH>
</TR>
<TR>
<TD><PRE> </PRE></TD>
```

```
<TD>
<TABLE BORDER="7" CELLSPACING="5">
<CAPTION ALIGN="BOTTOM">
The USS Enterprise arrives home
</CAPTION>
<TR>
<TD><IMG SRC="ee.jpg" ALT="Star Trek pic"></
TD>
</TR>
</TABLE>
</TD><TD><PRE> </PRE></TD>
</TR>
<TR>
<TD ALIGN=:LEFT"><B>Bold Text in a TD cell</
B></TD>
<TD><BR></TD>
<TD><I>Italic Text in a TD cell</I></TD>
</TR>
</TABLE>
```

COLOUR IN TABLES

In Tr Tag With Image

Example code

```
<TABLE BORDER="7"
CELLPADDING="7"CELLSPACING="10">
<TR BGCOLOUR="#00FF00">
<TD><IMG SRC="rrose.gif" ALT="rose"></TD>
<TD>Image is a transparent.gif.</TD>
</TR>
</TABLE>
```

Results of example code

Image is a
transparent.gif.

In Tr And Td/H Tags, Colspan And Rowspan

Example code

```
<TABLE BORDER="7" CELLPADDING="7"
```

```
CELLSPACING="10">
   <TR BGCOLOUR="#00FF00">
   <TD>A green row.</TD>
   <TD BGCOLOUR="#FFFF00">This cell should be
yellow, overriding the row colour.</TD>
   <TD>Back to the row colour.</TD>
   <TR BGCOLOUR="#0000FF">
   <TD>A blue row.</TD>
   <TD><PRE> </PRE></TD>
   <TD ROWSPAN="2">This cell takes the colour of
   the topmost row that it spans</TD>
   </TR>
   <TR BGCOLOUR="#FF0000">
   <TD>A red row.</TD>
   </TR>
   </TABLE>
```

Results of example code

A green row.	This cell should be yellow, overriding the row colour.	Back to the row colour.
A blue row.		This cell takes the colour of the topmost row that it spans.
	A red row.	

In Table And Tr Tags

Example code

```
<TABLE BGCOLOUR="#FF0000" BORDER="7"
CELLPADDING="7" CELLSPACING="10">
<TR>
<TD>The table has a red background</TD>
<TD><PRE> </PRE></TD>
</TR>
<TR>
<TD BGCOLOUR="#0000FF">BGCOLOUR in TD/H
```

```
or TR overrides BGCOLOUR in the TABLE
tag.</TD>
<TD><PRE> </PRE></TD>
</TR>
</TABLE>
```

Results of example code

The table has a red background

BGCOLOUR in TD/H or TR overrides BGCOLOUR in the TABLE tag.

In Table Tags, 1x1 Table Within A 1x1 Table, Borders=7 & 7

```
Example Code
<TABLE BORDER="7" CELLPADDING="10"
CELLSPACING="10" BGCOLOUR="#0000FF">
<CAPTION ALIGN="BOTTOM">Butterfly</CAPTION>
<TR>
<TD>
<TABLE BORDER="7" CELLPADDING="10"
CELLSPACING="10" BGCOLOUR=#FF0000>
<TR>
<TD><IMG SRC="bfly.gif" ALT="butterfly"></TD>
</TR></TABLE></TD>
</TR>
</TABLE>
```

Code Result

Butterfly

In Table Tags, Cellspacing Colouring

Example A: with an outer border

Example Code

```
<TABLE BORDER="0" CELLPADDING="0"
 CELLSPACING="0"BGCOLOUR="#0000FF">
<TR>
<TD>
<TABLE BORDER="5" CELLPADDING="10
CELLSPACING="10">
<TR>
<TD BGCOLOUR="#FFFFFE"> blah blah blah blah</
TD>
<TD BGCOLOUR="#FFFFFE"> more blah blah blah
blah</TD>
</TR>
</TABLE>
</TD>
</TR>
</TABLE>
```

Code Result

blah blah blah blah

more blah blah blah blah

Example B: with no outer border

Example Code

```
<TABLE BORDER="0" CELLPADDING="0"
CELLSPACING="0" BGCOLOUR="#0000FF">
<TR>
<TD>
<TABLE BORDER="0" CELLPADDING="10"
CELLSPACING="10">
<TR>
<TD BGCOLOUR="#FFFFFE"> blah blah blah blah</
TD><TD BGCOLOUR="#FFFFFE"> more blah blah blah
blah</TD>
</TR>
</TABLE>
</TD>
</TR>
```

```
</TABLE>
```

Code Result

blah blah blah blah

more blah blah blah blah

Table Colours With Font Colours

Example code

```
<TABLE BGCOLOUR="#FF0000" BORDER="0"
CELLPADDING="7" CELLSPACING="0">
<TR>
<TH BGCOLOUR="#FF8000"><FONT COLOUR=#804000"
SIZE="6">
H<BR>T<BR>M<BR>L<BR></FONT></TH>
<TH BGCOLOUR="#804000">
<FONT COLOUR=#FF8000" SIZE="5" FACE="ARIAL">
Mountain Dragon<BR>Web Designs</FONT></TH>
<TH BGCOLOUR="#FF8000"><PRE> </PRE></TH>
</TR>
</TABLE>
```

Results of example code

HTML

Mountain DragonWeb Designs

THE CAPTION TAG

A caption is like a title to your table which resides outside the border of the table. HTML tables start with an optional caption. The <CAPTION> tag is placed immediately after the <TABLE> tag. Place the text of the caption between the <CAPTION> tag and the </CAPTION> tag.

For example:

```
<TABLE>
<CAPTION>Favourite Foods</CAPTION>
</TABLE>
```

Example:

```
<table border="1" width="100%">
<caption>Table Caption</caption>
<tr>
<td>Left cell</td>
```

```
<td>Right cell</td>
</tr>
</table>
```

This will produce following result:

Left cell	Right cell

TABLE HEADER - TABLE ROW

HTML tables are organized by rows. Use the <TR> tag to start a table row, and use the </TR> tag to end the row. Now that you have specified a row, data or headings need to go into the cells that make up a row. The content of a cell is placed between the <TD> tag and the </TD> tag if data is to go into the cell or if a heading is to go into the cell, then the heading is placed between the <TH> tag and the </TH> tag. If you wish to have an empty cell, place the start marker and the end marker right next to each other with no space in between.

For example:

```
<TABLE>
<CAPTION>Favourite Foods</CAPTION>
<TR>
<TH>Italian</TH>
<TH>Fruits</TH>
</TR>
<TR>
<TD>Lasagna</TD>    <TD>Apples</TD>    </TR>
<TR>
<TD>Pizza</TD>      <TD>Bananas</TD>   </TR>
<TR>
<TD>Prosciutto</TD> <TD>Cherries</TD>  </TR>
<TR>
<TD>Ravioli</TD>    <TD>Figs</TD> </TR>
<TR>
<TD>Spaghetti</TD>  <TD>Grapes</TD>    </TR>
<TR>
<TD></TD>        <TD>Melon</TD></TR>
<TR>
<TD></TD>   <TD>Nectarines</TD>   </TR>
<TR>
```

```
<TD></TD>          <TD>Oranges</TD>    </TR>
<TR>
 <TD></TD>         <TD>Papaya</TD>     </TR>
</TABLE>
```

Would display this table on the user's screen

Table. Favourite Foods

Italian	**Fruits**
Lasagna	Apples
Pizza	Bananas
Prosciutto	Cherries
Ravioli	Figs
Spaghetti	Grapes
	Melon
	Nectarines
	Oranges
	Papaya

The difference between a table data element and a table header element is that the display of the information in the header cell will appear in a bolder type than in a data cell. Also, the default alignment of the information in the header cell is CENTER, while the default alignment of a data cell is LEFT.

TABLE ALIGNMENT

HTML tables can be aligned on the page, and cell content can be aligned within the cell. Both cases, the whole table and individual cells use the same attribute. This attribute is **ALIGN.** *To align a table on the page use the follow syntax within the <TABLE> tag:*

```
<TABLE ALIGN="alignment">
```

Where alignment can be one of the following options:

BLEEDLEFT	LEFT	CENTER	JUSTIFY	RIGHT	BLEEDRIGHT
Align to the leftmost edge of the window.	Align to the left text margin.	Align to the center of the window.	Adjust the table size to align to both text	Aligns to the right text margin. margins.	Aligns to the rightmost edge of the window.

To align the information within the cell use the ALIGN attribute within the <TD> marker or within the <TH> marker. Remember, the default alignment of the information in the header cell is CENTER, while the default alignment of a data cell is LEFT. So, the ALIGN attribute is optional. However, it was used in the table shown above to align the header and data cells.

ALIGN="LEFT"

Table aligned left

ALIGN="CENTER"

Table aligned center —Default setting.

ALIGN="RIGHT"

Table aligned right

TABLE WIDTH

- WIDTH="100%"
  Table expands...... to the entire window width.
- WIDTH="50%"
  Table expands... to fill half of the window's width.
- WIDTH="500"
  Table width set at.... 500 pixels.
- WIDTH="300"
  Table width set at...... 300 pixels.

TABLE WIDTH

One can specify the width of the table with the WIDTH attribute. For example:

```
<TABLE WIDTH="per cent">
```

Usually this is expressed as a percentage of the width of the text area of the page. Here are two table examples, the first one with WIDTH="10%" and the second one with WIDTH="100%".

```
<TABLE BORDER="1" WIDTH="10%">
<CAPTION>Example 1: TABLE WIDTH="10%"</
CAPTION>
<TR>
<TD>Apples</TD><TD>Bananas</TD> <TD>Cherries</
TD>
</TR>
```

```
<TR>
<TD>Nectarines</TD> <TD>Oranges</TD>
<TD>Papaya</TD>
</TR>
</TABLE>
```

Example: Table Width ="10%"

Apples	Bananas	Cherries
Nectarines	Oranges	Papaya

```
<TABLE BORDER="1" WIDTH="100%">
<CAPTION>Example 2: TABLE WIDTH="100%"</
CAPTION>
<TR>
<TD>Apples</TD> <TD>Bananas</TD>
<TD>Cherries</TD>
</TR>
<TR>
<TD>Nectarines</TD> <TD>Oranges</TD>
<TD>Papaya</TD>
</TR></TABLE>
```

Example: Table Width ="100%"

Apples	Bananas	Cherries
Nectarines	Oranges	Papaya

HTML will not always give you a table of the specified width because it has to fit the data into the cell. In Example 1 above, the table data is wider than 10% because the browser made the table wider in order to fit the data into the cell.

SPANNING MULTIPLE ROWS AND COLUMNS

Cells within HTML tables can span multiple rows and multiple columns. The cell default is one row and one column. However, with the ROWSPAN attribute a cell can span more than one row, and with the COLSPAN attribute a cell can span more than one column. Here are two table examples, the first one with cells spanning multiple columns using the COLSPAN attribute and the second one with cells spanning multiple rows using ROWSPAN attribute.

```
<TABLE BORDER="1">
```

```
<CAPTION>Example 1: COLSPAN</CAPTION>
<TR>
<TD>Apples</TD> <TD COLSPAN="2">Bananas</TD>
<TD COLSPAN="2">Cherries</TD>
</TR>
<TR>
<TD COLSPAN="3">Nectarines</TD> <TD>Oranges</
TD>
<TD>Papaya</TD>
</TR>
</TABLE>
```

Example 1: COLSPAN

Apples	Bananas	Cherries
Nectarines	Oranges	Papaya

```
<TABLE BORDER="1">
<CAPTION>
Example 2: ROWSPAN</CAPTION>
<TR>
<TD ROWSPAN="4">Apples</TD> <TD>Bananas</TD>
<TD ROWSPAN="4">Cherries</TD>
</TR>
<TR>
<TD>Nectarines</TD>
</TR>
<TR>
<TD>Oranges</TD>
</TR>
<TR>
<TD>Papaya</TD>
</TR>
</TABLE>
```

EXAMPLE

To the HTML file you have been working on, create a table, with a caption, using the lists and the same NASA button used in the exercise of the last chapter, similar to the example shown below.

```
<HTML>
<HEAD>
<TITLE>My Home Page</TITLE>
</HEAD>
<!— Written by me —>
<!— Created: yesterday —>
<!— Last modified: today —>
<BODY>
<TABLE BORDER="1" WIDTH="100%"
CELLPADDING="5">
<CAPTION>My Favourites</CAPTION>
<TR>
   <TH ROWSPAN="2">Web Site</TH>
   <TH COLSPAN="2">Foods</TH>
   <TH ROWSPAN="2">Cities</TH>
</TR>
<TR>
   <TH>Italian</TH> <TH>Fruits</TH>
</TR>
<TR>
<TD ALIGN="CENTER">
<A HREF="http://www.nri.gov">
<IMG SRC="images/btn.gif" ALT="logo"></A></TD>
<TD><UL>
    <LI>Lasagna     <LI>Pizza
    <LI>Prosciutto  <LI>Ravioli
    <Li>Papaya
   </UL>
</TD>
<TD><UL>
    <LI>Apples  <LI>Bananas
    <LI>Cherries    <LI>Figs
    <LI>Grapes  <LI>Melon
    <LI>Nectarines <LI>Oranges
    <LI>Papaya
   </UL>
</TD>
<TD><OL>
```

```
        <LI>Rio de Janeiro
    <LI>Paris
    <LI>Venice
       </OL>
   </TD>
   </TR>
   </TABLE>
   <P>
   <DL>
   <DT>
   <STRONG>favourite</STRONG>
   <DD>A person, or thing liked or prefered above
   all others; regarded with special favour;
special.
   </DL>
   </BODY>
   </HTML>
```

9

Forms within HTML

Forms are commonly used for questionnaires, order forms, data entry, and a wide variety of other applications. In this chapter we will learn about:

- The <FORM> tag.
- Different methods of form input
  - Text
  - Textarea
  - Checkbox
  - Hidden
  - Password
  - Radi
  - Reset
  - Select
  - Submit

THE FORM TAG

Forms are very common in web pages through out Internet. Web forms are mostly used to capture user entered data and post them back to the server. You can see signup forms, login forms, profile update forms and many more type of forms. Designing a form is based on the data format requirement. For example you want the users to tell about their sex. Here the user will enter one out of the two choices available, so one period button is to be provided for the user to select. Same way one input text box is to be provided for entering name of the joining member. Based on different data format requirements we can keep different form components.

Here we will discuss different types of components used to collect data and their possible use. Before that let us try to understand the basic form structure or syntax. The <FORM> tag resides within the body of the HTML document. To create a form, first start with the <FORM> tag with the following basic syntax:

```
<FORM METHOD="GET or POST" ACTION="URL">
```

Where URL is the URL of the file to access which will perform the action when the form is submitted. This URL is often a perl script, or a computer programme that acts on the information found on the form. The METHOD attribute is optional. The choices for METHOD are GET and POST. GET is the default. Use GET when you are only getting information from the server. Use POST when you want to send or post information to the server, such as updating a database entry. Also use POST when you are getting and posting information.

POST is preferred because the amount of information you can send is unlimited. End the form with the </FORM> tag, because otherwise you will get errors in your HTML code. Note that you can have more than one form in a document but you cannot have nested forms. Between the <FORM> tag and the </FORM> tag, you can have different ypes of input. These input tags provide the interface for the user to input data.

INPUT TYPE="TEXT"

The text box allows for one line of text to be entered by the viewer. It uses the following syntax:

```
<INPUT TYPE="TEXT" NAME="name of variable"
VALUE="value" SIZE="size" MAXLENGTH="length">
```

Where INPUT TYPE="TEXT"

specifies the input to be a text box. The NAME is the name of the variable. For example, NAME="postal_code". The user would input a number or a string of characters and that number or string would be the value assigned to the name of the variable "postal_code".

```
Only <INPUT TYPE="TEXT" NAME="name of
variable">
```

Is required syntax for the text box input. The other attributes are optional. If the VALUE attribute is specified that value will appear in the text box. This is used to save some typing. The user can override this. The SIZE attribute denotes the size of the text box. The SIZE is specified in number of characters. The default SIZE varies from browser to browser. The MAXLENGTH attribute limits the length of the input character string. MAXLENGTH can be greater than SIZE, in which case the text box will scroll, or MAXLENGTH can be less than or equal to SIZE.

Top of Form

Example:

```
Please enter country of residence:<BR><INPUT
TYPE="TEXT" NAME="country">
```

TEXTAREA

Text Area is nothing but multiline textbox. TextArea is mainly used when the user has to enter large amount of text. The text area allows for one or more lines of text to be entered by the viewer. It uses the following syntax:

```
<TEXTAREA NAME="name of variable" ROWS="number
of rows" COLS="number of columns">
```

Where TEXTAREA specifies the input is to be an area of text. The NAME is the name of the variable. For example, NAME="description".

The user would input a long character string such as a few sentences describing of an object. This long character string would be the value assigned to the name of the variable "description". ROWS specifies the number of rows of characters in the text area, and COLS specifies the number of columns, or characters in each row, in the text area.

ATTRIBUTES OF TEXTAREA FIELD

- *Name*: Specifies the name of the object through which it can be referenced.
- *Rows*: Specifies the height of the textarea in characters. Cols: Specifies the width of the textarea in characters.

- *Wrap*: Specifies how the text is wrapped when it reaches the right-hand edge of the textarea box. This attribute possibly takes the following values
- *Off*: If the wrap attribute is set to 'Off' then the text will not wrap and is submitted as it is entered by the user.
- *Readonly*: This attribute will not let the user change the contents of the field.

Example

```
<TextArea name="txtArea" rows=5 cols=35>
This is the default text
</TextArea>
```

These are required attributes, as is the </TEXTAREA> tag. Note that this is different than text box which did not require an ending tag.

Top of Form

Here is a basic example:

```
Please list your favourite foods:<BR>
<TEXTAREA NAME="foods" ROWS="3" COLS="40">
</TEXTAREA>
```

Bottom of Form

INPUT TYPE="RADIO"

Radio buttons are mainly used when the user has to select only one among a group of options.

Radio button has two states and can toggle between them. Several radio buttons can be grouped together so that only one radio button can be selected at any given time. We can group radio buttons by giving *same name* to all the radiobuttons.

A single radio button can be created as:

```
<input type="radio" name="radiogroupname"
value="value of the object" checked>
```

ATTRIBUTES OF RADIO BUTTON FIELD

- *Name*: Specifies the group name of the object.

- *Value*: Specifies the value of the radio button.
- *Checked*: If given, the radiobutton will be selected else, it will not be selected.
- *Align*: Specifies the alignment of the radio buttons.

EXAMPLE

Gender: <input type="radio" name="grpGender" value="Male" Checked> <input type="radio" name=" grpGender" value="Female">The above code places two radio buttons with a group name of "grpgender", one with a value "Male" and other one with value "Female". As the checked property is given for the first radio button it will be selected by default. This will give the output like:

Gender:

- Male
- Female

The radio button is used to select only one item from a list.

Please choose an ice cream flavour:

- Chocolate
- Grape
- Lemon
- Strawberry
- Vanilla

As you can see, you cannot have tutti-frutti. Radio buttons allow for only one selection. The input type is called "radio" because they act as push buttons on an old car radio.

SYNTAX

Radio buttons use the following syntax:

```
<INPUT TYPE="RADIO" NAME="name of variable"
VALUE="value of variable"> text description
```

Where VALUE will be assigned to NAME when the particular radio button is selected. Optionally you may add the CHECKED attribute. The CHECKED attribute will show the button as being pre-selected.

INPUT TYPE="CHECKBOX"

Checkboxes are objects of a HTML form which behaves

like a toggle switch. i.e, a checkbox can be in one of the two states, either checked or unchecked. Checkboxes are used to return a single specific value to a webserver i.e, either true or false or 1 or 0. The checkbox is identical to the radio button except that you may select one or more items from a list and the selections are marked with an X inside a square box.:

Please choose an ice cream flavour:

- Chocolate
- Grape
- Lemon
- Strawberry
- Vanilla

As you can see, you can have tutti-frutti. The checkbox syntax is very similar to that of radio. Here is the syntax:

```
<INPUT TYPE="CHECKBOX" NAME="name of variable"
VALUE="value of variable"> text description.
```

ATTRIBUTES

- *Name*: Specifies the name of the object through which it can be referenced.
- *Value*: Specifies the value of the checkbox. This value will be returned if the checkbox is checked.
- *Checked*: If given, the checkbox will be checked by default else, it will not be checked.

EXAMPLE

Favourite colours:

```
<input type="checkbox" name="blue" value="yes"
Checked>
<input type="Red" name="red" value="yes">
```

This will give the output like:

Favourite Colour(s): Blue Red

SELECT

Another way to enter data is through a pop-up box, where you select from a list of choices. The selection method is more complicated than RADIO or CHECKBOX, but it allows more flexibility.

Here is the syntax:

```
<SELECT NAME="variable name" MULTIPLE
SIZE="size">
<OPTION> text description
<OPTION SELECTED> text description
<OPTION VALUE="value"> text description
</SELECT>
```

Where <SELECT> marks the start and </SELECT> marks the end of the specification of the pop-up box. NAME is the same as NAME found in RADIO and CHECKBOX. It is the name of the variable. MULTIPLE is an optional attribute which, if included, allows for all options to be displayed. If MULTIPLE is not included, then only one option from the list will appear. SIZE represents the number of lines that will appear in the pop-up box.

The default is one line. OPTION is required. Each OPTION line is a line in the pop-up box. It is always good to have a "text description". Otherwise, you will have a blank line. SELECTED means that this particular OPTION wll appear in the pop-up box.

This is similar to the CHECKED attribute found in RADIO and CHECKBOX. VALUE is the value to be assigned to the selected option. If VALUE is not specified, then the "text description" will become the assigned value.

Here is an example:

```
Please choose an ice cream flavour.
<SELECT NAME="flavour">
<OPTION VALUE="chocolate"> chocolate
<OPTION SELECTED VALUE="grape"> grape
<OPTION VALUE="lemon"> lemon
<OPTION VALUE="strawberry"> strawberry
<OPTION VALUE="vanilla"> vanilla
</SELECT>
```

INPUT TYPE="PASSWORD"

Password type input is similar to that of the text box. Both allow for one line of text to be entered by the viewer. The difference is that the input is shown as asterisks.

It uses the following syntax:

```
<INPUT TYPE="PASSWORD" NAME="name of variable"
VALUE="value" SIZE="size" MAXLENGTH="length">
```

Where INPUT TYPE="PASSWORD" specifies the input to be a text box with text as asterisks. The NAME is the name of the variable.

For example, NAME="secret_code". The user would input a number or a string of characters and that number or string would be the value assigned to the name of the variable "secret_code".

```
Only <INPUT TYPE="PASSWORD" NAME="name of
variable">
```

Is required syntax for the input. The other attributes are optional. If the VALUE attribute is specified that value will appear in the text box. This is used to save some typing. The user can override this.

The SIZE attribute denotes the size of the text box. The SIZE is specified in number of characters. The default SIZE varies from browser to browser. The MAXLENGTH attribute limits the length of the input character string. MAXLENGTH can be greater than SIZE, in which case the text box will scroll, or MAXLENGTH can be less than or equal to SIZE.

Here is a basic example:

```
Please enter country of residence:<BR>
<INPUT TYPE="PASSWORD" NAME="country">
```

INPUT TYPE = SUBMIT

Submit buttons have a special purpose. i.e, when the submit button is clicked, then the form will be submitted to the page specified in the action attribute of the form tag along with its data.Submit button can be created as: <input type="Submit" name="<Name of the submit button >" value="valueof the button">

ATTRIBUTES OF SUBMIT BUTTON:

- *Name*: Specifies the name of the object through which it can be referenced.

- *Value*: Specifies the value of the submit button. this will be displayed on the submit button.

EXAMPLE:

```
    <input type="submit" name="submitbtn"
value="Submit">
```

This places a submit button within the HTML form, which can be referenced by using its name "submitbtn" The submit button will be displayed as below:

Submit

EXAMPLE

To the HTML file you have been working on, create a form inside the table, similar to the example shown below.

```
    <HTML>
    <HEAD>
    <TITLE>My Home Page</TITLE>
    </HEAD>
    <!— Written by me —>
    <!— Created: yesterday —>
    <!— Last modified: today —>
    <BODY>
    <FORM ACTION="exer9.htm" METHOD="POST">
    <TABLE BORDER="1" WIDTH="100%"
CELLPADDING="5">
    <CAPTION>What Are Your Favourites</CAPTION>
    <TR>
        <TH ROWSPAN="2">Web Site</TH>
        <TH COLSPAN="2">Foods</TH>
        <TH ROWSPAN="2">Cities</TH>
    </TR>
    <TR>
        <TH>Italian</TH> <TH>Fruits</TH>
    </TR>
    <TR>
    <TD ALIGN="CENTER">
        Please enter your favourite Web Site<BR>
        <INPUT TYPE="TEXT" NAME="web_site"
```

```
        VALUE="http://" SIZE="16">
    </TD>
    <TD>
        Please enter your favourite<BR>
        <SELECT NAME="italian_food" MULTIPLE>
        <OPTION VALUE="lasagna"> Lasagna
        <OPTION VALUE="pizza"> Pizza
        <OPTION SELECTED VALUE="prosciutto">
    Prosciutto
        <OPTION VALUE="ravioli"> Ravioli
        <OPTION VALUE="spaghetti"> Spaghetti
        </SELECT>
    </TD>
    <TD>
        Please enter your favourite<BR>
        <INPUT TYPE="CHECKBOX" NAME="fruit1"
    VALUE="apples"> Apples<BR>
        <INPUT TYPE="CHECKBOX" NAME="fruit2"
    VALUE="bananas"> Bananas<BR>
        <INPUT TYPE="CHECKBOX" NAME="fruit3"
    VALUE="cherries"> Cherries<BR>
        <INPUT TYPE="CHECKBOX" NAME="fruit4"
    VALUE="figs"> Figs<BR>
        <INPUT TYPE="CHECKBOX" NAME="fruit5"
    VALUE="grapes"> Grapes<BR>
        <INPUT TYPE="CHECKBOX" NAME="fruit6"
    VALUE="melon"> Melon<BR>
        <INPUT TYPE="CHECKBOX" NAME="fruit7"
    VALUE="nectarines"> Nectarines<BR>
        <INPUT TYPE="CHECKBOX" NAME="fruit8"
    VALUE="oranges"> Oranges<BR>
        <INPUT TYPE="CHECKBOX" NAME="fruit9"
    VALUE="papaya"> Papaya<BR>
    </TD>
    <TD>
        Please enter your favourite<BR>
           Rio de Janeiro
        <INPUT TYPE="RADIO" NAME="city"
```

```
    VALUE="rio"><BR>
          Paris
       <INPUT TYPE="RADIO" NAME="city"
    VALUE="par"><BR>
          Venice
       <INPUT TYPE="RADIO" NAME="city"
    VALUE="ven"><BR>
    </TD>
    </TR>
    </TABLE>
    <CENTER>
    <INPUT TYPE="RESET" VALUE=" Erase ">
    <INPUT TYPE="SUBMIT" VALUE=" Finished ">
    </CENTER>
    </FORM>
    <P>
    <DL>
    <DT><STRONG>favourite</STRONG>
    <DD>A person, or thing liked or prefered above
    all others;regarded with special favour;
special.
    </DL>
    </BODY>
    </HTML>
```

Results:

Table. Favourites

Web Site	**Foods**		**Cities**
Italian Fruits			
Please enter your favourite Web Site	Please enter your favourite	Please enter your favourite Apples Bananas Cherries Figs Grapes Melon Nectarines	Please enter your favourite Rio de Janeiro Paris Venice

Oranges
Papaya

Erase Finished

Bottom of Form

Attributes of Checkbox Field:

- *Name*: Specifies the name of the object through which it can be referenced.
- *Value*: Specifies the value of the checkbox. This value will be returned if the checkbox is checked.
- *Checked*: If given, the checkbox will be checked by default else, it will not be checked.

Example:

Favourite colours:

```
<input type="checkbox" name="blue" value="yes"
Checked> <input type="Red" name="red" value="yes">
```

This will give the output like:

Favourite Colour(s): Blue Red Bottom of Form

10

XML

INTRODUCTION

Because of the lack of SGML support in mainstream Web browsers, most applications that deliver SGML information over the Web convert the SGML to HTML. This down-translation removes much of the intelligence of the original SGML information. That lost intelligence virtually eliminates information flexibility and poses a significant barrier to reuse, interchange, and automation.For this reason, XML (Extensible Markup Language) was developed by the XML working group (known as the SGML Editorial Review Board) formed under the auspices of the World Wide Web Consortium (W3C) in 1996.

XML is a highly functional subset of SGML. The purpose of XML is to specify an SGML subset that works very well for delivering SGML information over the Web. When the mainstream Web browsers support XML, it is believed that it's going to be very easy to publish SGML information on the Web. It's actually misnamed because XML is not a single Markup Language.

It is a metalanguage to let users design their own markup language.XML is a public format and not a proprietary format of any company. The v 1.0 specifications was accepted by the W3C as Recommendation on February 10, 1998. XML was conceived as a means of regaining the power and flexibility of SGML without most of its complexity. While retaining the beneficial features of SGML, XML removes many of the more complex features of SGML that make the authoring and design of suitable software both difficult and costly. But XML also lacks some important capabilities of SGML that primarily affect document creation, not document delivery. That's because XML was not designed to replace SGML in every respect.The question that is open is not whether XML will succeed as a widespread data format, but rather how fast, to what level of success and with what products. The question of whether XML would enter the market was answered when Microsoft, Adobe, Netscape and other big market players not only supported the development of the new standard but began making sizable product investments to this new format.

The leading Web browser Products already support XML in their latest releases. The momentum building behind the XML effort means that XML is inevitably destined to become the mainstream technology for powering broadly functional and highly valuable business applications on the Internet, intranets, and extranets.

BASIC

WHAT IS XML

- XML stands for EXtensible Markup Language
- XML is a markup language much like HTML
- XML was designed to carry data, not to display data
- XML tags are not predefined. You must define your own tags
- XML is designed to be self-descriptive
- XML is a W3C Recommendation

XML: EXTENSIBLE MARKUP LANGUAGE

XML is a framework for defining markup languages:there is no fixed collection of markup tags - we may define our own tags, tailored for our kind of informationeach XML language is targeted at its own application domain, but the languages will share many featuresthere is a common set of generic tools for processing documentsXML is *not* a replacement for HTML:HTML should ideally be just another XML languagein fact, XHTML is just thatXHTML is a (very popular) XML language for hypertext markupXML is designed to:separate syntax from semantics to provide a common framework for structuring information (browser rendering semantics is completely defined by stylesheets);allow tailor-made markup for any imaginable application domainsupport internationalization (Unicode) and platform independencebe the future of structured information, including databases

Difference Between XML and HTML

XML is not a replacement for HTML.XML and HTML were designed with different goals:

- XML was designed to transport and store data, with focus on what data is.
- HTML was designed to display data, with focus on how data looks.

HTML is about displaying information, while XML is about carrying information.

Function of XML

Maybe it is a little hard to understand, but XML does not DO·anything. XML was created to structure, store, and transport information.

The following example is a note to Tove from Jani, stored as XML:

```
<note>
<to>Tove</to>
<from>Jani</from>
<heading>Reminder</heading>
<body>Don't forget me this weekend!</body>
</note>
```

The note above is quite self descriptive. It has sender and receiver information, it also has a heading and a message body. But still, this XML document does not DO anything. It is just pure information wrapped in tags. Someone must write a piece of software to send, receive or display it.

XML as Plain Text

XML is nothing special. It is just plain text. Software that can handle plain text can also handle XML.However, XML-aware applications can handle the XML tags specially. The functional meaning of the tags depends on the nature of the application.

XML Tags

The tags in the example above (like <to> and <from>) are not defined in any XML standard. These tags are "invented" by the author of the XML document.That is because the XML language has no predefined tags. The tags used in HTML (and the structure of HTML) are predefined. HTML documents can only use tags defined in the HTML standard (like <p>, <h1>, etc.).XML allows the author to define his own tags and his own document structure.

XML not a Replacement for HTML

XML is a complement to HTML.It is important to understand that XML is not a replacement for HTML. In most web applications, XML is used to transport data, while HTML is used to format and display the data.My best description of XML is this:

W3C Recommendation

XML became a W3C Recommendation 10. February 1998.To read more about the XML activities at W3C, please read our W3C Tutorial.

XML is Everywhere

We have been participating in XML development since its creation. It has been amazing to see how quickly the XML standard has developed, and how quickly a large number of software vendors has adopted the standard. XML is now as important for the Web as HTML was to the foundation of the Web.XML is everywhere. It is the most common tool for data transmissions between all sorts of applications, and is becoming more and more popular in the area of storing and describing information.

USING XML

XML is used in many aspects of web development, often to simplify data storage and sharing.

Separates Data from HTML

If you need to display dynamic data in your HTML document, it will take a lot of work to edit the HTML each time the data changes.With XML, data can be stored in separate XML files. This way you can concentrate on using HTML for layout and display, and be sure that changes in the underlying data will not require any changes to the HTML.With a few lines of JavaScript, you can read an external XML file and update the data content of your HTML.

Simplifying Data Sharing

In the real world, computer systems and databases contain data in incompatible formats.XML data is stored in plain text format. This provides a software- and hardware-independent way of storing data.This makes it much easier to create data that different applications can share.

Simplifies Data Transport

With XML, data can easily be exchanged between incompatible systems. One of the most time-consuming challenges for developers is to exchange data between incompatible systems over the Internet.Exchanging data as XML greatly reduces this complexity, since the data can be read by different incompatible applications.

Simplifies Platform Changes

Upgrading to new systems (hardware or software platforms), is always very time consuming. Large amounts of data must be converted and incompatible data is often lost.XML data is stored in text format. This makes it easier to expand or upgrade to new operating systems, new applications, or new browsers, without losing data.

Making Your Data Available

Since XML is independent of hardware, software and application, XML can make your data more available and useful.Different applications can access your data, not only in HTML pages, but also from XML data sources.With XML, your data can be available to all kinds of "reading machines" (Handheld computers, voice machines, news feeds, etc), and make it more available for blind people, or people with other disabilities.

Creating New Internet Languages

A lot of new Internet languages are created with XML.Here are some examples:

- XHTML the latest version of HTML
- WSDL for describing available web services
- WAP and WML as markup languages for handheld devices
- RSS languages for news feeds
- RDF and OWL for describing resources and ontology
- SMIL for describing multimedia for the web

XML TREE

XML documents form a tree structure that starts at "the root" and branches to "the leaves".

An Example XML Document

XML documents use a self-describing and simple syntax:

```
<?xml version="1.0" encoding="ISO-8859-1"?>
<note>
<to>Tove</to>
<from>Jani</from>
<heading>Reminder</heading>
<body>Don't forget me this weekend!</body>
</note>
```

The first line is the XML declaration. It defines the XML version (1.0) and the encoding used (ISO-8859-1 = Latin-1/West European character set).The next line describes the root element of the document (like saying: "this document is a note"):

```
<note>
```

The next 4 lines describe 4 child elements of the root (to, from, heading, and body):

```
<to>Tove</to>
```

```
<from>Jani</from>
<heading>Reminder</heading>
<body>Don't forget me this weekend!</body>
```

And finally the last line defines the end of the root element:

```
</note>
```

You can assume, from this example, that the XML document contains a note to Tove from Jani.Don't you agree that XML is pretty self-descriptive?

XML Documents Form a Tree Structure

XML documents must contain a root element. This element is "the parent" of all other elements.The elements in an XML document form a document tree. The tree starts at the root and branches to the lowest level of the tree.

All elements can have sub elements (child elements):

```
<root>
<child>
<subchild>.....</subchild>
</child>
</root>
```

The terms parent, child, and sibling are used to describe the relationships between elements. Parent elements have children. Children on the same level are called siblings (brothers or sisters).All elements can have text content and attributes (just like in HTML).

Example:

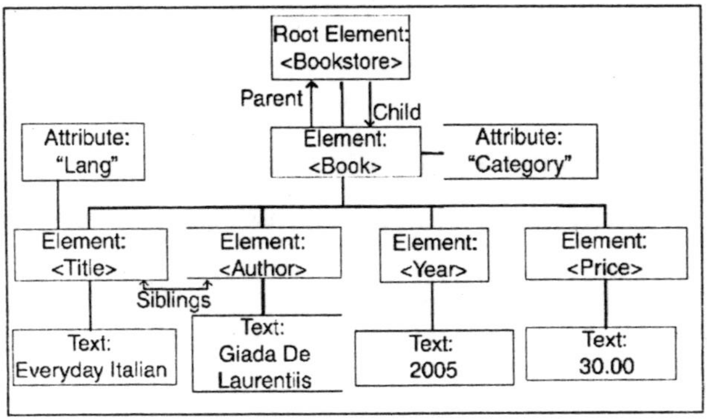

The image above represents one book in the XML below:

```
<bookstore>
 <book category="COOKING">
 <title lang="en">Everyday Italian</title>
      <author>Giada De Laurentiis</author>
      <year>2005</year>
      <price>30.00</price>
   </book>
   <book category="CHILDREN">
      <title lang="en">Harry Potter</title>
      <author>J K. Rowling</author>
      <year>2005</year>
      <price>29.99</price>
   </book>
   <book category="WEB">
      <title lang="en">Learning XML</title>
      <author>Erik T. Ray</author>
      <year>2003</year>
      <price>39.95</price>
   </book>
</bookstore>
```

The root element in the example is <bookstore>. All <book> elements in the document are contained within <bookstore>.

The <book> element has 4 children: <title>,< author>, <year>, <price>.

ML SYNTAX RULES

The syntax rules of XML are very simple and logical. The rules are easy to learn, and easy to use.

All XML Elements Must Have a Closing Tag

In HTML, you will often see elements that don't have a closing tag:

```
<p>This is a paragraph
<p>This is another paragraph
```

In XML, it is illegal to omit the closing tag. All elements must have a closing tag:

```
<p>This is a paragraph</p>
<p>This is another paragraph</p>
```

Note: You might have noticed from the previous example that the XML declaration did not have a closing tag. This is not an error. The declaration is not a part of the XML document itself, and it has no closing tag.

XML Tags are Case Sensitive

XML elements are defined using XML tags.XML tags are case sensitive. With XML, the tag <Letter> is different from the tag <letter>.

Opening and closing tags must be written with the same case:

```
<Message>This is incorrect</message>
<message>This is correct</message>
```

Note: "Opening and closing tags" are often referred to as "Start and end tags". Use whatever you prefer. It is exactly the same thing.

XML Elements Must be Properly Nested

In HTML, you might see improperly nested elements:

```
<b><i>This text is bold and italic</b></i>
```

In XML, all elements must be properly nested within each other:

```
<b><i>This text is bold and italic</i></b>
```

In the example above, "Properly nested" simply means that since the <i> element is opened inside the <b> element, it must be closed inside the <b> element.

XML Documents Must Have a Root Element

XML documents must contain one element that is the parent of all other elements. This element is called the root element.

```
<root>
 <child>
 <subchild>.....</subchild>
 </child>
</root>
```

XML Attribute Values Must be Quoted

XML elements can have attributes in name/value pairs just like in HTML.In XML the attribute value must always be quoted. Study the two XML documents below.

The first one is incorrect, the second is correct:

```
<note date=12/11/2007>
 <to>Tove</to>
 <from>Jani</from>
</note>
<note date="12/11/2007">
 <to>Tove</to>
 <from>Jani</from>
</note>
```

The error in the first document is that the date attribute in the note element is not quoted.

Entity References

Some characters have a special meaning in XML.If you place a character like "<" inside an XML element, it will generate an error because the parser interprets it as the start of a new element.

This will generate an XML error:

```
<message>if salary < 1000 then</message>
```

To avoid this error, replace the "<" character with an entity reference:

```
<message>if salary &lt; 1000 then</message>
```

There are 5 predefined entity references in XML:

<	<	Less than
>	>	Greater than
&	&	Ampersand
'	'	Apostrophe
"	"	Quotation mark

Note: Only the characters "<" and "&" are strictly illegal in XML. The greater than character is legal, but it is a good habit to replace it.

Comments in XML

The syntax for writing comments in XML is similar to that of HTML.

```
<!– This is a comment –>
```

White-space is Preserved in XML

HTML truncates multiple white-space characters to one single white-space:

HTML:	Hello my name is Tove
Output:	Hello my name is Tove.

With XML, the white-space in a document is not truncated.

XML Stores New Line as LF

In Windows applications, a new line is normally stored as a pair of characters: carriage return (CR) and line feed (LF). The character pair bears some resemblance to the typewriter actions of setting a new line. In Unix applications, a new line is normally stored as a LF character. Macintosh applications also use an LF to store a new line.

XML ELEMENT

WHAT IS AN XML ELEMENT

An XML element is everything from (including) the element's start tag to (including) the element's end tag.An element can contain other elements, simple text or a mixture of both. Elements can also have attributes.

```
<bookstore>
   <book category="CHILDREN">
      <title>Harry Potter</title>
      <author>J K. Rowling</author>
      <year>2005</year>
      <price>29.99</price>
   </book>
   <book category="WEB">
      <title>Learning XML</title>
```

```
        <author>Erik T. Ray</author>
        <year>2003</year>
        <price>39.95</price>
        </book>
</bookstore>
```

In the example above, <bookstore> and <book> have element contents, because they contain other elements. <author> has text content because it contains text.In the example above only <book> has an attribute (category="CHILDREN").

XML Naming Rules

XML elements must follow these naming rules:

- Names can contain letters, numbers, and other characters
- Names cannot start with a number or punctuation character
- Names cannot start with the letters xml (or XML, or Xml, etc)
- Names cannot contain spacesAny name can be used, no words are reserved.

Best Naming Practices

Make names descriptive. Names with an underscore separator are nice:

```
<first_name>, <last_name>.
```

Names should be short and simple, like this: <book_title> not like this: <the_title_of_the_book>.

Avoid "-" characters. If you name something "first-name," some software may think you want to subtract name from first.

Avoid "." characters. If you name something "first.name," some software may think that "name" is a property of the object "first."

Avoid ":" characters. Colons are reserved to be used for something called namespaces (more later).

XML documents often have a corresponding database. A good practice is to use the naming rules of your database for the elements in the XML documents.

Non-English letters like éòá are perfectly legal in XML, but watch out for problems if your software vendor doesn't support them.

XML Elements are Extensible

XML elements can be extended to carry more information.Look at the following XML example:

```
<note>
<to>Tove</to>
<from>Jani</from>
<body>Don't forget me this weekend!</body>
</note>
```

Let's imagine that we created an application that extracted the <to>, <from>, and <body> elements from the XML document to produce this output:

MESSAGE

To: Tove

From: Jani

Don't forget me this weekend!

Imagine that the author of the XML document added some extra information to it:

```
<note>
<date>2008-01-10</date>
<to>Tove</to>
<from>Jani</from>
<heading>Reminder</heading>
<body>Don't forget me this weekend!</body>
</note>
```

Should the application break or crash?

No. The application should still be able to find the <to>, <from>, and <body> elements in the XML document and produce the same output.One of the beauties of XML, is that it can often be extended without breaking applications.

XML ATTRIBUTES

From HTML you will remember this: <img src="computer.gif">. The "src" attribute provides additional information about the <img> element.

In HTML (and in XML) attributes provide additional information about elements:

```
<img src="computer.gif">
<a href="demo.asp">
```

Attributes often provide information that is not a part of the data. In the example below, the file type is irrelevant to the data, but important to the software that wants to manipulate the element:

```
<file type="gif">computer.gif</file>
```

XML Attributes Must be Quoted

Attribute values must always be enclosed in quotes, but either single or double quotes can be used. For a person's sex, the person tag can be written like this:

```
<person sex="female">
or like this:
<person sex='female'>
```

If the attribute value itself contains double quotes you can use single quotes, like in this example:

```
<gangster name='George "Shotgun" Ziegler'>
or you can use character entities:
<gangster name="George &quot;Shotgun&quot; Ziegler">
```

XML Elements vs. Attributes

Take a look at these examples:

```
<person sex="female">
    <firstname>Anna</firstname>
    <lastname>Smith</lastname>
</person>
<person>
    <sex>female</sex>
    <firstname>Anna</firstname>
    <lastname>Smith</lastname>
</person>
```

In the first example sex is an attribute. In the last, sex is an element. Both examples provide the same information. There are no rules about when to use attributes and when to use elements. Attributes are handy in HTML. In XML my advice is to avoid them. Use elements instead.

My Favourite Way

The following three XML documents contain exactly the same information:A date attribute is used in the first example:

```
<note date="10/01/2008">
<to>Tove</to>
<from>Jani</from>
<heading>Reminder</heading>
<body>Don't forget me this weekend!</body>
</note>
```

A date element is used in the second example:

```
<note>
<date>10/01/2008</date>
<to>Tove</to>
<from>Jani</from>
<heading>Reminder</heading>
<body>Don't forget me this weekend!</body>
</note>
```

An expanded date element is used in the third: (THIS IS MY FAVOURITE):

```
<note>
<date>
<day>10</day>
<month>01</month>
<year>2008</year>
</date>
<to>Tove</to>
<from>Jani</from>
<heading>Reminder</heading>
<body>Don't forget me this weekend!</body>
</note>
```

Avoid XML Attributes

Some of the problems with using attributes are:

- Attributes cannot contain multiple values (elements can)

- Attributes cannot contain tree structures.
- Attributes are not easily expandable.

Attributes are difficult to read and maintain. Use elements for data. Use attributes for information that is not relevant to the data.

Don't end up like this:

```
<note day="10" month="01" year="2008"
to="Tove" from="Jani" heading="Reminder"
body="Don't forget me this weekend!">
</note>
```

XML Attributes for Metadata

Sometimes ID references are assigned to elements. These IDs can be used to identify XML elements in much the same way as the ID attribute in HTML.

This example demonstrates this:

```
<messages>
 <note id="501">
   <to>Tove</to>
   <from>Jani</from>
   <heading>Reminder</heading>
   <body>Don't forget me this weekend!</body>
 </note>
 <note id="502">
   <to>Jani</to>
   <from>Tove</from>
   <heading>Re: Reminder</heading>
   <body>I will not</body>
 </note>
</messages>
```

The ID above is just an identifier, to identify the different notes. It is not a part of the note itself.What I'm trying to say here is that metadata (data about data) should be stored as attributes, and that data itself should be stored as elements.

XML VALIDATION

XML with correct syntax is "Well Formed" XML.XML validated against a DTD is "Valid" XML.

WELL FORMED XML DOCUMENTS

A "Well Formed" XML document has correct XML syntax. *The syntax rules were described in the previous chapters*:

- XML documents must have a root element
- XML elements must have a closing tag
- XML tags are case sensitive
- XML elements must be properly nested
- XML attribute values must be quoted

```
<?xml version="1.0" encoding="ISO-8859-1"?>
<note>
<to>Tove</to>
<from>Jani</from>
<heading>Reminder</heading>
<body>Don't forget me this weekend!</body>
</note>
```

Valid XML Documents

A "Valid" XML document is a "Well Formed" XML document, which also conforms to the rules of a Document Type Definition (DTD):

```
<?xml version="1.0" encoding="ISO-8859-1"?>
<!DOCTYPE note SYSTEM "Note.dtd"><note>
<to>Tove</to>
<from>Jani</from>
<heading>Reminder</heading>
<body>Don't forget me this weekend!</body>
</note>
```

The DOCTYPE declaration in the example above, is a reference to an external DTD file. The content of the file is shown in the paragraph below.

XML DTD

The purpose of a DTD is to define the structure of an XML document. It defines the structure with a list of legal elements:

```
<!DOCTYPE note
[
<!ELEMENT note (to,from,heading,body)>
```

```
<!ELEMENT to (#PCDATA)>
<!ELEMENT from (#PCDATA)>
<!ELEMENT heading (#PCDATA)>
<!ELEMENT body (#PCDATA)>
]>
```

If you want to study DTD, you will find our DTD tutorial on our homepage.

XML Schema

W3C supports an XML-based alternative to DTD, called XML Schema:

```
<xs:element name="note">
<xs:complexType>
 <xs:sequence>
 <xs:element name="to" type="xs:string"/>
 <xs:element name="from" type="xs:string"/
>
 <xs:elementname="heading"type="xs:string"/
>
    <xs:elementname="body" type="xs:string"/
    >
 </xs:sequence>
</xs:complexType>
</xs:element>
```

If you want to study XML Schema, you will find our Schema tutorial on our homepage.

A General XML Validator

To help you check the syntax of your XML files, we have created an XML validator to syntax-check your XML.

XML VALIDATOR

Use our XML validator to syntax-check your XML.

XML Errors Will Stop You

Errors in XML documents will stop your XML applications.The W3C XML specification states that a programme should stop processing an XML document if it finds an error. The reason is that XML software should be small, fast, and compatible.HTML browsers will display documents with errors (like missing end tags). HTML browsers are big and incompatible because they have a lot of unnecessary code to deal with (and display) HTML errors. With XML, errors are not allowed.

Syntax-Check Your XML

To help you syntax-check your XML, we have created an XML validator.Paste your XML into the text area below, and syntax-check it by clicking the "Validate" button.

```
<?xml version="1.0" ?> <note> <to>Tove</to>
<from>Jani</Ffrom> <heading>Reminder</heading>
<body>Don't forget me this weekend!</body> </
note>
```

Top of Form

Bottom of Form

Note: This only checks if your XML is "Well formed". If you want to validate your XML against a DTD, see the last paragraph on this page.

Syntax-Check an XML File

You can syntax-check an XML file by typing the URL of the file into the input field below, and then click the "Validate" button:Top of FormBottom of FormNote: If you get an "Access denied" error, it's because your browser security does not allow file access across domains.The file "note_error.xml" demonstrates your browsers error handling. If you want see an error free message, substitute the "note_error.xml" with "cd_catalog.xml".

Validate Your XML Against a DTD

If you know DTD, you can validate your XML in the text area below.Just add the DOCTYPE declaration to your XML and click the "Validate" button:

VIEWING XML FILES

```
<?xml version="1.0" encoding="ISO-8859-1"?>
```

```
- <note>
    <to>Tove</to>
    <from>Jani</from>
    <heading>Reminder</heading>
    <body>Don't forget me this weekend!</body>
  </note>
```

Look at this XML file: note.xmlThe XML document will be displayed with colour-coded root and child elements. A plus (+) or minus sign (–) to the left of the elements can be clicked to expand or collapse the element structure.

To view the raw XML source (without the + and - signs), select "View Page Source" or "View Source" from the browser menu.

Note: In Chrome, Opera, and Safari, only the element text will be displayed. To view the raw XML, you must right click the page and select "View Source"

Viewing an Invalid XML File

If an erroneous XML file is opened, the browser will report the error.Look at this XML file: note_error.xml

Other XML Examples

Viewing some XML documents will help you get the XML feeling. An XML CD catalogThis is a CD collection, stored as XML data.

An XML plant catalog. This is a plant catalog from a plant shop, stored as XML data.A Simple Food MenuThis is a breakfast food menu from a restaurant, stored as XML data.

Why Does XML Display Like This

XML documents do not carry information about how to display the data.Since XML tags are "invented" by the author of the XML document, browsers do not know if a tag like <table> describes an HTML table or a dining table.

Without any information about how to display the data, most browsers will just display the XML document as it is.In the next chapters, we will take a look at different solutions to the display problem, using CSS, XSLT and JavaScript.

DISPLAYING XML WITH CSS

With CSS (Cascading Style Sheets) you can add display information to an XML document.

Displaying your XML Files with CSS

It is possible to use CSS to format an XML document. Below is an example of how to use a CSS style sheet to format an XML document:Take a look at this XML file: The CD catalogThen look at this style sheet: The CSS fileFinally, view: The CD catalog formatted with the CSS fileBelow is a fraction of the XML file. The second line links the XML file to the CSS file:

```
<?xml version="1.0" encoding="ISO-8859-1"?>
<?xml-stylesheet type="text/css"
href="cd_catalog.css"?>
<CATALOG>
 <CD>
    <TITLE>Empire Burlesque</TITLE>
    <ARTIST>Bob Dylan</ARTIST>
    <COUNTRY>USA</COUNTRY>
    <COMPANY>Columbia</COMPANY>
    <PRICE>10.90</PRICE>
    <YEAR>1985</YEAR>
 </CD>
 <CD>
    <TITLE>Hide your heart</TITLE>
    <ARTIST>Bonnie Tyler</ARTIST>
    <COUNTRY>UK</COUNTRY>
    <COMPANY>CBS Records</COMPANY>
    <PRICE>9.90</PRICE>
    <YEAR>1988</YEAR>
 </CD>
 .
 .
 .
</CATALOG>
```

Formatting XML with CSS is not the most common method.W3C recommend using XSLT instead. See the next chapter.

DISPLAYING XML WITH XSLT

XSLT is the recommended style sheet language of XML.XSLT (eXtensible Stylesheet Language Transformations) is far more sophisticated than CSS.XSLT can be used to transform XML into HTML, before it is displayed by a browser:Display XML with XSLTIf you want to learn more about XSLT, find our XSLT tutorial on our homepage.

Transforming XML with XSLT on the Server

In the example above, the XSLT transformation is done by the browser, when the browser reads the XML file.Different browsers may produce different result when transforming XML with XSLT. To reduce this problem the XSLT transformation can be done on the server.View the result.Note that the result of the output is exactly the same, either the transformation is done by the web server or by the web browser.

XML JAVASCRIPT

With an XMLHttpRequest you can communicate with your server from inside a web page.

WHAT IS THE XMLHTTPREQUEST OBJECT

The XMLHttpRequest object is the developer's dream, because you can:

- Update a web page with new data without reloading the page
- Request and receive new data from a server after the page has loaded
- Communicate with a server in the background

XMLHttpRequest Example

When you type in the input box below, an HTTP request is sent to the server and name suggestions are returned from a name list:

Type a letter in the input box:
First Name

Suggestions:
no suggestion

Creating an XMLHttpRequest Object

Creating an XMLHttpRequest object is done with one single line of JavaScript.

In all modern browsers:

```
var xmlhttp=new XMLHttpRequest()
```

In older Microsoft browsers (IE 5 and 6):

var xmlhttp=new ActiveXObject("Microsoft.XMLHTTP")

In the next chapter, we will use the XMLHttpRequest object to retrieve XML information from a server.

Is the XMLHttpRequest Object a W3C Standard

The XMLHttpRequest object is not specified in any W3C recommendation.However, the W3C DOM Level 3 "Load and Save" specification contains some similar functionality, but these are not implemented in any browsers yet.

XML PARSER

The XML DOM contains methods (functions) to traverse XML trees, access, insert, and delete nodes.However, before an XML document can be accessed and manipulated, it must be loaded into an XML DOM object.An XML parser reads XML, and converts it into an XML DOM object that can be accessed with JavaScript.Most browsers have a built-in XML parser.

Load An Xml Document

The following JavaScript fragment loads an XML document ("books.xml"):

Example:

```
if (window.XMLHttpRequest)
 {
 xhttp=new XMLHttpRequest();
 }
else// Internet Explorer 5/6
 {
```

```
 xhttp=new ActiveXObject("Microsoft.XMLHTTP");
 }
xhttp.open("GET","books.xml",false);
xhttp.send("");
xmlDoc=xhttp.responseXML;
```

Code explained:

- Create an XMLHTTP object
- Open the XMLHTTP object
- Send an XML HTTP request to the server
- Set the response as an XML DOM object

Load an XML String

The following code loads and parses an XML string:

Example

```
if (window.DOMParser)
 {
 parser=new DOMParser();
 xmlDoc=parser.parseFromString(text,"text/
xml");
 }
else// Internet Explorer
 {
 xmlDoc=new ActiveXObject("Microsoft.XMLDOM";
 xmlDoc.async="false";
 xmlDoc.loadXML(text);
 }
```

Note: Internet Explorer uses the loadXML() method to parse an XML string, while other browsers use the DOMParser object.

Access Across Domains

For security reasons, modern browsers do not allow access across domains.This means, that both the web page and the XML file it tries to load, must be located on the same server.The examples on W3Schools all open XML files located on the W3Schools domain.If you want to use the example above on one of your web pages, the XML files you load must be located on your own server.

THE XML DOM

The XML DOM (XML Document Object Model) defines a standard way for accessing and manipulating XML documents.The DOM views XML documents as a tree-structure. All elements can be accessed through the DOM tree. Their content (text and attributes) can be modified or deleted, and new elements can be created. The elements, their text, and their attributes are all known as nodes.In the examples below we use the following DOM reference to get the text from the <to> element:

xmlDoc.getElementsByTagName("to")[0].childNodes[0].nodeValue

- *XmlDoc*: The XML document created by the parser.
- *GetElementsByTagName("to")[0]*: The first <to> element
- *ChildNodes[0]*: The first child of the <to> element (the text node)
- *NodeValue*: The value of the node (the text itself)You can learn more about the XML DOM in our XML DOM tutorial.

The Html Dom

The HTML DOM (HTML Document Object Model) defines a standard way for accessing and manipulating HTML documents.All HTML elements can be accessed through the HTML DOM.

In the examples below we use the following DOM reference to change the text of the HTML element where id="to":

Document.getElementById("to").innerHTML=

- Document - the HTML document
- GetElementById("to") - the HTML element where id="to"
- InnerHTML - the inner text of the HTML element

You can learn more about the HTML DOM in our HTML DOM tutorial.

Load an XML File- A Cross Browser Example

```
<html>
```

```
<body>
<h1>W3Schools Internal Note</h1>
<p><b>To:</b> <span id="to"></span><br/>
<b>From:</b> <span id="from"></span><br/>
<b>Message:</b> <span id="message"></span>
<script type="text/javascript">
if (window.XMLHttpRequest)
 {
 xhttp=new XMLHttpRequest()
 }
else
 {
 xhttp=new ActiveXObject("Microsoft.XMLHTTP")
 }
xhttp.open("GET","note.xml",false);
xhttp.send("");
xmlDoc=xhttp.responseXML;
document.getElementById("to").innerHTML=
xmlDoc.getElementsByTagName("to")[0].childNodes[0].
nodeValue;
document.getElementById("from").innerHTML=
xmlDoc.getElementsByTagName("from")[0].
childNodes[0].nodeValue;
document.getElementById("message").innerHTML=
xmlDoc.getElementsByTagName("body")[0].child
Nodes[0].nodeValue;
</script>
</body>
</html>
```

Example

The following code loads an XML document ("node.XMl")into the XML parser:

Important Note

To extract the text "Jani" from the XML,the syntx is:

```
getElementByTagName("from")[0].childNodes[0]
nodeValue
```

In the XML example there is only one <from> tag, but you

still have to specify the array index [o], because the XML paraser method get Element By Tag Name()return an array of all <from> nodes.

Load an XML String - A Cross browser Example

The following code loads and parses an XML string:

Example

```
<html>
<body>
<h1>W3Schools Internal Note</h1>
<p><b>To:</b> <span id="to"></span><br/>
<b>From:</b> <span id="from"></span><br/>
<b>Message:</b> <span id="message"></span></
p>
<script>
text="<note>";
text=text+"<to>Tove</to>";
text=text+"<from>Jani</from>";
text=text+"<heading>Reminder</heading>";
text=text+"<body>Don't forget me this
weekend!</body>";
text=text+"</note>";
if (window.DOMParser)
 {
 parser=new DOMParser();
 xmlDoc=parser.parseFromString(text,"text/
xml");
 }
else// Internet Explorer
 {
 xmlDoc=new ActiveXObject("Microsoft.
 XMLDOM");
 xmlDoc.async="false";
 xmlDoc.loadXML(text);
 }
document.getElementById("to").innerHTML=
xmlDoc.getElementsByTagName("to")[0].childNodes[0].
nodeValue;
```

```
document.getElementById("from").innerHTML=
xmlDoc.getElementsByTagName("from")[0].childNodes[0].
nodeValue;
document.getElementById("message").innerHTML=
xmlDoc.getElementsByTagName("body")[0].childNodes[0].
nodeValue;
</script>
</body>
</html>
```

XML TO HTML

Display XML Data in HTML

In the example below, we loop through an XML file (cd_catalog.xml), and display each CD element as an HTML table row:

Example

```
<html>
<body>
<script type="text/javascript">
if (window.XMLHttpRequest)
 {
 xhttp=new XMLHttpRequest();
 }
else// Internet Explorer 5/6
 {
 xhttp=new ActiveXObject("Microsoft.
 XMLHTTP");
 }
 xhttp.open("GET","cd_catalog.xml",false);
 xhttp.send("");
 xmlDoc=xhttp.responseXML;
document.write("<table border='1'>");
var x=xmlDoc.getElementsByTagName("CD");
for (i=0;i<x.length;i++)
 {
 document.write("<tr><td>");
 document.write(x[i].getElementsByTagName("ARTIST")[0].
 childNodes[0].nodeValue);
```

```
 document.write("</td><td>");
document.write(x[i].getElementsByTagName("TITLE")[0].
 childNodes[0].nodeValue);
 document.write("</td></tr>");
 }
document.write("</table>");
</script>
</body>
</html>
```

Example Explained

- We check the browser, and load the XML using the correct parser (explained in the previous chapter)
- We create an HTML table with <table border="1">
- We use getElementsByTagName() to get all XML CD nodes
- For each CD node, we display data from ARTIST and TITLE as table data.
- We end the table with </table>

XML APPLICATION

The XML Example Document

Look at the following XML document ("cd_catalog.xml"), that represents a CD catalog:

```
<?xml version="1.0" encoding="ISO-8859-1"?>
<CATALOG>
 <CD>
     <TITLE>Empire Burlesque</TITLE>
     <ARTIST>Bob Dylan</ARTIST>
     <COUNTRY>USA</COUNTRY>
     <COMPANY>Columbia</COMPANY>
     <PRICE>10.90</PRICE>
     <YEAR>1985</YEAR>
 </CD>
.
.
.
```

Load the XML Document

To load the XML document (cd_catalog.xml), we use the same code as we used in the XML Parser chapter:

```
if (window.XMLHttpRequest)
 {
 xhttp=new XMLHttpRequest();
 }
else// Internet Explorer 5/6
 {
 xhttp=new ActiveXObject("Microsoft.
 XMLHTTP");
 }
xhttp.open("GET","cd_catalog.xml",false);
xhttp.send("");
xmlDoc=xhttp.responseXML;
```

After the execution of this code, xmlDoc is an XML DOM object, accessible by JavaScript.

Display XML Data as an HTML Table

The following code displays an HTML table filled with data from the XML DOM object:

Example:

```
document.write("<table border='1'>");
var x=xmlDoc.getElementsByTagName("CD");
for (i=0;i<x.length;i++)
 {
 document.write("<tr><td>");
 document.write(x[i].getElementsByTag
 Name("ARTIST")[0].childNodes[0].nodeValue);
 document.write("</td><td>");
 document.write(x[i].getElementsByTagName
 ("TITLE")[0].childNodes[0].nodeValue);
 document.write("</td></tr>");
 }
document.write("</table>");
```

For each CD element in the XML document, a table row is created. Each table row contains two table data with ARTIST and TITLE from the current CD element.

Display XML Data in any HTML Element

XML data can be copied into any HTML element that can display text.The code below is part of the <head> section of the HTML file. It gets the XML data from the first <CD> element and displays it in the HTML element with the id="show":

Example

```
var x=xmlDoc.getElementsByTagName("CD");
i=0;
function display()
{
artist=(x[i].getElementsByTagName("ARTIST")[0].
childNodes[0].nodeValue);
title=(x[i].getElementsByTagName("TITLE")[0].
childNodes[0].nodeValue);
year=(x[i].getElementsByTagName("YEAR")[0].
childNodes[0].nodeValue);
txt="Artist: " + artist + "<br/>Title: " +
title + "<br/>Year:"+year;
document.getElementById("show").innerHTML=txt;
}
```

The body of the HTML document contains an onload event attribute that calls the display() function when the page is loaded. It also contains a <div id='show'> element to receive the XML data.

```
<body onload="display()">
<div id='show'></div>
</body>
```

In the example above, you will only see data from the first CD element in the XML document. To navigate to the next CD element, you have to add some more code.

Add a Navigation Script

To add navigation to the example above, create two functions called next() and previous():

Example

```
function next()
{
```

```
if (i<x.length-1)
 {
 i++;
 display();
    }
}
function previous()
{
if (i>0)
 {
 i-;
 display();
 }
}
```

The next() function displays the next CD, unless you are on the last CD element.

The previous() function displays the previous CD, unless you are at the first CD element.

The next() and previous() functions are called by clicking next/previous buttons:

```
<input type="button" onclick="previous()"
value="previous"/>
<input type="button" onclick="next()"
value="next"/>
```

All Together Now

With a little creativity you can create a full application.If you use what you have learned on this page, and a little imagination, you can easily develop this into a full application.

XML ADVANCED

XML NAMESPACES

Name Conflicts

In XML, element names are defined by the developer. This often results in a conflict when trying to mix XML documents from different XML applications.

This XML carries HTML table information:

```
<table>
 <tr>
     <td>Apples</td>
     <td>Bananas</td>
 </tr>
</table>
```

This XML carries information about a table (a piece of furniture):

```
<table>
 <name>African Coffee Table</name>
 <width>80</width>
 <length>120</length>
</table>
```

If these XML fragments were added together, there would be a name conflict. Both contain a <table> element, but the elements have different content and meaning.An XML parser will not know how to handle these differences.

Solving the Name Conflict Using a Prefix

Name conflicts in XML can easily be avoided using a name prefix.

This XML carries information about an HTML table, and a piece of furniture:

```
<h:table>
 <h:tr>
     <h:td>Apples</h:td>
     <h:td>Bananas</h:td>
 </h:tr>
</h:table>
<f:table>
 <f:name>African Coffee Table</f:name>
 <f:width>80</f:width>
 <f:length>120</f:length>
</f:table>
```

In the example above, there will be no conflict because the two <table> elements have different names.

XML Namespaces - The xmlns Attribute

When using prefixes in XML, a so-called namespace for the prefix must be defined.The namespace is defined by the xmlns attribute in the start tag of an element.The namespace declaration has the following syntax. xmlns:*prefix="URI"*.

```
<root>
<h:table xmlns:h="http://www.w3.org/TR/html4/
">
 <h:tr>
     <h:td>Apples</h:td>
     <h:td>Bananas</h:td>
 </h:tr>
</h:table>
<f:table xmlns:f="http://www.w3schools.com/
furniture">
 <f:name>African Coffee Table</f:name>
 <f:width>80</f:width>
 <f:length>120</f:length>
</f:table>
</root>
```

In the example above, the xmlns attribute in the <table> tag give the h: and f: prefixes a qualified namespace.When a namespace is defined for an element, all child elements with the same prefix are associated with the same namespace.

Namespaces can be declared in the elements where they are used or in the XML root element:

```
<root
xmlns:h="http://www.w3.org/TR/html4/"
xmlns:f="http://www.w3schools.com/furniture">
<h:table>
 <h:tr>
     <h:td>Apples</h:td>
     <h:td>Bananas</h:td>
 </h:tr>
</h:table>
<f:table>
 <f:name>African Coffee Table</f:name>
```

```
 <f:width>80</f:width>
 <f:length>120</f:length>
 </f:table>
</root>
```

Note: The namespace URI is not used by the parser to look up information.The purpose is to give the namespace a unique name. However, often companies use the namespace as a pointer to a web page containing namespace information.

Uniform Resource Identifier (URI)

A Uniform Resource Identifier (URI) is a string of characters which identifies an Internet Resource.The most common URI is the Uniform Resource Locator (URL) which identifies an Internet domain address. Another, not so common type of URI is the Universal Resource Name (URN).In our examples we will only use URLs.

Default Namespaces

Defining a default namespace for an element saves us from using prefixes in all the child elements. It has the following syntax:

```
xmlns="namespaceURI"
This XML carries HTML table information:
<table xmlns="http://www.w3.org/TR/html4/">
 <tr>
     <td>Apples</td>
     <td>Bananas</td>
 </tr>
</table>
```

This XML carries information about a piece of furniture:

```
<table xmlns="http://www.w3schools.com/
furniture">
  <name>African Coffee Table</name>
  <width>80</width>
  <length>120</length>
</table>
```

Namespaces in Real Use

XSLT is an XML language that can be used to transform

XML documents into other formats, like HTML.In the XSLT document below, you can see that most of the tags are HTML tags.

The tags that are not HTML tags have the prefix xsl, identified by the namespace:

```
xmlns:xsl="http://www.w3.org/1999/XSL/
Transform":
<?xml version="1.0" encoding="ISO-8859-1"?>
<xsl:stylesheet version="1.0"
xmlns:xsl="http://www.w3.org/1999/XSL/
Transform">
<xsl:template match="/">
<html>
<body>
 <h2>My CD Collection</h2>
 <table border="1">
     <tr>
     <th align="left">Title</th>
     <th align="left">Artist</th>
     </tr>
     <xsl:for-each select="catalog/cd">
     <tr>
     <td><xsl:value-of select="title"/></
 td>
     <td><xsl:value-of select="artist"/>
     </td>
     </tr>
     </xsl:for-each>
 </table>
</body>
</html>
</xsl:template>
</xsl:stylesheet>
```

XML CDATA

All text in an XML document will be parsed by the parser.But text inside a CDATA section will be ignored by the parser.

PCDATA - Parsed Character Data

XML parsers normally parse all the text in an XML document.When an XML element is parsed, the text between the XML tags is also parsed:

```
<message>This text is also parsed</message>
```

The parser does this because XML elements can contain other elements, as in this example, where the <name> element contains two other elements (first and last):

```
<name><first>Bill</first><last>Gates</last></name>
```

and the parser will break it up into sub-elements like this:

```
<name>
    <first>Bill</first>
    <last>Gates</last>
</name>
```

Parsed Character Data (PCDATA) is a term used about text data that will be parsed by the XML parser.

CDATA - (Unparsed) Character Data

The term CDATA is used about text data that should not be parsed by the XML parser.

Characters like "<" and "&" are illegal in XML elements.

- "<" will generate an error because the parser interprets it as the start of a new element.
- "&" will generate an error because the parser interprets it as the start of an character entity.

Some text, like JavaScript code, contains a lot of "<" or "&" characters. To avoid errors script code can be defined as CDATA.Everything inside a CDATA section is ignored by the parser.A CDATA section starts with "<![CDATA[" and ends with "]]>":

```
<script>
<![CDATA[
function matchwo(a,b)
{
if(a<b &&a < 0)then
 {
 return 1;
```

```
    }
  else
    {
    return 0;
    }
  }
  ]]>
  </script>
```

In the example above, everything inside the CDATA section is ignored by the parser.

Notes on CDATA sections:

A CDATA section cannot contain the string "]]>". Nested CDATA sections are not allowed.The "]]>" that marks the end of the CDATA section cannot contain spaces or line breaks.

XML ENCODING

XML documents can contain non ASCII characters, like Norwegian æ ø å, or French ê è é.To avoid errors, specify the XML encoding, or save XML files as Unicode.

XML Encoding Errors

If you load an XML document, you can get two different errors indicating encoding problems:An invalid character was found in text content.You get this error if your XML contains non ASCII characters, and the file was saved as single-byte ANSI (or ASCII) with no encoding specified.Single byte XML file with encoding attribute. Same single byte XML file with no encoding attribute.Switch from current encoding to specified encoding not supported.You get this error if your XML file was saved as double-byte Unicode (or UTF-16) with a single-byte encoding (Windows-1252, ISO-8859-1, UTF-8) specified.

You also get this error if your XML file was saved with single-byte ANSI (or ASCII), with double-byte encoding (UTF-16) specified.Double byte XML file without encoding.Same double byte XML file with single byte encoding.

Windows Notepad

Windows Notepad save files as single-byte ANSI (ASCII)

by default.If you select "Save as...", you can specify double-byte Unicode (UTF-16).Save the XML file below as Unicode (note that the document does not contain any encoding attribute):

```
<?xml version="1.0"?>
<note>
<from>Jani</from>
<to>Tove</to>
<message>Norwegian: æøå. French: êèé</message>
</note>
```

The file above, note_encode_none_u.xml will NOT generate an error. But if you specify a single-byte encoding it will.

The following encoding (open it), will give an error message:

```
<?xml version="1.0" encoding="windows-1252"?>
```

The following encoding (open it), will give an error message:

```
<?xml version="1.0" encoding="ISO-8859-1"?>
```

The following encoding (open it), will give an error message:

```
<?xml version="1.0" encoding="UTF-8"?>
```

The following encoding (open it), will NOT give an error:

```
<?xml version="1.0" encoding="UTF-16"?>
```

Conclusion

- Always use the encoding attribute
- Use an editor that supports encoding
- Make sure you know what encoding the editor uses
- Use the same encoding in your encoding attribute

XML ON THE SERVER

XML files are plain text files just like HTML files.XML can easily be stored and generated by a standard web server.

Storing XML Files on the Server

XML files can be stored on an Internet server exactly the same way as HTML files.

Start Windows Notepad and write the following lines:

```
<?xml version="1.0" encoding="ISO-8859-1"?>
<note>
```

```
  <from>Jani</from>
  <to>Tove</to>
  <message>Remember me this weekend</message>
</note>
```

Save the file on your web server with a proper name like "note.xml".

Generating XML with ASP

XML can be generated on a server without any installed XML software.

To generate an XML response from the server - simply write the following code and save it as an ASP file on the web server:

```
<%
response.ContentType="text/xml"
response.Write("<?xml version='1.0'
encoding='ISO-8859-1'?>")
response.Write("<note>")
response.Write("<from>Jani</from>")
response.Write("<to>Tove</to>")
response.Write("<message>Remember me this
weekend</message>")
response.Write("</note>")
%>
```

Note that the content type of the response must be set to "text/xml".See how the ASP file will be returned from the server.If you want to study ASP, you will find our ASP tutorial on our homepage.

Generating XML with PHP

To generate an XML response from the server using PHP, use following code:

```
<?php
header("Content-type: text/xml");
echo "<?xml version='1.0' encoding='ISO-8859-
1'?>";
echo "<note>";echo "<from>Jani</from>";
echo "<to>Tove</to>";
echo "<message>Remember me this weekend</
```

```
message>";
    echo "</note>";
    ?>
```

Note that the content type of the response header must be set to "text/xml".

Generating XML From a Database

XML can be generated from a database without any installed XML software.

To generate an XML database response from the server, simply write the following code and save it as an ASP file on the web server:

```
    <%
    response.ContentType = "text/xml"
    set conn  =Server.Create Object
("ADODB.Connection")
    conn.provider="Microsoft.Jet.OLEDB.4.0;"
    conn.open server.mappath("/db/database.mdb")
    sql="select fname,lname from tblGuestBook"
    set rs=Conn.Execute(sql)
    response.write("<?xml version='1.0'
encoding='ISO-8859-1'?>")
    response.write("<guestbook>")while (not
rs.EOF)
    response.write("<guest>")
    response.write("<fname>" & rs("fname") & "</
    fname>")
    response.write("<lname>" & rs("lname") & "</
    lname>")
    response.write("</guest>")
    rs.MoveNext()
    wend
    rs.close()
    conn.close()
    response.write("</guestbook>")
    %>
```

The example above uses ASP with ADO.If you want to study ASP and ADO, you will find the tutorials on our homepage.

Transforming XML with XSLT on the Server

This ASP transforms an XML file to XHTML on the server:

```
<%
'Load XML
set xml = Server.CreateObject
("Microsoft.XMLDOM")
xml.async = falsexml.
load(Server.MapPath("simple.xml"))
'Load XSL
set xsl = Server. Create Object
("Microsoft.XMLDOM")
xsl.async =false
xsl.load(Server.MapPath("simple.xsl"))'
Transform file
Response.Write(xml.transformNode(xsl))
%>
```

Example explained

- The first block of code creates an instance of the Microsoft XML parser (XMLDOM), and loads the XML file into memory.
- The second block of code creates another instance of the parser and loads the XSL file into memory.
- The last line of code transforms the XML document using the XSL document, and sends the result as XHTML to your browser. Nice!

Saving XML To a File Using ASP

This ASP example creates a simple XML document and saves it on the server:

```
<%
text="<note>"
text=text & "
<to>Tove</to>"
text=text & "<from>Jani</from>"
text=text & "<heading>Reminder</heading>"
text=text & "<body>Don't forget me this
weekend!</body>"
```

```
    text=text & "</note>
    "set xmlDoc     =Server.Create
Object("Microsoft.XMLDOM")
    xmlDoc.async="false"
    xmlDoc.loadXML(text)
    xmlDoc.Save("test.xml")
    %>
```

XML DOM ADVANCED

The XML DOM (Document Object Model) defines a standard way for accessing and manipulating XML documents.

The XML DOM

The DOM views XML documents as a tree-structure. All elements can be accessed through the DOM tree. Their content (text and attributes) can be modified or deleted, and new elements can be created. The elements, their text, and their attributes are all known as nodes.In an earlier chapter of this tutorial we introduced the XML DOM, and used the XML DOM getElementsByTagName() method to retrieve data from a DOM tree.In this chapter we will describe some other commonly used XML DOM methods. In the examples below, we have used the XML file: books.xml.

Get the Value of an Element

The following code retrieves the text value of the first <title> element:

Example

```
x=xmlDoc.getElementsByTagName("title")[0]
.child Nodes[0];txt=x.nodeValue;
```

Get the Value of an Attribute

The following code retrieves the text value of the "lang" attribute of the first <title> element:

Example

```
txt=xmlDoc.getElementsByTagName("title")[0].
getAttribute("lang");
```

Change the Value of an Element

The following code changes the text value of the first <title> element:

Example

```
x=xmlDoc.getElementsByTagName("title")[0]
.childNodes[0];x.nodeValue="Easy Cooking";
```

Change the Value of an Attribute

The setAttribute() method can be used to change the value of an existing attribute, or to create a new attribute.The following code adds a new attribute called "edition" (with the value "first") to each <book> element:

Example

```
x=xmlDoc.getElementsByTagName("book");
for(i=0;i<x.length;i++)
 {
 x[i].setAttribute("edition","first");
 }
```

Create an Element

The createElement() method creates a new element node.

The createTextNode() method creates a new text node.

The appendChild() method adds a child node to a node (after the last child). To create a new element with text content, it is necessary to create both an element node and a text node.

The following code creates an element (<edition>), and adds it to the first <book> element:

Example

```
newel=xmlDoc.createElement("edition");
newtext=xmlDoc.createTextNode("First");
newel.appendChild(newtext);
x=xmlDoc.getElementsByTaName("book");
x[0].appendChild(newel);
```

Example explained:

- Create an <edition> element
- Create a text node with value = "First"
- Append the text node to the <edition> element

- Append the <edition> element to the first <book> element

Remove an Element

The removeChild() method removes a specified node (or element).The following code fragment will remove the first node in the first <book> element:

Example

```
x=xmlDoc.getElementsByTagName("book")[0];
x.removeChild(x.childNodes[0]);
```

Note: The result of the example above may be different depending on what browser you use. Firefox treats new lines as empty text nodes, Internet Explorer don't. You can read more about this and how to avoid it in the XML DOM tutorial.

XML DON'T

Here are some technologies you should try to avoid when using XML.

Internet Explorer - XML Data Islands

What is it? An XML data island is XML data embedded into an HTML page.

Why avoid it? XML Data Islands only works with Internet Explorer browsers.

What to use instead? You should use JavaScript and XML DOM to parse and display XML in HTML.For more information about JavaScript and XML DOM, visit our XML DOM tutorial.

XML Data Island Example

This example uses the XML document "cd_catalog.xml". Bind the XML document to an <xml> tag in the HTML document. The id attribute defines an id for the data island, and the src attribute points to the XML file:

Example

This example only works in IE

```
<html>
<body>
```

```
<xml id="cdcat" src="cd_catalog.xml"></xml>
<table border="1" datasrc="#cdcat">
<tr>
<td><span datafld="ARTIST"></span></td>
<td><span datafld="TITLE"></span></td>
</tr>
</table>
</body>
</html>
```

The datasrc attribute of the <table> tag binds the HTML table to the XML data island.The <span> tags allow the datafld attribute to refer to the XML element to be displayed. In this case, "ARTIST" and "TITLE". As the XML is read, additional rows are created for each <CD> element.

Internet Explorer – Behaviours

What is it? Internet Explorer 5 introduced behaviours. Behaviours are a way to add behaviours to XML (or HTML) elements with the use of CSS styles.

Why avoid it? The behaviour attribute is only supported by Internet Explorer.

What to use instead? Use JavaScript and XML DOM (or HTML DOM) instead.

Example 1 - Mouseover Highlight

The following HTML file has a <style> element that defines a behaviour for the <h1> element:

```
<html>
<head>
<style type="text/css">
h1 { behaviour: url(behave.htc) }
</style>
</head>
<body>
<h1>Mouse over me!!!</h1>
</body>
</html>
```

The XML document "behave.htc" is shown below:

```
<attach for="element" event="onmouseover"
```

```
handler="hig_lite"/>
    <attach for="element" event="onmouseout"
handler="low_lite"/>
    <script type="text/javascript">
    function hig_lite()
    {
    element.style.colour='red';
    }
    function low_lite()
    {
    element.style.colour='blue';
    }
    </script>
```

The behaviour file contains a JavaScript and event handlers for the elements.

Example 2 - Typewriter Simulation

The following HTML file has a <style> element that defines a behaviour for elements with an id of "typing":

```
<html>
<head>
<style type="text/css">
#typing
{
behaviour:url(typing.htc);
font-family:'courier new';
}
</style>
</head>
<body>
<span id="typing" speed="100">IE5 introduced
DHTML behaviours.
Behaviours are a way to add DHTML functionality
to HTML elements with the ease of CSS.<br
/><br/>How do      behaviours work?<br/>By
using XML we can link behaviours to any element
in a web pageand manipulate that element.</
p>v </span>
</body>
```

```
</html>
```

The XML document "typing.htc" is shown below:

```
<attach for="window" event="onload"
handler="beginTyping"/>
<method name="type"/>
<script type="text/javascript">
var i,text1,text2,textLength,t;
function beginTyping()
{
i=0;
text1=element.innerText;
textLength=text1.length;
element.innerText="";
text2="";
t=window.setInterval(element.id+".type()",speed);
}
function type()
{
text2=text2+text1.substring(i,i+1);
element.innerText=text2;
i=i+1;
if (i==textLength)
 {
 clearInterval(t);
 }
}
</script>
```

XML IN REAL LIFE

Some examples of how XML can be used to exchange information.

Example: XML News

XMLNews is a specification for exchanging news and other information.

Using such a standard makes it easier for both news producers and news consumers to produce, receive, and archive any kind of news information across different hardware, software, and programming languages.

An example XMLNews document:

```
<?xml version="1.0" encoding="ISO-8859-1"?>
<nitf>
 <head>
 <title>Colombia Earthquake</title>
 </head>
 <body>
 <headline>
 <hl1>143 Dead in Colombia Earthquake
     </hl1>
 </headline>
 <byline>
 <bytag>By Jared Kotler, Associated
Press Writer</bytag>
 </byline>
 <dateline>
 <location>Bogota, Colombia</location>
 <date>Monday January 25 1999 7:28
ET</date>
 </dateline>
 </body>
</nitf>
```

Example: XML Weather Service

An example of an XML national weather service from NOAA (National Oceanic and Atmospheric Administration):

```
<?xml version="1.0" encoding="ISO-8859-1" ?>
<current_observation>
<credit>NOAA's National Weather Service</
credit>
<credit_URL>http://weather.gov/</credit_URL>
<image>
    <url>http://weather.gov/images/xml_logo.
    gif</url>
 <title>NOAA's National Weather Service</
title>
 <link>http://weather.gov</link>
</image>
<location>New York/John F. Kennedy Intl
```

```
Airport, NY</location>
    <station_id>KJFK</station_id>
    <latitude>40.66</latitude>
    <longitude>-73.78</longitude>
    <observation_time_rfc822>Mon, 11 Feb 2008
06:51:00 -0500     EST
    </observation_time_rfc822>
    <weather>A Few Clouds</weather>
    <temp_f>11</temp_f>
    <temp_c>-12</temp_c>
    <relative_humidity>36</relative_humidity>
    <wind_dir>West</wind_dir>
    <wind_degrees>280</wind_degrees>
    <wind_mph>18.4</wind_mph>
    <wind_gust_mph>29</wind_gust_mph>
    <pressure_mb>1023.6</pressure_mb>
    <pressure_in>30.23</pressure_in>
    <dewpoint_f>-11</dewpoint_f>
    <dewpoint_c>-24</dewpoint_c>
    <windchill_f>-7</windchill_f>
    <windchill_c>-22</windchill_c>
    <visibility_mi>10.00</visibility_mi>
    <icon_url_base>http://weather.gov/weather/
images/fcicons/</icon_url_base>
    <icon_url_name>nfew.jpg</icon_url_name>
    <disclaimer_url>http://weather.gov/
disclaimer.html</disclaimer_url>
    <copyright_url>http://weather.gov/
disclaimer.html</copyright_url>
    </current_observation>
```

XML EDITORS

If you are serious about XML, you will benefit from using a professional XML Editor.

XML is Text-based

XML is a text-based markup language.One great thing about XML is that XML files can be created and edited using a simple text-editor like Notepad.However, when you start working with XML, you will soon find that it is better to edit XML documents using a professional XML editor.

Why Not Notepad

Many web developers use Notepad to edit both HTML and XML documents because Notepad is included with the most common OS and it is simple to use. Personally I often use Notepad for quick editing of simple HTML, CSS, and XML files.But, if you use Notepad for XML editing, you will soon run into problems.Notepad does not know that you are writing XML, so it will not be able to assist you.

Why an XML Editor

Today XML is an important technology, and development projects use XML-based technologies like:

- XML Schema to define XML structures and data types
- XSLT to transform XML data
- SOAP to exchange XML data between applications
- WSDL to describe web services
- RDF to describe web resources
- XPath and XQuery to access XML data
- SMIL to define graphics

To be able to write error-free XML documents, you will need an intelligent XML editor!

XML Editors

Professional XML editors will help you to write error-free XML documents, validate your XML against a DTD or a schema, and force you to stick to a valid XML structure.

An XML editor should be able to:

- Add closing tags to your opening tags automatically
- Force you to write valid XML
- Verify your XML against a DTD
- Verify your XML against a Schema
- Colour code your XML syntax

At W3Schools we have been using XMLSpy for many years. XMLSpy is our favourite XML editor.

These are some of the features we especially like:

- Easy to use
- Syntax colouring and pretty printing
- Built in validation & well-formedness checking
- Easy switching between text view and grid view
- Graphical XML Schema editor
- Database import and export for all major databases
- Built in templates for many XML document types
- Intelligent XPath 1.0/2.0 auto-completion
- XSLT 1.0/2.0 editor, profiler, and debugger
- XQuery editor, profiler, and debugger
- SOAP client and debugger
- Graphical WSDL editor
- XBRL validation & taxonomy editing
- Support for Office 2007/ OOXML
- Code generation in Java, C++, and C#

HTML VS. XML

Consider the HTML recipe collection again:

```
<h1>Rhubarb Cobbler</h1>
<h2>Maggie.Herrick@bbs.mhv.net</h2>
<h3>Wed, 14 Jun 95</h3>
Rhubarb Cobbler made with bananas as the main
sweetener. It was delicious. Basicly it was
<table>
<tr><td> 2 1/2 cups <td> diced rhubarb
<tr><td> 2 tablespoons <td> sugar
<tr><td> 2 <td> fairly ripe bananas
<tr><td> 1/4 teaspoon <td> cinnamon
<tr><td> dash of <td> nutmeg
</table>
Combine all and use as cobbler, pie, or crisp.
Related recipes: <a
href="#GardenQuiche">Garden      Quiche</a>
```

With XML, we can instead define our own "recipe markup language" where the markup tags directly correspond to concepts in the world of recipes:

```
<recipe id="117" category="dessert">
```

```
    <title>Rhubarb Cobbler</title>
    <author><e-mail>Maggie.Herrick@bbs.mhv.net</
    e-mail></author>
    <date>Wed, 14 Jun 95</date>
    <description>
    Rhubarb Cobbler made with bananas as the
 main sweetener. It was delicious.
    </description>
    <ingredients>
    <item><amount>2 1/2 cups</amount><type>diced
 rhubarb</type></item>
    <item><amount>2 tablespoons</amount><type>
 sugar</type></item>
    <item><amount>2</amount><type>fairly ripe
 bananas</type></item>
    <item><amount>1/4teaspoon<amount><type>
 cinnamon</type></item>
    <item><amount>dash of</amount><type>nutmeg</
    type></item>
    </ingredients>
    <preparation>
    Combine all and use as cobbler, pie, or
 crisp.
    </preparation>
    <related url="#GardenQuiche">Garden Quiche</
    related>
   </recipe>
```

This example illustrates:

The markup tags are chosen purely for logical structurethis is just one choice of markup detail levelwe need to define which XML documents we regard as "recipe collections"we need a stylesheet to define browser presentation semanticswe need to express queries in a general wayLater:

XML Schema will later be used to define our class of recipe documents XSLT will be used to transform the XML document into XHTML (or HTML), including automatic construction of index, references, etc.XLink, XPointer, and XPath could be used to create cross-references XQuery will be used to express queries.

A CONCEPTUAL VIEW OF XML

An XML document is an ordered, labeled tree:character data leaf nodes contain the actual data (text strings)usually, character data nodes must be non-empty and non-adjacent to other character data nodeselements nodes, are each labeled witha name (often called the element *type*), anda set of attributes, each consisting of a name and a value,and these nodes can have child nodes

A tree view of the XML recipe collection:

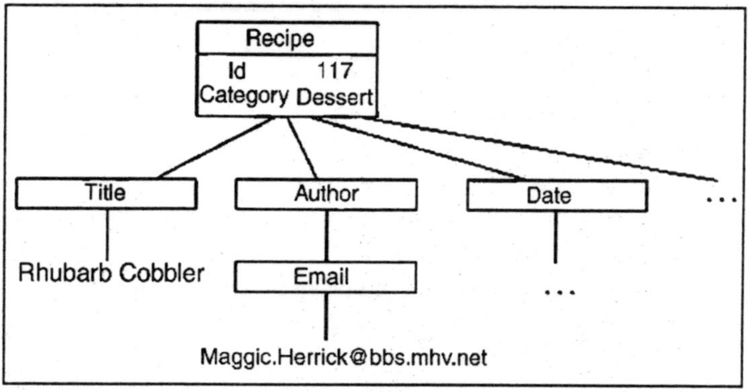

The tree structure of a document can be examined in the Explorer and Mozilla browsers.In addition, XML trees may contain other kinds of leaf nodes:

Processing instructions: Annotations for various processors

Comments: As in programming languages

Document type declaration: Described later

A CONCRETE VIEW OF XML

An XML document is a (Unicode) text with markup tags and other meta-information.

Markup tags denote elements:

```
...<foo attr="val"...>...</foo>...
```

| | | |

| | | A matching *element end* tag

| | The *contents* of the element

| An attribute with name attr and value val, values enclosed by ' or " an *element start* tag with name foo

There is a short-hand notation for empty elements:

```
...<foo attr="val".../>...
```

An XML document must be well-formed:start and end tags must matchelement tags must be properly nested+ some more subtle syntactical requirements

Note: XML is *case sensitive*!Special characters can be escaped using Unicode *character references*

:< and < both yield <

& and & both yield &

CDATA Sections are an alternative to escaping many characters:

```
<![CDATA[<greeting>Hello, world!</greeting>]]>
```

The strange syntax is a legacy from SGML...White-space (blanks, newlines, etc.) is used both for indentation and actual contents. (xml:space attribute provides some control.)Other meta-information:

```
<?target data...?>
```

An instruction for a processor, target identifies the processor for which it is directed, data is a string containing the instruction

```
<!– comment –>
```

A comment, will be ignored by all processors

```
<!DOCTYPE...>
```

APPLICATIONS OF XML

There are already hundreds of serious applications of XML.XHTML

W3C's XMLization of HTML 4.0. Example XHTML document:

```
<?xml version="1.0" encoding="UTF-8"?>
<html xmlns="http://www.w3.org/1999/xhtml"
xml:lang="en">
  <head><title>Hello world!</title></head>
  <body><p>foobar</p></body>
</html>
```

CML

Chemical Markup Language. Example CML document snippet:

```
<molecule id="METHANOL">
 <atomArray>
```

```
    <stringArray builtin="elementType">C O H
    H H H</stringArray>
    <floatArray builtin="x3" units="pm">
    -0.748 0.558 -1.293 -1.263 -0.699 0.716
    </floatArray>
    </atomArray>
   </molecule>
```

WML

Wireless Markup Language for WAP services:

```
<?xml version="1.0"?>
<wml>
 <card id="Card1" title="Wap-UK.com">
 <p>
 Hello World
 </p>
 </card>
</wml>
```

ThML

Theological Markup Language:

```
<h3 class="s05" id="One.2.p0.2">Having a
Humble Opinion of Self</h3>
<p class="First" id="One.2.p0.3">EVERY man
naturally desires knowledge
 <note place="foot" id="One.2.p0.4">
 <p class="Footnote" id="One.2.p0.5">
    <added id ="One.2.p0.6">
 <name id="One.2.p0.7">Aristotle</name>,
 Metaphysics, i.1.
 </added></p>
 </note>;
 but what good is knowledge without fear of
 God? Indeed   a humble rustic who serves God
 is better than a proud intellectual who
neglects his soul to study the course of
the stars.
 <added id="One.2.p0.8"><note place="foot"
id="One.2.p0.9">
 <p class="Footnote" id="One.2.p0.10">
```

```
Augustine, Confessions V. 4.
</p>
</note></added>
</p>
```

THE RECIPE EXAMPLE

Consider again recipes, such as in this example (raw text file).We design an XML version of a recipe collection:recipes consist of ingredients, steps for preparation, possibly some comments, and a specification of its nutritionan ingredient can be simple or compositea simple ingredient has a name, an amount (possibly unspecified), an a unit (unless amount is dimensionless)a composite ingredient is recursively a recipe with ingredients and preparation

This example (formatted XML file) contains five recipes. Abbreviated version:

```
<?xml version="1.0" encoding="UTF-8"?>
<collection>
 <description>
 Some recipes used for the XML tutorial.
 </description>
 <recipe>
 <title>Beef Parmesan with Garlic Angel
 Hair Pasta</title>
 <ingredient name="beef cube steak"
amount="1.5"unit="pound"/>
...
 <preparation>
 <step>
    Preheat oven to 350 degrees F (175
 degrees C).
 </step>
...
 </preparation>
 <comment>
 Make the meat ahead of time, and
refrigerate over night, the acid in
the tomato sauce will tenderize the       meat
```

```
even more. If you do this, save  the mozzarella
till the last minute.
     </comment>
     <nutrition calories="1167" fat="23"
 carbohydrates ="45" protein="32"/>
     </recipe>
    ...
    </collection>
```

FROM SGML TO SML

DocHeads vs. Simpletons, a process of simplification SGML (Standard Generalized Markup Language)ISO standard, 1985huge amount of "document archive" applications in government, military, industry, academia...a successfull well-known application: HTML is designed as a simple application of SGML.

|

V

XML

W3C Recommendation 1998

A simple subset of SGML, targeted for Web applicationsnow de facto standard

|

V

MinML (Minimal XML, previously known as SML - Simple Markup Language)Web community discussions and collaborations, started 1999simplifies the XML spec: no DTDs, processing instructions, or comments, UTF-8 and UTF-16 only, considerations on element attributes, white-space...

Canonical XML: W3C Recommendation, March 2001intended as simplification of general XML documents, *not as a simplified XML spec*"canonical" representationremoves document type declarations, imposes ordering on attributes, UTF-8 encoding, etc.

SGML RELICS

Only a fool does not fear "external general parsed entities"As an unfortunate heritage from SGML, the header of an XML document may contain a document type declaration:

```
<?xml version="1.0"?>
<!DOCTYPE greeting [
 <!ELEMENT greeting (#PCDATA)>
 <!ATTLIST greeting style (big|small)
"small">
 <!ENTITY hi "Hello">
]>
<greeting> &hi; world! </greeting>
```

This part can contain:

DTD (Document Type Definition) information:element type declarations (ELEMENT)attribute-list declarations (ATTLIST)(described later...)entity declarations (ENTITY) - a simple macro mechanismnotation declarations (NOTATION) - data format specifications Avoid all these features whenever possible!Unfortunately, they cannot always be ignored - all XML processors (even non-validating ones) are required to:normalize attribute values (prune white-space etc.)handle internal entity references (*e.g.* expand &hi; in greeting)insert default attribute values (*e.g.* insert style="small" in greeting)

XML TECHNOLOGIES

XML is: Hot ($$$)the standard for representation of Web informationby itself, just a notation for hierarchically structured textBut a notation for tree structures is not enough:the real force of XML is generic languages and tools!by building on XML, you get a massive infrastructure for freeThe XML vision offers:common extensions to the core XML specificationa namespace mechanism, document inclusion, etc.schemas grammars to define classes of documentslinking between documentsa generalization of HTML anchors and linksaddressing parts of read-only documentsflexible and robust pointers into documentstransformationconversion from one document class to anotherqueryingextraction of information, generalizing relational databases

To "use XML": Define your XML language (use *e.g.* XML Schema to define its syntax)exploit the generic XML tools (*e.g.*

XSLT and XQuery processors), the generic protocols, and the generic programming frameworks (*e.g.* DOM or SAX) to build application tools

XML ACTIVITY

Development and application activity in the XML community:

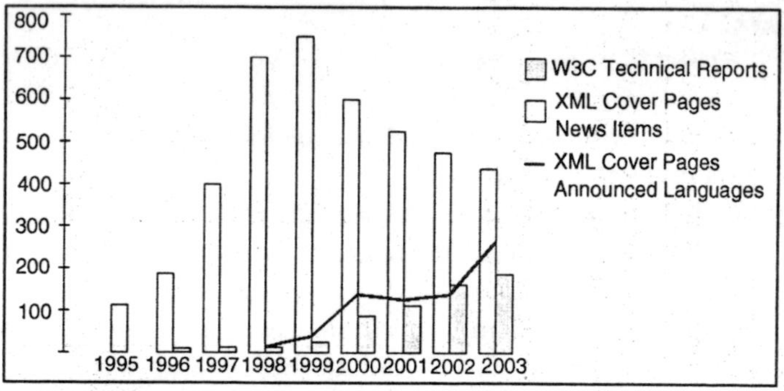

(Rough unscientific measure based on XML Cover Pages news items and W3C reports.) As the development of core XML technologies is stabilizing, their use is taking off.The core XML technologies are now mostly Recommendations, and W3C focuses on building higher-level layers.

11

XML Base

LANGUAGES

MIXING XML LANGUAGES

Consider an XML language WidgetML which uses XHTML as a sublanguage for help messages:

```
<widget type="gadget">
 <head size="medium"/>
 <big><subwidget ref="gizmo"/></big>
 <info>
 <head>
 <title>Description of gadget</title>
 </head>
 <body>
 <h1>Gadget</h1>
 A gadget contains a big gizmo
 </body>
 </info>
</widget>
```

A problem: the meaning of head and big depends on the context!This complicates things for processors and might even cause ambiguities.The root of the problem is: one common name space.

QUALIFYING NAMES

Simple solution: qualify names with URIs (Universal Resource Identifiers)

```
<{http://www.w3.org/TR/xhtml1}head>
```

\/ \/

qualifying URI local name

Do not be confused by the use of URIs for namespaces:

They are not supposed to point to anythingit is simply the cheapest way of getting unique nameswe rely on existing organizations that control domain names

NAMESPACE DECLARATIONS

Namespaces are declared by special attributes and associated prefixes:

```
<...xmlns:foo="http://www.w3.org/TR/xhtml1">
...
 <foo:head>...</foo:head>
...
</...>
```

xmlns:*prefix="URI"* declares a namespace with a prefix and a URI:

The scope of declaration is lexical, the element containing the declaration and all descendants can be overridden by nested declarationboth element and attribute names can be qualified with namespacesthe name of the prefix is irrelevant - applications should use only the URIFor backward compatibility and simplicity, unprefixed element names are assigned a default namespace:

- *Declaration*: xmlns="*URI*"
- *Default value*: "" (means: treat as unqualified name)

Does *not* affect unprefixed attribute names (they belong to the containing elements)

WidgetML *with namespaces:*

```
<widget xmlns="http://www.widget.org"
 xmlns:xhtml="http://www.w3.org/TR/xhtml1"
 type="gadget">
 <head size="medium"/>
 <big><subwidget ref="gizmo"/></big>
 <info>
 <xhtml:head>
    <xhtml:title>Description of gadget</
```

```
  xhtml:title>
    </xhtml:head>
    <xhtml:body>
     <xhtml:h1>Gadget</xhtml:h1>
     A gadget contains a big gizmo
    </xhtml:body>
  </info>
</widget>
```

NAMESPACES IN XML

We envision applications of Extensible Markup Language (XML) where a single XML document may contain elements and attributes (here referred to as a "markup vocabulary") that are defined for and used by multiple software modules.

One motivation for this is modularity: if such a markup vocabulary exists which is well-understood and for which there is useful software available, it is better to re-use this markup rather than re-invent it.Such documents, containing multiple markup vocabularies, pose problems of recognition and collision.

Software modules need to be able to recognize the elements and attributes which they are designed to process, even in the face of "collisions" occurring when markup intended for some other software package uses the same element name or attribute name.

These considerations require that document constructs should have names constructed so as to avoid clashes between names from different markup vocabularies. This specification describes a mechanism, *XML namespaces,* which accomplishes this by assigning expanded names to elements and attributes.

A NOTE ON NOTATION AND USAGE

Where *emphasized,* the key words *must, must not, required, should, should not, may* in this document are to be interpreted as described in [Keywords].Note that many of the nonterminals in the productions in this specification are defined not here but in the XML specification [XML]. When nonterminals defined here have the same names as nonterminals defined in the XML specification, the productions here in all cases match a subset of the strings matched by the corresponding ones there.In this document's productions, the NSC is a "Namespace Constraint", one of the rules that documents conforming to this specification *must* follow.

XML NAMESPACES

BASIC CONCEPTS

Definition: An XML namespace is identified by a URI reference [RFC3986]; element and attribute names may be placed in an XML namespace using the mechanisms described in this specification.][Definition: An expanded name is a pair consisting of a namespace name and a local name.] [Definition: For a name *N* in a namespace identified by a URI *I*, the namespace name is *I*.

For a name *N* that is not in a namespace, the namespace namehas no value.] [Definition: In either case the local name is *N*.] It is this combination of the universally managed IRI namespace with the vocabulary's local names that is effective in avoiding name clashes.

URI references can contain characters not allowed in names, and are often inconveniently long, so expanded names are not used directly to name elements and attributes in XML documents.

Instead qualified names are used. [Definition: A qualified name is a name subject to namespace interpretation.] In documents conforming to this specification, element and attribute names appear as qualified names. Syntactically, they are either prefixed names or unprefixed names.

An attribute-based declaration syntax is provided to bind prefixes to namespace names and to bind a default namespace that applies to unprefixed element names; these declarations are scoped by the elements on which they appear so that different bindings may apply in different parts of a document. Processors conforming to this specification *must* recognize and act on these declarations and prefixes.

Use of URIs as Namespace Names

The empty string, though it is a legal URI reference, cannot be used as a namespace name.The use of relative URI references, including same-document references, in namespace declarations is deprecated.

Note: This deprecation of relative URI references was decided on by a W3C XML Plenary Ballot [Relative URI deprecation]. It also declares that "later specifications such as DOM, XPath, etc. will define no interpretation for them".

Comparing URI References

URI references identifying namespaces are compared when determining whether a name belongs to a given namespace, and whether two names belong to the same namespace. [Definition: The two URIs are treated as strings, and they are identical if and only if the strings are identical, that is, if they are the same sequence of characters.] The comparison is case-sensitive, and no%-escaping is done or undone.

A consequence of this is that URI references which are not identical in this sense may resolve to the same resource. Examples include URI references which differ only in case or%-escaping, or which are in external entities which have different base URIs (but note that relative URIs are deprecated as namespace names).In a namespace declaration, the URI reference is the normalized value of the attribute, so replacement of XML character and entity references has already been done before any comparison.

Examples:

The URI references below are all different for the purposes of identifying namespaces, since they differ in case:

http://www.example.org/wine

http://www.Example.org/wine

http://www.example.org/Wine

The IRI references below are also all different for the purposes of identifying namespaces:

http://www.example.org/~wilbur

```
http://www.example.org/%7ewilbur
http://www.example.org/%7Ewilbur
```

Because of the risk of confusion between URIs that would be equivalent if dereferenced, the use of%-escaped characters in namespace names is strongly discouraged.

DECLARING NAMESPACES

Definition: A namespace (or more precisely, a namespace binding) is declared using a family of reserved attributes. Such an attribute's name must either be xmlns or begin xmlns:. These attributes, like any other XML attributes, may be provided directly or by default.

Attribute Names for Namespace Declaration

[1]	NSAttName	::=	PrefixedAttName | DefaultAttName	
[2]	Prefixed AttName	::=	'xmlns:' NCName	[NSC:Reserved Prefixes and Namespace Names]
[3]	Default AttName	::=	'xmlns'	
[4]	NCName	::=	NCName StartChar NC NameChar*	*/* An XML Name, minus the ":" */*
[5]	NCName Char	::=	NameChar - ':'	
[6]	NCName StartChar	::=	Letter | '_'	

The attribute's normalized value *must* be either a URI reference — the namespace name identifying the namespace — or an empty string. The namespace name, to serve its intended purpose, *should* have the characteristics of uniqueness and persistence.

It is not a goal that it be directly usable for retrieval of a schema (if any exists). Uniform Resource Names [RFC2141]is an example of a syntax that is designed with these goals in mind. However, it should be noted that ordinary URLs can be managed in such a way as to achieve these same goals.

[*Definition*: If the attribute name matches Prefixed AttName, then the NCName gives the namespace prefix, used to associate element and attribute names with the namespace name in the attribute value in the scope of the element to which the declaration is attached. In such declarations, the namespace name may not be empty.]

[*Definition*: If the attribute name matches DefaultAttName, then the namespace name in the attribute value is that of the default namespace in the scope of the element to which the declaration is attached.] Default namespaces and overriding of declarations are discussed in 6 Applying Namespaces to Elements and Attributes.An example namespace declaration, which associates the namespace prefix edi with the namespace namehttp://ecommerce.example.org/schema:

```
<x xmlns:edi='http://ecommerce.example.org/
schema'>
  <!– the "edi" prefix is bound to http://
 ecommerce.example.org/schema for the "x"
 element and contents –>
</x>
```

Namespace Constraint

Reserved Prefixes and Namespace Names

The prefix xml is by definition bound to the namespace name http://www.w3.org/XML/1998/namespace. It *may*, but need not, be declared, and *must not* be bound to any other namespace name. Other prefixes *must not* be bound to this namespace name, and it *must not* be declared as the default namespace.The prefix xmlns is used only to declare namespace bindings and is by definition bound to the namespace namehttp://www.w3.org/2000/xmlns/.

It *must not* be declared. Other prefixes *must not* be bound to this namespace name, and it *must not* be declared as the default namespace. Element names *must not* have the prefix xmlns.All other prefixes beginning with the three-letter sequence x, m, l, in any case combination, are reserved. This means that:users *should not* use them except as defined by later specificationsprocessors *must not* treat them as fatal errors.Though they are not themselves reserved, it is inadvisable to use prefixed names whose LocalPart begins with the letters x, m, l, in any case combination, as these names would be reserved if used without a prefix.

QUALIFIED NAMES

In XML documents conforming to this specification, some names (constructs corresponding to the nonterminal Name) *must* begiven as qualified names, defined as follows:

Qualified Name:

[7]	QName	::=	PrefixedName | UnprefixedName
[8]	PrefixedName	::=	Prefix ':' LocalPart
[9]	UnprefixedName	::=	LocalPart
[10]	Prefix	::=	NCName
[11]	LocalPart	::=	NCName

The Prefix provides the namespace prefix part of the qualified name, and *must* be associated with a namespace URI reference in a namespace declaration. [Definition: The LocalPart provides the local part of the qualified name.]Note that the prefix functions *only* as a placeholder for a namespace name. Applications *should* use the namespace name, not the prefix, in constructing names whose scope extends beyond the containing document.

USING QUALIFIED NAMES

In XML documents conforming to this specification, element names are given as qualified names, as follows:

Element Names:

[12]	STag	::=	'<' QName (S Attribute) * S? '>'	[NSC: Prefix Declared]
[13]	ETag	::=	'</' QName S? '>'	[NSC: Prefix Declared]
[14]	Empty ElemTag	::=	'<' QName (S Attribute) * S? '/>'	[NSC: Prefix Declared]

An example of a qualified name serving as an element name:

```
<!– the 'price' element's namespace is http:/
/ecommerce.example.org/schema –>
<edi:price xmlns:edi='http://
ecommerce.example.org/schema'
units='Euro'>32.18</edi:price>
```

Attributes are either namespace declarations or their names are given as qualified names:

Attribute:

[15]	Attribute	::=	NSAttName Eq AttValue	
			| QName Eq AttValue	[NSC: Prefix Declared]

An example of a qualified name serving as an attribute name:

```
<x xmlns:edi='http://ecommerce.example.org/
schema'>
  <!– the 'taxClass' attribute's namespace is
  http://ecommerce.example.org/schema –>
  <lineItem edi:taxClass="exempt">Baby food</
  lineItem>
</x>
```

Namespace Constraint: Prefix Declared

The namespace prefix, unless it is xml or xmlns, *must* have been declared in a namespace declaration attribute in either the start-tag of the element where the prefix is used or in an ancestor element (*i.e.* an element in whose content the prefixed markup occurs).This constraint may lead to operational difficulties in the case where the namespace declaration attribute is provided, not directly in the XML document entity, but via a default attribute declared in an external entity.

Such declarations may not be read by software which is based on a non-validating XML processor. Many XML applications, presumably including namespace-sensitive ones, fail to require validating processors. If correct operation with such applications is required, namespace declarations *must*be provided either directly or via default attributes declared in the internal subset of the DTD.Element names and attribute names are also given as qualified names when they appear in declarations in the DTD:

Qualified Names in Declarations:

<table>
<tr><td>[16]</td><td>doctypedecl</td><td>::=</td><td>'<!DOCTYPE' S QName (SExternalID)? S? ('[' (markupdecl | PEReference | S)* ']' S?)? '>'</td></tr>
<tr><td>[17]</td><td>elementdecl</td><td>::=</td><td>'<!ELEMENT' S QName S contentspec S? '>'</td></tr>
<tr><td>[18]</td><td>cp</td><td>::=</td><td>(QName | choice | seq) ('?' | '*' | '+')?</td></tr>
<tr><td>[19]</td><td>Mixed</td><td>::=</td><td>'(' S? '#PCDATA' (S? '|' S? QName)* S? ')*'
| '(' S? '#PCDATA' S? ')'</td></tr>
<tr><td>[20]</td><td>AttlistDecl</td><td>::=</td><td>'<!ATTLIST' S QName AttDef* S? '>'</td></tr>
<tr><td>[21]</td><td>AttDef</td><td>::=</td><td>S (QName | NSAttName) S AttType S Defaulted</td></tr>
</table>

Note that DTD-based validation is not namespace-aware in the following sense: a DTD constrains the elements and attributes that may appear in a document by their uninterpreted names, not by (namespace name, local name) pairs. To validate a document that uses namespaces against a DTD, the same prefixes must be used in the DTD as in the instance. A DTD may however indirectly constrain the namespaces used in a valid document by providing #FIXED values for attributes that declare namespaces.

APPLYING NAMESPACES TO ELEMENTS AND ATTRIBUTES

Namespace Scoping

The scope of a namespace declaration declaring a prefix extends from the beginning of the start-tag in which it appears to the end of the corresponding end-tag, excluding the scope of any inner declarations with the same NSAttName part. In the case of an empty tag, the scope is the tag itself.Such a namespace declaration applies to all element and attribute names within its scope whose prefix matches that specified in the declaration.The expanded name corresponding to a prefixed element or attribute name has the URI to which the prefix is bound as its namespace name, and the local part as its local name.

```
<?xml version="1.0"?>
<html:html xmlns:html='http://www.w3.org/1999/
xhtml'>
 <html:head><html:title>Frobnostication</
html:title></html:head>
 <html:body><html:p>Moved to
 <html:ahref='http://frob.example.
com'>here.</html:a></html:p></html:body>
</html:html>
```

Multiple namespace prefixes can be declared as attributes of a single element, as shown in this example:

```
<?xml version="1.0"?>
<!– both namespace prefixes are available
throughout –>
<bk:book xmlns:bk='urn:loc.gov:books'
 xmlns:isbn='urn:ISBN:0-395-36341-6'>
 <bk:title>Cheaper by the Dozen</bk:title>
 <isbn:number>1568491379</isbn:number>
</bk:book>
```

NAMESPACE DEFAULTING

The scope of a default namespace declaration extends from the beginning of the start-tag in which it appears to the end of the corresponding end-tag, excluding the scope of any inner default namespace declarations. In the case of an empty tag, the scope is the tag itself.

A default namespace declaration applies to all unprefixed element names within its scope. Default namespace declarations do not apply directly to attribute names; the interpretation of unprefixed attributes is determined by the element on which they appear.If there is a default namespace declaration in scope, the expanded name corresponding to an unprefixed element name has the URI of the default namespace as its namespace name. If there is no default namespace declaration in scope, the namespace name has no value. The namespace name for an unprefixed attribute name always has no value. In all cases, the local name islocal part (which is of course the same as the unprefixed name itself).

```
<?xml version="1.0"?>
<!– elements are in the HTML namespace, in
this case by default –>
<html xmlns='http://www.w3.org/1999/xhtml'>
 <head><title>Frobnostication</title></head>
 <body><p>Moved to
   <a href='http://frob.example.com'>here</
   a>.</p></body>
</html>
<?xml version="1.0"?>
<!– unprefixed element types are from "books"
–>
<book xmlns='urn:loc.gov:books'
 xmlns:isbn='urn:ISBN:0-395-36341-6'>
   <title>Cheaper by the Dozen</title>
   <isbn:number>1568491379</isbn:number>
</book>
```

A larger example of namespace scoping:

```
<?xml version="1.0"?>
<!– initially, the default namespace is "books"
–>
<book xmlns='urn:loc.gov:books'
 xmlns:isbn='urn:ISBN:0-395-36341-6'>
 <title>Cheaper by the Dozen</title>
 <isbn:number>1568491379</isbn:number>
 <notes>
 <!– make HTML the default namespace for
some commentary –>
   <p xmlns='http://www.w3.org/1999/xhtml'>
    This is a <i>funny</i> book!
 </p>
 </notes>
</book>
```

The attribute value in a default namespace declaration *may* be empty. This has the same effect, within the scope of the declaration, of there being no default namespace.

```
<?xml version='1.0'?>
<Beers>
 <!— the default namespace inside tables is
 that of HTML —>
 <table xmlns='http://www.w3.org/1999/xhtml'>
 <th><td>Name</td><td>Origin</td>
<td>Description</td></th>
 <tr>
 <!— no default namespace inside table
cells —>
   <td><brandName xmlns="">Huntsman</
 brandName></td>
   <td><origin xmlns="">Bath, UK</origin></
   td>
   <td>
    <details xmlns=""><class>Bitter<
class>          <hop>Fuggles</hop>
    <pro>Wonderful hop, light alcohol, good
    summer beer</pro>
    <con>Fragile; excessive variance pub to
    pub</con>
    </details>
 </td>
 </tr>
 </table>
</Beers>
```

Uniqueness of Attributes

In XML documents conforming to this specification, no tag may contain two attributes which:

Have identical names, orhave qualified names with the same local part and with prefixes which have been bound to namespace names that are identical.This constraint is equivalent to requiring that no element have two attributes with the same expanded name.

For example, each of the bad empty-element tags is illegal in the following:

```
<!– http://www.w3.org is bound to n1 and n2 –
>
<x xmlns:n1="http://www.w3.org"
 xmlns:n2="http://www.w3.org" >
 <bad a="1" a="2"/>
 <bad n1:a="1" n2:a="2"/>
</x>
```

However, each of the following is legal, the second because the default namespace does not apply to attribute names:

```
<!– http://www.w3.org is bound to n1 and is
the default–>
<x xmlns:n1="http://www.w3.org"
 xmlns="http://www.w3.org" >
 <good a="1"    b="2"/>
 <good a="1"    n1:a="2"/>
</x>
```

CONFORMANCE OF DOCUMENTS

This specification applies to XML 1.0 documents. To conform to this specification, a document *must* be well-formed according to the XML 1.0 specification [XML10].In XML documents which conform to this specification, element and attribute names *must* match the production for QName and*must* satisfy the "Namespace Constraints". All other tokens in the document which are *required*, for XML 1.0 well-formedness, to match the XML production for Name *must* match this specification's production for NCName.[Definition: A document is namespace-well-formed if it conforms to this specification.]

It follows that in a namespace-well-formed document:All element and attribute names contain either zero or one colon;No entity names, processing instruction targets, or notation names contain any colons.In addition, a namespace-well-formed document may also be namespace-valid.[Definition: A namespace-well-formed document is namespace-valid if it is valid according to the XML 1.0

specification, and all tokens other than element and attribute names which are *required,* for XML 1.0 validity, to match the XML production for Name match this specification's production for NCName.]It follows that in a namespace-valid document:No attributes with a declared type of ID, IDREF(S), ENTITY(IES), or NOTATION contain any colons.

CONFORMANCE OF PROCESSORS

To conform to this specification, a processor *must* report violations of namespace well-formedness, with the exception that it is not *required* to check that namespace names are legal URIs.[Definition: A validating XML processor that conforms to this specification is namespace-validating if in addition it reports violations of namespace validity.]

A Normative References

- *Keywords*: *RFC 2119: Key words for use in RFCs to Indicate Requirement Levels,* S. Bradner, ed. IETF (Internet Engineering Task Force), March 1997. Available at http://www.rfc-editor.org/rfc/rfc2119.txt
- *RFC 2141: URN Syntax,* R. Moats, ed. IETF (Internet Engineering Task Force), May 1997. Available at http://www.rfc-editor.org/rfc/rfc2141.txt.
- *RFC3986*: *Uniform Resource Identifier (URI): Generic Syntax,* T. Berners-Lee, R. Fielding, and L. Masinter, eds. IETF (Internet Engineering Task Force), January 2005. Available at http://www.rfc-editor.org/rfc/rfc3986.txt
- *RFC 3629: UTF-8, a transformation format of ISO 10646,* F. Yergeau, ed. IETF (Internet Engineering Task Force), November 2003. Available at http://www.rfc-editor.org/rfc/rfc3629.txt
- XML: *Extensible Markup Language (XML) 1.0 (Fourth Edition),* Tim Bray, Jean Paoli, C. M. Sperberg-McQueen, Eve Maler, and François Yergeau eds. W3C (World Wide Web Consortium), 16 August 2006. Available at http://www.w3.org/TR/2006/REC-xml-20060816/.

B Other references (Non-Normative)

1.0 Errata
Namespaces in XML Errata. W3C (World Wide Web Consortium). Available at http://www.w3.org/XML/xml-names-19990114-errata.

Relative URI deprecation
Results of W3C XML Plenary Ballot on relative URI References In namespace declarations 3-17 July 2000, Dave Hollander and C. M. Sperberg-McQueen, 6 September 2000. Available at http://www.w3.org/2000/09/xppa.

C The Internal Structure of XML Namespaces (Non-Normative)

This appendix has been deleted.

D Changes since version 1.0 (Non-Normative)

This version incorporates the errata as of 1 June 2006 [1.0 Errata].There are several editorial changes, including a number of terminology changes and additions intended to produce greater consistency. The non-normative appendix "The Internal Structure of XML Namespaces" has been removed.

E Acknowledgements (Non-Normative)

This work reflects input from a very large number of people, including especially the participants in the World Wide Web Consortium XML Working Group and Special Interest Group and the participants in the W3C Metadata Activity. The contributions of Charles Frankston of Microsoft were particularly valuable.

SPECIFICATION CONTROVERSIES

- How should a relative URI be interpreted?
- Relative to the base URI?
- Relative to the document URI?
- Just as a string?

This innocent question spawned a controversy that resulted in leaving the matter undefined (by deprecating such namespaces).Other controversies:

Does the choice of prefix matter, or is

```
<a:widget xmlns:a="www.widget.org"/> the
same as
<b:widget xmlns:b="www.widget.org"/>?
```

is <a:widget size="big"/> the same as

```
<a:widget a:size="big"/>?
```

Unfortunately, according to the spec, the choice of prefix *may* matter, and an unqualified attribute generally does *not* just inherit the namespace from its element.

XINCLUDE - COMBINING XML DOCUMENTS

INTRODUCTION

Many programming languages provide an inclusion mechanism to facilitate modularity. Markup languages also often have need of such a mechanism. This specification introduces a generic mechanism for merging XML documents (as represented by their information sets) for use by applications that need such a facility. The syntax leverages existing XML constructs - elements, attributes, and URI references.

Relationship to XLink

XInclude differs from the linking features described in the [XML Linking Language], specifically links with the attribute valueshow="embed". Such links provide a media-type independent syntax for indicating that a resource is to be embedded graphically within the display of the document. XLink does not specify a specific processing model, but simply facilitates the detection of links and recognition of associated metadata by a higher level application.XInclude, on the other hand, specifies a media-type specific (XML into XML) transformation.

It defines a specific processing model for merging information sets. XInclude processing occurs at a low level, often by a generic XInclude processor which makes the resulting information set available to higher level applications.Simple information item inclusion as described in this specification differs from transclusion, which preserves contextual information such as style.

Relationship to XML External Entities

There are a number of differences between XInclude and [XML 1.0] or [XML 1.1] external entities which make them complementary technologies.Processing of external entities (as with the rest of DTDs) occurs at parse time. XInclude operates on information sets and thus is orthogonal to parsing.Declaration of external entities requires a DTD or internal subset. This places a set of dependencies on inclusion, for instance, the syntax for the DOCTYPE declaration requires that the document element be named - orthogonal to inclusion in many cases. Validating parsers must have a complete content model defined.

XInclude is orthogonal to validation and the name of the document element.External entities provide a level of indirection - the external entity must be declared and named, and separately invoked. XInclude uses direct references. Applications which generate XML output incrementally can benefit from not having to pre-declare inclusions.Failure to load an external entity is normally a fatal error. XInclude allows the author to provide default content that will be used if the remote resource cannot be loaded.The syntax for an internal subset is cumbersome to many authors of simple well-formed XML documents. XInclude syntax is based on familiar XML constructs.

Relationship to DTDs

XInclude defines no relationship to DTD validation. XInclude describes an infoset-to-infoset transformation and not a change in XML parsing behaviour. XInclude does not define a mechanism for DTD validation of the resulting infoset.

Relationship to XML Schemas

XInclude defines no relationship to the augmented infosets produced by applying an XML schema. Such an augmented infoset can be supplied as the input infoset, or such augmentation might be applied to the infoset resulting from the inclusion.

Relationship to Grammar-Specific Inclusions

Special-purpose inclusion mechanisms have been introduced into specific XML grammars. XInclude provides a generic mechanism for recognizing and processing inclusions, and as such can offer a simpler overall authoring experience, greater performance, and less code redundancy.

TERMINOLOGY

[Definition: The key words must, must not, required, shall, shall not, should, should not, recommended, may, andoptional in this specification are to be interpreted as described in [IETF RFC 2119].][Definition: The term information set refers to the output of an [XML 1.0] or [XML 1.1] processor, expressed as a collection of information items and properties as defined by the [XML Information Set] specification.] In this document the term *infoset* is used as a synonym for *information set*.[Definition: The term fatal error refers to the presence of factors that prevent normal processing from continuing.] [Definition: The term resource error refers to a failure of an attempt to fetch a resource from a URL.] XInclude processors must stop processing when encountering errors other than resource errors, which must be handled as described in 4.4 Fallback Behaviour.

SYNTAX

XInclude defines a namespace associated with the URI. The XInclude namespace contains two elements with the local names include and fallback. For convenience, within this specification these elements are referred to as xi:include and xi:fallback respectively.The following (non-normative) XML schema [XML Schemas] illustrates the content model of the xi namespace:

```
<xs:schema xmlns:xs="http://www.w3.org/2001/
XMLSchema"
 xmlns:xi="http://www.w3.org/2001/XInclude"
```

```
    targetNamespace="http://www.w3.org/2001/
 Include"
    finalDefault="extension">
    <xs:element name="include" type="xi
:includeType"/>
    <xs:complexType name="includeType"
 mixed="true">
    <xs:choice minOccurs='0' maxOccurs
   ='unbounded' >
    <xs:element ref='xi:fallback'/>
    <xs:any namespace='##other' process
 Contents='lax'/>
    <xs:any namespace='##local' process
 Contents='lax'/ >
    </xs:choice>
    <xs:attribute name="href" use="optional"
   type="xs:anyURI"/>
    <xs:attribute name="parse" use="optional"
   default="xml"
   type="xi:parseType"/>
    <xs:attribute name="xpointer" use="
    optional" type="xs:string"/>
    <xs:attribute name="encoding" use="
      optional" type="xs:string"/>
    <xs:attribute name="accept" use="
      optional" type="xs:string"/>
    <xs:attribute name="accept-language"
use="optional"
type="xs:string"/>
    <xs:anyAttributenamespace="##other"
    procesContents="lax"/>
    </xs:complexType>
    <xs:simpleType name="parseType">
       <xs:restriction base="xs:token">
       <xs:enumeration value="xml"/>
       <xs:enumeration value="text"/>
      </xs:restriction>
    </xs:simpleType>
```

```
    <xs:element name="fallback" type
="xi:fallbackType"/>
    <xs:complexType name="fallbackType"
mixed="true">
       <xs: choiceminOccurs="0" maxOccurs
    ="unbounded">
          <xs:element ref="xi:include"/>
          <xs:anynamespace="##other" process
Contents="lax"/>
          <xs:any namespace="##local" process
       Contents="lax"/>
       </xs:choice>
    <xs:anyAttributenamespace="##other"process
    Contents="lax"/>
    </xs:complexType>
   </xs:schema>
   XI:include Element
```

The xi:include element has the following attributes:

Hhref

A value which, after appropriate escaping (4.1.1 Escaping of href attribute values) has been performed, results in a URI reference or an IRI reference specifying the location of the resource to include. The href attribute is optional; the absence of this attribute is the same as specifying href="", that is, the reference is to the same document. If the hrefattribute is absent when parse="xml", the xpointer attribute must be present. Fragment identifiers must not be used; their appearance is a fatal error. A value that results in a syntactically invalid URI or IRI should be reported as a fatal error, but some implementations may find it impractical to distinguish this case from a resource error.

Note: A URI ending in # is considered by [IETF RFC 2396] to have an empty fragment identifier. Such a URI would result in afatal error as described above.

Note: A key feature of XInclude is that it allows a resource to be cast to a user-specifed type for inclusion (XML or text). The returned media type is therefore essentially ignored for the purposes of inclusion processing, and the syntax of the fragment identifier of the returned media type will generally not be applicable to the user-specified type.

Forparse="xml" inclusions, sub-resources are identified by a separate xpointer attribute, which is applied after the casting takes place. While this does not prevent subresources of XML documents to be identified by URI (Architecture of the World Wide Web [Identification]), it does preclude the use of these identifiers directly within XInclude.

Parse

Indicates whether to include the resource as parsed XML or as text. The parse attribute allows XInclude to give the author of the including document priority over the server of the included document in terms of how to process the included content.

A value of "xml" indicates that the resource must be parsed as XML and the infosets merged. A value of "text" indicates that the resource must be included as the character information items. This attribute is optional. When omitted, the value of "xml" is implied (even in the absence of a default value declaration). Values other than "xml" and "text" are a fatal error.

Note: For interoperability between validating and non-validating systems, whitespace should not appear in the parse attribute.

Xpointer

When parse="xml", the XPointer ([XPointer Framework]) contained in the xpointer attribute is evaluated to identify a portion of the resource to include. This attribute is optional; when omitted, the entire resource is included. The xpointerattribute must not be present when parse="text". If the xpointer attribute is absent, the href attribute must be present.

Note: Since the xpointer attribute is not a URI reference, and%-escaping is not done in XPointers, '%' is an ordinary character in the value of the xpointer attribute.

Encoding

When parse="text", it is sometimes impossible to correctly detect the encoding of the text resource. The encoding attribute specifies how the resource is to be translated. The value of this attribute should be a valid encoding name. The encodingattribute has no effect when parse="xml".

Accept

The value of the accept attribute may be used by the XInclude processor to aid in content negotiation. When the XInclude processor fetches a resource via HTTP, it should place the value of the accept attribute, if one exists, in the HTTP request as an Accept header as described in section 14.1 of [IETF RFC 2616]. Values containing characters outside the range #x20 through #x7E must be flagged as fatal errors.

Accept-language

The value of the accept-language attribute may be used by the XInclude processor to aid in content negotiation. When the XInclude processor fetches a resource via HTTP, it should place the value of the accept-language attribute, if one exists, in the HTTP request as an Accept-Language header as described in section 14.4 of [IETF RFC 2616]. Values containing characters outside the range #x20 through #x7E are disallowed in HTTP headers, and must be flagged as fatal errors.Attributes other than those listed above may be placed on the xi:include element.

Unprefixed attribute names are reserved for future versions of this specification, and must be ignored by XInclude 1.0 processors.

The *children* property of the xi:include element may include a single xi:fallback element; the appearance of more than onexi:fallback element, an xi:include element, or any other element from the XInclude namespace is a fatal error. Other content (text, processing instructions, comments, elements not in the XInclude namespace, descendants of child elements) is not constrained by this specification and is ignored by the XInclude processor, that is, it has no effect on include processing, and does not appear in the *children* properties of the result infoset. Such content might be used by applications analyzing a pre-inclusion infoset, or be made available to an application post-inclusion through means other than the normal infoset properties.The following (non-normative) DTD fragment illustrates a sample declaration for the xi:include element:

```
    <!ELEMENT xi:include (xi:fallback?)>
    <!ATTLIST xi:include
    xmlns:xi   CDATA     #FIXED "http://
          www.w3.org/
2001/XInclude"
    href    CDATA    #IMPLIED
    parse (xml|text)     "xml"
    xpointer    CDATA     #IMPLIED
    encoding    CDATA    #IMPLIED
    accept      CDATA     #IMPLIED
    accept-language CDATA    #IMPLIED>
```

XI:fallback Element

The xi:fallback element appears as a child of an xi:include element. It provides a mechanism for recovering from missing resources. When a resource error is encountered, the xi:include element is replaced with the contents of the xi:fallbackelement. If the xi:fallback element is empty, the xi:include element is removed from the result.

If the xi:fallback element is missing, a resource error results in a fatal error.The xi:fallback element can appear only as a child of an xi:include element. It is a fatal error for an xi:fallback element to appear in a document anywhere other than as the direct child of the xi:include (before inclusion processing on the contents of the element.)

It is a fatal error for the xi:fallback element to contain any elements from the XInclude namespace other thanxi:include. Attributes may be placed on the xi:fallback element. Unprefixed attribute names are reserved for future versions of this specification, and must be ignored by XInclude 1.0 processors.The content of xi:fallback elements are ignored unless a resource error occurs while processing the surrounding xi:includeelement.

In particular, apparent fatal errors caused by the presence, absence, or content of elements and attributes inside thexi:fallback element must not be reported in xi:fallback elements that are ignored.The following (non-normative) DTD fragment illustrates a sample declaration for the xi:fallback element:

```
<!ELEMENT xi:fallback ANY>
<!ATTLIST xi:fallback
xmlns:xi CDATA #FIXED "http://www.w3.org/2001/
      XInclude">
```

PROCESSING MODEL

Inclusion as defined in this document is a specific type of [XML Information Set] transformation.[Definition: The input for the inclusion transformation consists of a source infoset.] [Definition: The output, called the result infoset, is a new infoset which merges the source infoset with the infosets of resources identified by URI references or IRI references appearing in xi:include elements.] Thus a mechanism to resolve URIs or IRIs and return the identified resources as infosets is assumed. Well-formed XML entities that do not have defined infosets (*e.g.* an external entity with multiple top-level elements) are outside the scope of this specification, either for use as a source infoset or the result infoset.xi:include elements in the source infoset serve as inclusion transformation instructions. [Definition: The information items located by the xi:include element are called the top-level included items]. [Definition: The top-level included items together with their attributes, namespaces, and descendants, are called the included items]. The result infoset is essentially a copy of the source infoset, with each xi:include element and its descendants replaced by its corresponding included items.

The Include Location

The value of the href attribute, after escaping according to 4.1.1 Escaping of href attribute values, is interpreted as either a URI reference or an IRI reference. The base URI for relative URIs or IRIs is the base URI of the xi:include element as specified in[XML Base]. [Definition: The URI or IRI resulting from resolution of the normalized value of the href attribute (or the empty string if no attribute appears) to absolute URI or IRI form is called the include location.]The absence of a value for the href attribute, either by the appearance of href="" or by the absence of the href attribute, represents a case which may be incompatible with certain implementation strategies.

For instance, an XInclude processor might not have a textual representation of the source infoset to include as parse="text", or it may be unable to access another part of the document using parse="xml" and an xpointer because of streamability concerns. An implementation may choose to treat any or all absences of a value for the href attribute as resource errors. Implementations should document the conditions under which such resource errors occur.

Escaping of Href Attribute Values

The value of this attribute is an XML resource identifer as defined in [XML 1.1] section 4.2.2 "External Entities", which is interpreted as [Definition: an IRI Reference as defined in RFC 3987 [IETF RFC 3987]], after the escaping procedure described in[XML 1.1] section 4.2.2 is applied. If necessary for the implementation, the value may be further converted to a URI reference as described in [XML 1.1].

Using XInclude with Content Negotiation

The use of a mechanism like HTTP [IETF RFC 2616] content negotiation introduces an additional level of potential complexity into the use of XInclude. Developers who use XInclude in situations where content negotiation is likely or possible should be aware of the possibility that they will be including content that may differ structurally from the content they expected, even if that content is XML. For example, a single URI or IRI may variously return a raw XML representation of the resource, an XSL-FO [XSL-FO]representation, or an XHTML [XHTML] representation, as well as versions in different character encodings or languages.Authors whose XInclude processing depends on the receipt of a particular vocabulary of XML should use the accept and accept-language attributes to increase the probability that the resource is provided in the expected format.

Included Items when parse="xml"

When parse="xml", the include location is dereferenced, the resource is fetched, and an infoset is created by parsing the resource as if the media type were application/xml (including character encoding determination).

Note: The specifics of how an infoset is created are intentionally unspecified, to allow for flexibility by implementations and to avoid defining a particular processing model for components of the XML architecture. Particulars of whether DTD or XML schema validation are performed, for example, are not constrained by this specification.

Note: The character encodings of the including and included resources can be different. This does not affect the resulting infoset, but might need to be taken into account during any subsequent serialization.Resources that are unavailable for any reason (for example the resource doesn't exist, connection difficulties or security restrictions prevent it from being fetched, the URI scheme isn't a fetchable one, the resource is in an unsupported encoding, or the resource is determined through implementation-specific mechanisms not to be XML) result in a resource error. Resources that contain non-well-formed XML result in a fatal error.

Note: The distinction between a resource error and a fatal error is somewhat implementation-dependent. Consider an include location returning an HTML document, perhaps as an error page.

One processor might determine that no infoset can be created from the resource (by examining the media type, for example) and raise a resource error, enabling fallback behaviour. Another processor with no such heuristics might attempt to parse the non-XML resource as XML and encounter a well-formedness (fatal) error.

[*Definition*: xi:include elements in this infoset are recursively processed to create the acquired infoset. For an intra-document reference (via xpointer attribute) the source infoset is used as the acquired infoset.]

[*Definition*: The portion of the acquired infoset to be included is called the inclusion target.] The *document information item* of the acquired infoset serves as the inclusion target unless the xpointer attribute is present and identifies a subresource. XPointers of the forms described in [XPointer Framework] and [XPointer element() scheme] must be supported. XInclude processors optionally support other forms of XPointer such as that described in [XPointer xpointer() Scheme]. An error in the XPointer is aresource error.The [XPointer xpointer() Scheme] is not specified in terms of the [XML Information Set], but instead is based on the [XPath 1.0]Data Model, because the XML Information Set had not yet been developed. The mapping between XPath node locations and information items is straightforward. However, xpointer() assumes that all entities have been expanded. Thus it is a fatal error to attempt to resolve an xpointer() scheme on a document that contains *unexpanded entity reference information items*.The set of top-level included items is derived from the acquired infoset as follows.

Document Information Items

The inclusion target might be a *document information item* (for instance, no specified xpointer attribute, or an XPointer specifically locating the document root.) In this case, the set of top-level included items is the *children* of the acquired infoset'sdocument information item, except for the *document type declaration information item* child, if one exists.

Note: The XML Information Set specification does not provide for preservation of white space outside the document element. XInclude makes no further provision to preserve this white space.

Multiple Nodes

The inclusion target might consist of more than a single

node. In this case the set of top-level included items is the set of information items from the acquired infoset corresponding to the nodes referred to by the XPointer, in the order in which they appear in the acquired infoset.

Range Locations

The inclusion target might be a location set that represents a range or a set of ranges.Each range corresponds to a set of information items in the acquired infoset.

[Definition: An information item is said to beselected by a range if it occurs after (in document order) the starting point of the range and before the ending point of the range.] [Definition: An information item is said to be partially selected by a range if it contains only the starting point of the range, or only the ending point of the range.] By definition, a character information item cannot be partially selected.

The set of top-level included items is the union, in document order with duplicates removed, of the information items eitherselected or partially selected by the range. The *children* property of selected information items is not modified. The *children*property of partially selected information items is the set of information items that are in turn either selected or partially selected, and so on.

Point Locations

The inclusion target might be a location set that represents a point. In this case the set of included items is empty.

Element, Comment, and Processing Instruction Information Items

The inclusion target might be an element node, a comment node, or a processing instruction node, respectively representing anelement information item.

A comment information item, or a processing instruction information item. In this case the set of top-level included items consists of the information item corresponding to the element, comment, or processing instruction node in theacquired infoset.

Attribute and Namespace Declaration Information Items

It is a fatal error for the inclusion target to be an attribute node or a namespace node.

Inclusion Loops

When recursively processing an xi:include element, it is a fatal error to process another xi:include element with an include location and xpointer attribute value that have already been processed in the inclusion chain.

In other words, the following are all legal:

An xi:include element may reference the document containing the include element, when parse="text".An xi:include element may identify a different part of the same local resource (same href, different xpointer).Two non-nested xi:include elements may identify a resource which itself contains an xi:include element.

The following are illegal:

An xi:include element pointing to itself or any ancestor thereof, when parse="xml".An xi:include element pointing to any include element or ancestor thereof which has already been processed at a higher level.

Included Items when Parse="text"

When parse="text", the include location is dereferenced and the resource is fetched and transformed to a set of character information items.

This feature facilitates the inclusion of working XML examples, as well as other text-based formats.Resources that are unavailable for any reason (for example the resource doesn't exist, connection difficulties or security restrictions prevent it from being fetched, the URI scheme isn't a fetchable one, or the resource is in an unsupported encoding) result in a resource error.

The encoding of such a resource is determined by:

External encoding information, if available, otherwiseif the media type of the resource indicates, according to XML Media Types [IETF RFC 3023], that the resource is XML, for example text/xml or application/xml or matches text/*+xml or application/*+xml, then the encoding is determined as specified in [XML 1.0] or [XML 1.1] section 4.3.3, as appropriate, otherwisethe value of the encoding attribute if one exists, otherwiseUTF-8.Byte sequences outside the range allowed by the encoding are a fatal error.

Characters that are not permitted in XML documents also are a fatal error.Each character obtained from the transformation of the resource is represented in the top-level included items as a *character information item* with the *character code* set to the character code in ISO 10646 encoding, and the *element content whitespace*set to false.When the first character is U+FEFF and is interpreted as a Byte-Order Mark, it should be discarded. It is interpreted as a BOM in UTF-8, UTF-16, and UTF-32 encodings; it is not interpreted as a BOM in the UTF-16LE, UTF-16BE, UTF-32LE, and UTF-32BE encodings.The [Character Model] discusses normalization of included text.

Fallback Behaviour

XInclude processors must perform fallback behaviour in the event of a resource error, as follows:If the *children* of the xi:include element information item in the source infoset contain exactly one xi:fallback element, the top-level included items consist of the information items corresponding to the result of performing XInclude processing on the *children*of the xi:fallback element. It is a fatal error if there is zero or more than one xi:fallback element.

Note: Fallback content is not dependent on the value of the parse attribute. The xi:fallback element can contain markup even when parse="text". Likewise, it can contain a simple string when parse="xml".

Creating the Result Infoset

The result infoset is a copy of the source infoset, with each xi:include element processed as follows:The information item for the xi:include element is found. [Definition: The *parent* property of this item refers to an information item called the include parent.] The *children* property of the include parent is modified by replacing the xi:include element information item with the top-level included items. The *parent* property of each included item is set to the include parent.It is a fatal error to attempt to replace an xi:include element appearing as the document (top-level) element in the source infoset with something other than a list of zero or more comments, zero or more processing instructions, and one element.Some processors may not be able to represent an element's *in-scope namespaces* property if it does not include bindings for all the prefixes bound in its parent's *in-scope namespaces.*

Such processors may therefore include additional namespace bindings inherited from the include parent in the *in-scope namespaces* of the included items.The inclusion history of each top-level included item is recorded in the extension property *include history.* The *include history*property is a list of *element information items,* representing the xi:include elements for recursive levels of inclusion. If an *include history* property already appears on a top-level included item, the xi:include element information item is prepended to the list.If no *include history* property exists, then this property is added with the single value of the xi:include element information item.The included items will all appear in the result infoset.

This includes *unexpanded entity reference information items* if they are present.Intra-document references within xi:include elements are resolved against the source infoset. The effect of this is that the order in which xi:include elements are processed does not affect the result.In the following example, the second include always points to the first xi:include element and not to itself, regardless of the order in which the includes are processed. Thus the result of this inclusion is two copies of something.xml, and does not produce an inclusion loop error.

```
<x xmlns:xi="http://www.w3.org/2001/XInclude">
 <xi:include href="something.xml"/>
 <xi:include xpointer="xmlns(xi=http://
www.w3.org/2001/XInclude)xpointer(x/
xi:include[1])"parse="xml"/>
</x>
```

An XInclude processor may, at user option, suppress xml:base and/or xml:lang fixup.

Unparsed Entities

Any *unparsed entity information item* appearing in the *references* property of an attribute on the included items or any descendant thereof is added to the *unparsed entities* property of the result infoset's *document information item*, if it is not a duplicate of an existing member. Duplicates do not appear in the result infoset.Unparsed entity items with the same *name, system identifier, public identifier, declaration base URI, notation name,* and*notation* are considered to be duplicate. An application may also be able to detect that unparsed entities are duplicate through other means. For instance, the URI resulting from combining the system identifier and the declaration base URI is the same.It is a fatal error to include unparsed entity items with the same name, but which are not determined to be duplicates.

Notations

Any *notation information item* appearing in the *references* property of an attribute in the included items or any descendant thereof is added to the *notations* property of the result infoset's *document information item,* if it is not a duplicate of an existing member. Likewise, any notation referenced by an unparsed entity added as described in 4.5.1 Unparsed Entities, is added unless it is a duplicate. Duplicates do not appear in the result infoset.Notation items with the same *name, system identifier, public identifier,* and *declaration base URI* are considered to be duplicate. An application may also be able to detect that notations are duplicate through other means. For instance, the URI resulting from combining the system identifier and the declaration base URI is the same.It is a fatal error to include notation items with the same name, but which are not determined to be duplicates.

References Property Fixup

During inclusion, an *attribute information item* whose *attribute type* property is IDREF or IDREFS has a *references* property with zero or more element values from the source or included infosets. These values must be adjusted to correspond to element values that occur in the result infoset. During this process, XInclude also corrects inconsistencies between the *references* property and the *attribute type* property, which might arise in the following circumstances:

A document fragment contains an IDREF pointing to an element in the included document but outside the part being included. In this case there is no element in the result infoset that corresponds to the element value in the original *references*property.

A document or document fragment is not self-contained. That is, it contains IDREFs which do not refer to an element within that document or document fragment, with the intention that these references will be realised after inclusion. In this case, the value of the *references* property is unknown or has no value.

The result infoset has ID clashes - that is, more than one attribute with *attribute type* ID with the same *normalized value*. In this case, attributes with *attribute type* IDREF or IDREFS with the same *normalized value* might have different values for their *references* properties.In resolving these inconsistencies, XInclude takes the *attribute type* property as definitive. In the result infoset, the value of the*references* property of an *attribute information item* whose *attribute type* property is IDREF or IDREFS is adjusted as follows:For each token in the *normalized value* property, the *references* property contains an *element information item* with the same properties as the *element information item* in the result infoset with an attribute with *attribute type* ID and *normalized value* equal to the token. The order of the elements in the *references* property is the same as the order of the tokens appearing in the*normalize value*. If for any of the token values, no element or more than one element is found, the *references* property has no value.

Namespace Fixup

The *in-scope namespaces* property ensures that namespace scope is preserved through inclusion. However, after inclusion, the*namespace attributes* property might not provide the full list of namespace declarations necessary to interpret qualified names in attribute or element content in the result. It is therefore not recommended that XInclude processors expose *namespace attributes*in the result. If this is unavoidable, the implementation may add *attribute information items* to the *namespace attributes* property in order to approximate the information conveyed by *in-scope namespaces.*

Base URI Fixup

The base URI property of the acquired infoset is not changed as a result of merging the infoset, and remains unchanged after merging. Thus relative URI references in the included infoset resolve to the same URI despite being included into a document with a potentially different base URI in effect. xml:base attributes are added to the result infoset to indicate this fact.

Each *element information item* in the top-level included items which has a different *base URI* than its include parent has an*attribute information item* added to its *attributes* property. This attribute has the following properties:

A *namespace name* of namespace.

A *local name* of base.A *prefix* of xml.A *normalized value* equal to either the *base URI* of the element, or an equivalent URI reference relative to the *base URI* of the include parent. The circumstances in which a relative URI is desirable, and how to compute such a relative URI, are implementation-dependent.A *specified* flag indicating that this attribute was actually specified in the start-tag of its element.An *attribute type* of CDATA.A *references* property with no value.An *owner element* of the information item of the element.If an xml:base attribute information item is already present, it is replaced by the new attribute.

Language Fixup

While the xml:lang attribute is described as inherited by XML, the XML Information Set makes no provision for preserving the inheritance of this property through document composition such as XInclude provides. This section introduces a *language*property which records the scope of xml:lang information in order to preserve it during inclusion.An XInclude processor should augment the source infoset and the acquired infoset by adding the *language* property to each*element information item*.

The value of this property is the *normalized value* of the xml:lang attribute appearing on that element if one exists, with xml:lang="" resulting in no value, otherwise it is the value of the *language* property of the element's parent element if one exists, otherwise the property has no value.Each *element information item* in the top-level included items which has a different value of *language* than its include parent(taking case-insensitivity into account per [IETF RFC 3066]), or that has a value if its include parent is a *document information item,* has an *attribute information item* added to its *attributes* property.

This attribute has the following properties:

A *namespace name* of http://www.w3.org/XML/1998/namespace.A *local name* of lang.A *prefix* of xml.A *normalized value* equal to the *language* property of the element. If the *language* property has no value, the normalized value is the empty string.A *specified* flag indicating that this attribute was actually specified in the start-tag of its element.An *attribute type* of CDATA.A *references* property with no value.An *owner element* of the information item of the element.If an xml:lang attribute information item is already present, it is replaced by the new attribute.

Note: The xml:space attribute is not treated specially by XInclude.

Properties Preserved by the Infoset

As an infoset transformation, XInclude operates on the logical structure of XML documents, not on their text serialization. All properties of an information item described in [XML Information Set] other than those specifically modified by this specification are preserved during inclusion. The *include history* and *language* properties introduced in this specification is also preserved. Extension properties such as [XML Schemas] Post Schema Validation Infoset (PSVI) properties are discarded by default.

However, an XInclude processor may, at user option, preserve these properties in the resulting infoset if they are correct according to the specification describing the semantics of the extension properties.For instance, the PSVI *validity* property describes the conditions of ancestors and descendants.

Modification of ancestors and descendants during the XInclude process can render the value of this property inaccurate. By default, XInclude strips this property, but by user option the property could be recalculated to obtain a semantically accurate value. Precisely how this is accomplished is outside the scope of this specification.

CONFORMANCE

Markup Conformance

An *element information item* conforms to this specification if it meets the structural requirements for include elements defined in this specification. This specification imposes no particular constraints on DTDs or XML schemas; conformance applies only to elements and attributes.

Application Conformance

An application conforms to XInclude if it:supports [XML 1.0] and [Namespaces in XML] or [XML 1.1] and [Namespaces in XML 1.1], the [XML Information Set], [XML Base], the [XPointer Framework], and the [XPointer element() scheme];stops processing when a fatal error is encountered;observes the mandatory conditions (must) set forth in this specification, and for any optional conditions (should and may) it chooses to observe, observes them in the way prescribed; andperforms markup conformance testing according to all the conformance constraints appearing in this specification.Support for the [XPointer xpointer() Scheme] is not mandatory for full XInclude conformance. Authors are advised that use of xpointer() and other XPointer schemes than element() might not be supported by all conformant XInclude implementations.

XML Information Set Conformance

This specification conforms to the [XML Information Set]. The following information items must be present in the input infosets to enable correct processing:Document information items with children and base URI properties.

Element information items with namespace name, local name, children, attributes, base URI and parent properties.Attribute information items with namespace name, local name and normalized value properties.

Additionally, XInclude processing might generate the following kinds of information items in the result:Character information items with character code, element content whitespace and parent properties.

XInclude extends the infoset with the property include history, which may appear on the following types of information items in the result:Element information items.

Processing instruction information items.Comment information items.Character information items.XInclude also extends the infoset with the property language, which may appear on element information items in the result.

EXAMPLES (NON-NORMATIVE)

Basic Inclusion Example

The following XML document contains an xi:include element which points to an external document. Assume the base URI of this document is http://www.example.org/document.xml.

```
<?xml version='1.0'?>
 document xmlns:xi="http://www.w3.org/2001/
XInclude">
 <p>120 Mz is adequate for an average home
user.</p>
 <xi:include href="disclaimer.xml"/>
</document>
```

Disclaimer.xml contains:

```
<?xml version='1.0'?>
<disclaimer>
```

```
  <p>The opinions represented herein
represent those of the individual and
should not be interpreted as official
policy endorsed by this organization.</p>
  </disclaimer>
```

The infoset resulting from resolving inclusions on this document is the same (except for the *include history* and *language*properties) as that of the following document:

```
  <?xml version='1.0'?>
  <document xmlns:xi="http://www.w3.org/2001/
XInclude">
   <p>120 Mz is adequate for an average home
user.</p>
   <disclaimer xml:base="http://www.example.
   org/disclaimer.xml">
   <p>The opinions represented herein represent
   those of the individual and should not be
interpreted as official policy endorsed by
this organization.</p>
  </disclaimer>
  </document>
```

Textual Inclusion Example

The following XML document includes a "working example" into a document:

```
  <?xml version='1.0'?>
  <document xmlns:xi="http://www.w3.org/2001/
  XInclude">
   <p>This document has been accessed
   <xi:include href="count.txt" parse="text"/>
      times.</p>
  </document>
```

Where count.txt contains:

324387

The infoset resulting from resolving inclusions on this document is the same (except for the *include history* and *language*properties) as that of the following document:

```
<?xml version='1.0'?>
<document xmlns:xi="http://www.w3.org/2001/
XInclude">
  <p>This document has been accessed 324387
times.</p>
</document>
```

Textual Inclusion of XML Example

The following XML document includes a "working example" into a document:

```
<?xml version='1.0'?>
<document xmlns:xi="http://www.w3.org/2001/
XInclude">
  <p>The following is the source of the
"data.xml" resource:</p>
  <example><xi:include href="data.xml"
parse="text"/></example>
</document>
```

data.xml contains:

```
<?xml version='1.0'?>
<data>
  <item><![CDATA[Brooks & Shields]]></item>
</data>
```

The infoset resulting from resolving inclusions on this document is the same (except for the *include history* and *language*properties) as that of the following document:

```
<?xml version='1.0'?>
<document xmlns:xi="http://www.w3.org/2001/
XInclude">
  <p>The following is the source of the
"data.xml" resource:</p>
  <example>&lt;?xml version='1.0'?&gt;
&lt;data&gt;
  &lt;item&gt;&lt;![CDATA[Brooks &amp;
Shields]]&gt;&lt;/item&gt;
&lt;/data&gt;</example>
</document>
```

Fragment Inclusion Example

The following illustrates the results of including fragments of another XML document.

Assume the base URI of the document is:

```
http://www.example.com/JoeSmithQuote.xml.
<?xml version='1.0'?>
<price-quote xmlns:xi="http://www.w3.org/2001/
 XInclude">
 <prepared-for>Joe Smith</prepared-for>
 <good-through>20040930</good-through>
 <xi:include href="price-list.xml"
xpointer="w002-description"/>
 <volume>40</volume>
 <xi:include href="price-list.xml"
 xpointer=" element(w002-prices/2)"/>
</price-quote>
```

Price-list.xml references a DTD which declares the id attributes as type ID, and contains:

```
<?xml version='1.0'?>
<!DOCTYPE price-list SYSTEM "price-list.dtd">
<price-list xml:lang="en-us">
 <item id="w001">
 <description id="w001-description">
 <p>Normal Widget</p>
     </description>
     <prices id="w001-prices">
     <price currency="USD" volume="1+">
     39.95</    price>
     <price currency="USD" volume="10+">
     34.95</price>
     <pricecurrency="USD" volume="100+">
     29.95</price>
 </prices>
 </item>
 <item id="w002">
 <description id="w002-description">
     <p>Super-sized widget with bells
```

```
<i>and</i> whistles.</p>
    </description>
    <prices id="w002-prices">
    <price currency="USD" volume="1+">
        59.95</price>
        <price currency="USD" volume="10+">
         54.95</price>
        <pricecurrency="USD" volume="100+">
        49.95</price>
        </prices>
    </item>
   </price-list>
```

The infoset resulting from resolving inclusions on this document is the same (except for the *include history* and *language*properties) as that of the following document:

```
<?xml version='1.0'?>
<price-quote xmlns:xi="http://www.w3.org/2001/
XInclude">
 <prepared-for>Joe Smith</prepared-for>
 <good-through>20040930</good-through>
 <description id="w002-description"
xml:lang="en-us"
     xml:base="http://www.example.com/price-
       list.xml">
 <p>Super-sized widget with bells <i>and</
i> whistles.</p>
 </description>
 <volume>40</volume>
 <price currency="USD" volume="10+" xml
:lang="en-us"
     xml:base="http://www.example.com/price-
      list.xml">54.95</price>
</price-quote>
```

Range Inclusion Example

The following illustrates the results of including a range specified by an XPointer. Assume the base URI of the document ishttp://www.example.com/document.xml.

```
<?xml version='1.0'?>
<document>
 <p>The relevant excerpt is:</p>
 <quotation>
 <include xmlns="http://www.w3.org/2001/
XInclude"
   href="source.xml" xpointer="  xpointer
(string-range(chapter/
p[1],'Sentence 2')/ range-to(string-
range(/chapter/p[2]/i,'3.',1,2)))"/>
 </quotation>
</document>
```

Source.xml contains:

```
<chapter>
 <p>Sentence 1. Sentence 2.</p>
 <p><i>Sentence 3. Sentence 4.</i> Sentence
 5.</p>
</chapter>
```

The infoset resulting from resolving inclusions on this document is the same (except for the *include history* and *language*properties) as that of the following document:

```
<?xml version='1.0'?>
<document>
 <p>The relevant excerpt is:</p>
 <quotation>
 <p xml:base="http://www.example.com
source.xml">Sentence 2.</p>
 <p xml:base="http://www.example.com/
source.xml"><i>Sentence 3.</i></p>
 </quotation>
</document>
```

Fallback Example

The following XML document relies on the fallback mechanism to succeed in the event that the resources example.txt andfallback-example.txt are not available..

```
<?xml version='1.0'?>
<div>
```

```
    <xi:include href="example.txt" parse="text"
    xmlns:xi="http://www.w3.org/2001/
XInclude">
    <xi:fallback><xi:include href="fallback-
   example.txt"        parse="text">
    <xi:fallback><a href="mailto:bob@
   example.org">Report    error</a></xi:
        fallback>
    </xi:include></xi:fallback>
    </xi:include>
   </div>
```

If neither example.txt nor fallback-example.txt are available, the infoset resulting from resolving inclusions on this document is the same (except for the *include history* and *language* properties) as that of the following document:

```
   <?xml version='1.0'?>
   <div>
    <a href="mailto:bob@example.org">Report
error</a>
   </div>
```

COMBINING XML DOCUMENTS

To enhance reuse and modularity, a technique for constructing new XML documents from existing ones is desirable.XInclude provides a simple inclusion mechanism.Why yet another specification?many XML documents and languages can benefit from modularityas for the namespace solution, a generic approach can be implemented in generic toolsApplication conformance: Think of XML as if Namespaces, XInclude, and XML Base were parts of the basic XML specification. (Caveat: the latter two are not widely implemented yet.)

AN XINCLUDE EXAMPLE

A document containing:

```
   <foo xmlns:xi="http://www.w3.org/2001/
XInclude">
    <xi:include href="somewhere.xml"/>
```

```
</foo>
```

where somewhere.xml contains:

```
<bar>...</bar>
```

is equivalent to:

```
<foo xmlns:xi="http://www.w3.org/2001/
XInclude">
 <bar>...</bar>
</foo>
```

http://www.w3.org/2001/XInclude is the official XInclude namespacethe include element name in that namespace is an inclusion directiveright after parsing and before other processing, an XInclude processor performs the inclusion (tree substitution)the original and the resulting document should be considered equivalentit is an error to have cyclic includes

XINCLUDE DETAILS

How is the included resource denoted?with XPointer (described later...) - an extension of URLs that can address document nodes, node sets, or character data rangesOther issues:with parse="text" and encoding="..." attributes, a resource can be transformed into a character data node before inclusionXInclude processors may need to create namespace declaration attributes to ensure equivalenceMany XInclude processors support only whole-document URIs, not full XPointer.

XML BASE - RESOLVING RELATIVE URIS XML BASE

INTRODUCTION

The XML Linking Language [XLink] defines Extensible Markup Language (XML) 1.0 [XML] constructs to describe links between resources. One of the stated requirements on XLink is to support HTML [HTML 4.01] linking constructs in a generic way. The HTML BASE element is one such construct which the XLink Working Group has considered. BASE allows authors to explicitly specify a document's base URI for the purpose of resolving relative URIs in links to external images, applets, form-processing programs, style sheets, and so on.This document describes a mechanism for providing base URI services to XLink, but as a modular specification so that other XML applications benefiting from additional control over relative URIs but not built upon XLink can also make use of it.

The syntax consists of a single XML attribute named xml:base.The deployment of XML Base is through normative reference by new specifications, for example XLink and the XML Infoset.

Applications and specifications built upon these new technologies will natively support XML Base. The behaviour of xml:baseattributes in applications based on specifications that do not have direct or indirect normative reference to XML Base is undefined.This specification does not attempt to specify which text strings in a document are to be interpreted as URIs.

That is the responsibility of each XML vocabulary. The question addressed by this specification is: given a relative URI in an XML document, what base URI is it resolved against?It is expected that a future RFC for XML Media Types will specify XML Base as the mechanism for establishing base URIs in the media types it defines.

TERMINOLOGY

[Definition: The key words must, must not, required, shall, shall not, should, should not, recommended, may, andoptional in this specification are to be interpreted as described in [RFC 2119].]The terms base URI and relative URI are used in this specification as they are defined in [RFC 3986].

3 XML:BASE ATTRIBUTE

The attribute xml:base may be inserted in XML documents to specify a base URI other than the base URI of the document or external entity.

The value of this attribute is interpreted as a Legacy Extended IRI (LEIRI) as defined in the W3C Note "Legacy extended IRIs for XML resource identification" [LEIRI].In namespace-aware XML processors, the "xml" prefix is bound to the namespace name as described in Namespaces in XML

[XML Names]. Note that xml:base can be still used by non-namespace-aware processors. An example of xml:base in a simple document containing XLinks follows. XLink normatively references XML Base for interpretation of relative URI references in xlink:href attributes.

```
<?xml version="1.0"?>
<doc xml:base="http://example.org/today/"
 xmlns:xlink="http://www.w3.org/1999/
xlink">
 <head>
 <title>Virtual Library</title>
 </head>
 <body>
 <paragraph>See <link xlink:type="simple"
 xlink:href="new.xml">what's new</link>!</
 paragraph>
 <paragraph>Check out the hot picks of
    the   day!</paragraph>
    <olist xml:base="/hotpicks/">
    <item>
      <link xlink:type="simple" xlink
:href="pick1.xml">Hot Pick #1</link>
    </item>
    <item>
      <link xlink:type="simple" xlink
:href="pick2.xml">Hot Pick #2</link>
    </item>
    <item>
      <link xlink:type="simple" xlink
:href="pick3.xml">Hot    Pick #3
      </link>
 </item>
 </olist>
 </body>
</doc>
```

The URIs in this example resolve to full URIs as follows:

"what's new" resolves to the URI "http://example.org/today/new.xml"

```
"Hot Pick #1" resolves to the URI
 "http://example.org/hotpicks/pick.xml"
"Hot Pick #2" resolves to the URI
 "http://example.org/hotpicks/pick2.xml"
"Hot Pick#3" resolves to the URI
 "http://example/org/hotpicks/pick3.xml"
```

Note: This specification does not give the xml:base attribute any special status as far as XML validity is concerned. In a valid document the attribute must be declared in the DTD, and similar considerations apply to other schema languages.

URI REFERENCE ENCODING AND ESCAPING

The value of an xml:base attribute is a Legacy Extended IRI (LEIRI) and may contain characters not allowed in URIs. (However, some characters allowed in LEIRIs are not legal XML characters, and cannot therefore appear in xml:base values.)In accordance with the principle that per cent-encoding must occur as late as possible in the processing chain, applications which provide access to the base URI of an element should calculate and return the value without escaping.In the example below, the base URI of element e2 should be returned as "http://example.org/wine/rosé".

```
<?xml version="1.0"?>
<e1 xml:base="http://example.org/wine/">
 <e2 xml:base="rosé"/>
</e1>
```

RESOLVING RELATIVE URIS

Relation to RFC 3986

RFC 3986 [RFC 3986] provides for base URI information to be embedded within a document. The rules for determining the base URI can be summarized as follows (highest priority to lowest):The base URI is embedded in the document's content.The base URI is that of the encapsulating entity (message, document, or none).The base URI is the URI used to retrieve the entity.The base URI is defined by the context of the application.

Note: The term "entity" in points #2 and #3 above uses the RFC 3986 meaning of the term. Elsewhere in this document the term "entity" is used in the XML sense.This document specifies the details of rule #1 for embedding base URI information in the specific case of XML documents.

Granularity of base URI information

Relative URIs appearing in an XML document are always resolved relative to either an element, a document entity, or an external entity. There is no provision for finer granularity, such as per-attribute, per-character, or per-entity base information. Neither internal entities, whether declared in the internal subset or in an external DTD, nor freestanding text (text not enclosed in an element) in an external entity, are considered to set a base URI separate from the base URI in scope for the entity reference.The base URI of a document entity or an external entity is determined by RFC 3986 rules, namely, that the base URI is the URI used to retrieve the document entity or external entity.

The base URI of an element is:

The base URI specified by an xml:base attribute on the element, if one exists, otherwisethe base URI of the element's parent element within the document entity or external entity, if one exists, otherwisethe base URI of the document entity or external entity containing the element.

Note: It follows that the base URI specified by an xml:base attribute is inherited by descendant elements within the same entity until another element with an xml:base attribute is encountered.The base URI of an element bearing an xml:base attribute with a value that is not a valid Legacy Extended IRI is application dependent.

Matching URIs with base URIs

The base URI corresponding to a given relative URI appearing in an XML document is determined as follows:The base URI for a URI reference appearing in text content is the base URI of the element containing the text.The base URI for a URI reference appearing in an xml:base attribute is the base

URI of the parent element of the element bearing the xml:base attribute, if one exists within the document entity or external entity, otherwise the base URI of the document entity or external entity containing the element.The base URI for a URI reference appearing in any other attribute value, including default attribute values, is the base URI of the element bearing the attribute.

The base URI for a URI reference appearing in the content of a processing instruction is the base URI of the parent element of the processing instruction, if one exists within the document entity or external entity, otherwise the base URI of the document entity or external entity containing the processing instruction.

Note: The presence of xml:base attributes might lead to unexpected results in the case where the attribute value is provided, not directly in the XML document entity, but via a default attribute. For instance, such a declaration in an external entity might not be read by software which is based on a non-validating XML processor.

Defaulting attributes through an external mechanism such as XML Schema may also lead to unexpected results; even if a validating processor is used by the application, the addition of defaulted attributes subsequent to creation of the infoset can cause xml:base attributes to get out of sync with the [base URI] infoset property. For these reasons, xml:base values should be provided either directly in the XML document instance or via default attributes declared in the internal subset of the DTD.

Interpretation of Same-Document References

RFC 3986 defines certain relative URI references, in particular the empty string and those of the form #fragment, as *same-document references*. Dereferencing of same-document references is handled specially. However, their use as the value of anxml:base attribute does not involve dereferencing, and XML Base processors should resolve them in the usual way. In particular,xml:base="" does not reset the base URI to that of the containing document.

Note: Some existing processors *do* treat these xml:base values as resetting the base URI to that of the containing document, so the use of such values is strongly discouraged.The published errata have been incorporated;The definition of URI reference has been switched from RFC2396 to 3986;The xml:base attribute has been redescribed as a Legacy Extended IRI, but this does not change its syntax (the December 2006 PER used the term "XML Resource Identifier" which was to be defined in an XLink revision, but that plan has been superseded by the definition of LEIRI in the W3C Note);Implementations are now encouraged to return base "URIs" without escaping non-URI characters;The meanings of xml:base="" and xml:base="#frag" have been clarified;The expected reference to XML Base in the forthcoming XML Media Types RFC ("son of 3023") has been noted;It has been clarified that normal validity rules apply to the xml:base attribute;The out-of-date appendix describing effects on other standards has been removed;Various minor editorial changes have been made.

A URI identifies a resource:

http://somewhere/somefile.xml is an absolute URI

somefile.xml is a relative URI

Inspired by the <base href="..."> mechanism in HTML, XML Base provides a uniform way of resolving relative URIs.

In the following example:

```
<... xml:base="http://www.daimi.au.dk/">
 <... href="~mis/mn/index.html".../>
</...>
```

The value of href attribute can be interpreted as the absolute URI *http://www.daimi.au.dk/~mis/mn/index.html*.the xml namespace prefix is hardwired by the Namespace specificationxml:base has lexical scope (as namespace declarations)the URI used to access the document is used as default URI baseExamples of applications:XLink (requires XML Base support)XHTML (will use XML Base)Namespaces (does not conform to XML Base, but it ought to...)your future XML languageFuture XML parsers will support Namespaces, XInclude, and XML Base.

12

DTD and DSD

OVERVIEW

LANGUAGES

A schema is a definition of the syntax of an XML-based language (*i.e.*, it defines a class of XML documents).A schema language is a formal language for expressing schemas.Schema processing: Given an XML document and a schema, a schema processorchecks for validity, *i.e* that the document conforms to the schema requirementsif the document is valid, a normalized version is output: default attributes and elements are inserted, parsing information may be added, etc.

Why bother formalizing the syntax with a schema?a formal definition can provide a precise but human-readable referenceschema processing can be done with existing implementationsyour own tools for your languages can benefit: by piping input documents through a schema processor, you can assume that the input is valid and defaults have been insertedSchemas are similar to grammars for programming languages, however, context-free grammars are not expressive enough for XML.The term "schema" comes from the database community.

CHOOSING LANGUAGE

There have been many schema language proposals.W3C proposals:

DTD

XML-Data, January 1998 DCD (Document Content

Description), July 1998 DDML (Document Definition Markup Language), January 1999 SOX (Schema for Object-oriented XML), July 1999

XML Schema

Non-W3C proposals:

Assertion Grammars by Dave RaggettSchematron by Rick JellifeTREX (Tree Regular Expressions for XML) by James ClarkExamplotron by Eric van der VlistRELAX by Makoto Murara/ RELAX NG by Murata and Clark

DSD (Document Structure Description)

Unlike for many other XML technologies, it has proved difficult to reach a consensus - probably because:it is an inherently difficult problempeople have different needs from a schema languagethe official (W3C) proposals are not very goodhowever, most schema languages have many similarities.We shall look at W3C's DTD and XML Schema proposals and at the DSD proposal developed by BRICS and AT&T.

XML-DATA

Shemas define the characteristics of classes of objects. This paper describes an XML vocabulary for schemas, that is, for defining and documenting object classes. It can be used for classes which as strictly syntactic (for example, XML) or those which indicate concepts and relations among concepts (as used in relational databases, KR graphs and RDF). The former are called "syntactic schemas;" the latter "conceptual schemas."For example, an XML document might contain a "book" element which lexically contains an "author" element and a "title" element.

An XML-Data schema can describe such syntax. However, in another context, we may simply want to represent more abstractly that books have titles and authors, irrespective of any syntax. XML-Data schemas can describe such conceptual relationships. Further, the information about books, titles and authors might be stored in a relational database, in which XML-Data schemas describe row types and key relationships.One immediate implication of the ideas in this paper is that XML document types can now be described using XML itself, rather than DTD systax. Another is that XML-Data schemas provide a common vocabulary for ideas which overlap between syntactic, database and conceptual schemas. All features can be used together as appropriate.

Schemas are composed principally of declarations for:

- Concepts
- Classes of objects
- Class hierarchies
- Properties
- Constraints
- Relationships
- Indicated by primary key to foreign key matching
- Indicated by URI

XML DTD Grammars and Compatibilitygrammatical rules governing the valid nesting of the elements and attributesattributes of elementsinternal and external entities, represented by intEntityDecl and extEntityDeclnotations, represented by notationDclDatatypes giving parsing rules and implementation formats.Mapping rules allowing abbreviated grammars to map to a conceptual data model.

The Schema Element Type

All schema declarations are contained within a schema element, like this:

```
<?XML version='1.0' ?>
<?xml:namespace name="urn:uuid:BDC6E3F0-6DA3-
11d1-A2A3-00AA00C14882/" as="s"/?>
<s:schema id='ExampleSchema'>
 <!— schema goes here. —>
</ε:schema>
```

The namespace of the vocabulary described in this document is named "urn:uuid:BDC6E3F0-6DA3-11d1-A2A3-00AA00C14882/".

The ElementType Declaration

The heart of an XML-Data schema is the *elementType*

declaration, which defines a class of objects (or "type of element" in XML terminology). The *id* attribute serves a dual role of identifying the definition, and also naming the specific class.

```
<elementType id="author"/>
```

Within an elementType, the *description* subelement may be used to provide a human-readable description of the element's purpose.

```
<elementType id="author">
 <description>The person, natural or
otherwise,who    wrote the book.</description>
</elementType >
```

Properties and Content Models

Subelements within *elementType* define characteristics of the class's members. An XML "content model" is a description of the contents that may validly appear within a particular element type in a document instance.

```
<elementType id="author">
 <string/>
</elementType>
<elementType id="Book">
 <element type="#author"occurs="ONEORMORE"/>
</elementType>
```

The example above defines two elements, author and book, and says that a book has one or more authors. The author element may contain a string of character data (but no other elements). For example, the following is valid:

```
<Book>
    <author>Henry Ford</author>
    <author>Samuel Crowther</author>
</Book>
```

Within an elementType, various specialized subelements (element, group, any, empty, string etc.) indicate which subelements (properties) are allowed/required. Ordinarily, these imply not only the cardinality of the subelements but also their sequence. (We discuss a means to relax sequence later.)

Element

Element indicates the containment of a single element type (property). Each *element* contains an *href* attribute referencing another *elementType*, thereby including it in the content model syntacticly, or declaring it to be a property of the object class conceptually. The element may be required or optional, and may occur multiple times, as indicated by its *occurs* attribute having one of the four values "REQUIRED", "OPTIONAL", "ZEROORMORE" or "ONEORMORE". It has a default of "REQUIRED".

```
<elementType id="Book">
 <element type="#title" occurs="OPTIONAL"/>
 <element type="#author" occurs="ONEORMORE"/
 >
</elementType>
```

The example above describes a book element type. Here, each instance of a book *may* contain a title, and *must* contain one or more authors.

```
<Book>
 <author>Henry Ford</author>
 <author>Samuel Crowther</author>
   <title>My Life and Work</title>
</Book>
```

When we discuss type hierarchies, later, we will see that an element type may have subtypes. If so, inclusion of an element type in a content model permits elements of that type directly and all its subtypes.

Empty, Any, String, and Mixed Content

Empty and *any* content are expressed using predefined elements *empty* and *any*. (*Empty* may be omitted.) *String* means any character string not containing elements, known as "PCDATA" in XML. *Any* signals that any mixture of subelements is legal, but no free characters. *Mixed* content (a mixture of parsed character data and one or more elements) is identified by a *mixed* element, whose content identifies the element types allowed in addition to parsed character data.

When the content model is mixed, any number of the listed elements are allowed, in any order.

```
<?XML version='1.0' ?>
<?xml:namespace name="urn:uuid:BDC6E3F0-6DA3-
11d1-A2A3-00AA00C14882/" as="s"/?>
<s:schema>
 <elementType id="name">
 <string/>
 </elementType>
 <elementType id="Person">
 <any/>
 </elementType>
 <elementType id="author">
 <string/>
 </elementType> <elementType id="titlePart">
 <string/>
 </elementType> <elementType id="title">
 <mixed><element type="#titlePart"/>
   </mixed>
 </elementType>
 <elementType id="Book">
 <element type="#title" occurs="OPTIONAL"/
>
  <element type="#author" occurs
="ONEORMORE"/>
  </elementType>
 </s:schema>
 ...
 <Book>
  <author>Henry Ford</author>
  <author>Samuel Crowth_r</author>
  <title>My Life and<titlePart>Work</
titlePart></title>
 </Book>
```

Here, *book* is defined to have an optional *title* and one or more *authors*. The *name* element has content model of *any*, meaning that free text is not allowed, but any arrangement of subelements is valid. The *content model* of *title* is *mixed*, allowing a free intermixture of characters and any number of *titleParts*. The author, *name* and *titleParts* elements have a *content model* of *string*.

Group

Group indicates a set or sequence of elements, allowing alternatives or ordering among the elements by use of the groupOrder attribute. The group as a whole is treated similarly to an element.

```
<elementType id="Book">
 <element type="#title"/>
 <element type="#author" occurs="ONEORMORE"/
 >
 <group occurs="OPTIONAL">
 <element type="#preface"/>
 <element type="#introduction"/>
 </group>
</elementType>
```

In the above example, if a preface or introduction appears, both must, with the preface preceding the introduction.

Each of the following is valid:

```
<Book>
 <author>Henry Ford</author>
</Book>
<Book>
 <author>Henry Ford</author>
 <preface>Prefatory text</preface>
 <introduction>This is a swell book.</
introduction>
</Book>
```

Sometimes a schema designer wants to relax the ordering restrictions among elements, allowing them to appear in any order. This is indicated by setting the groupOrder attribute to "AND":

```
<elementType id="Book">
 <element type="#title"/>
 <element type="#author"occurs="ONEORMORE"/
>
```

```
<group groupOrder="AND" occurs="OPTIONAL">
<element type="#preface"/>
<element type="#introduction"/>
</group>
</elementType>
```

Now the following is also valid:

```
<Book>
 <author>Henry Ford</author>
 <introduction>This is a swell book.</
introduction>
 <preface>Prefatory text</preface>
</Book>
```

Finally, a schema can indicate that any one of a list of elements (or groups) is needed. For example, either a preface *or* an introduction. The groupOrder attribute value "OR" signals this.

```
<elementType id="Book">
 <element type="#title"/>
 <element type="#author" occurs="ONEORMORE"/
 >
 <group groupOrder="OR">
 <element type="#preface"/>
 <element type="#introduction"/>
 </group>
</elementType>
```

Now each of the following is valid:

```
<Book>
 <author>Henry Ford</author>
 <preface>Prefatory text</preface>
</Book>
<Book>
 <author>Henry Ford</author>
 <introduction>This is a swell book.</
introduction>
</Book>
```

Open and Closed Content Models

XML typically does not allow an element to contain

content unless that content was listed in the model. This is useful in some cases, but overly in others in which we would like the listed content model to govern the cardinality and other aspects of whichever subelements are explicitly named, while allowing that other subelements can appear in instances as well.

The distinction is effected by the *content* attribute taking the values "OPEN" and "CLOSED." The default is "OPEN" meaning that all element types not explicitly listed are valid, without order restrictions. (This idea has a close relation to the Java concept of a final class.)For example, the following instance data for a book, including the unmentioned element *copyrightDate* would be valid given the content models declared so far, because they have all been *open*.

```
<Book>
 <author>Henry Ford</author>
 <author>Samuel Crowther</author>
 <title>My Life and Work</title>
 <copyrightDate>1922</copyrightDate>
</Book>
```

However, had the content model been declared closed, as follows, the *copyrightDate* element would be invalid.

```
<elementType id="Book" content="CLOSED">
 <element type="#title"/>
 <element type="#author" occurs="ONEORMORE"/
 >
 <group groupOrder="SEQ" occurs="OPTIONAL">
 <element type="#preface"/>
 <element type="#introduction"
occurs="REQUIRED"/>
 </group>
</elementType>
```

A closed content model does not allow instances to contain any elements or attributes beyond those explicitly listed in the elementType declaration.

Default Values

An element with occurs of REQUIRED or OPTIONAL (but

not ONEORMORE or ZEROORMORE) can have a default value specified.

```
<elementType id="Book">
 <element type="#title"/>
 <element type="#author" occurs="ONEORMORE"/
 >
 <element type="#ageGrp" occurs
="OPTIONAL">
 <default>adult</default>
 </element>
</elementType>
```

The default value is implied for all element *instances* in which it is syntactically omitted.To indicate that the default value is the only allowed value, the *presence* attribute is set to "FIXED".

```
<elementType id="Book">
 <element type="#title"/>
 <element type="#author" occurs="ONEORMORE"/
 >
 <element type="#ageGrp" occurs="OPTIONAL"
presence="FIXED">
 <default>ADULT</default>
 </element>
</elementType>
```

Presence has values of "IMPLIED," "SPECIFIED," "REQUIRED," and "FIXED" with the same meanings as defined in XML DTD.

Aliases and Correlatives

ElementTypes can be know be different names in different languages or domains. The equivalence of several names is effected by the sameAs attribute, as in

```
<elementTypeEquivalent id="livre"
type="#Book"/>
<elementTypeEquivalent id="auteur"
type="#author"/>
```

Elements are used to represent both primary object types (nouns) and also properties, relations and so forth. Relations are often known by two names, each reflecting one direction of the relationship. For example, husband and wife, above and below, earlier and later, etc.

The correlative element identifies such a pairing.

```
<elementType id= "author">
 <string/>
</elementType>
<elementType id= "wrote">
 <correlative type="#author"/>
 <string/>
</elementType>
```

This indicates that "wrote" is another name for the "author" relation, but from the perspective of the person, not the book.

That is, the two fragments below express the same fact:

```
<Person>
 <name>Henry Ford</name>
</Person>
<Book>
 <title>My Life and Work</title>
 <author>Henry Ford</author>
</Book>
...
<Person>
 <name>Henry Ford</name>
 <wrote>My Life and Work</wrote>
</Person>
<Book>
 <title>My Life and Work</title>
</Book>
```

A correlative may be defined simply to document the alternative name for the relation. However, it may also be used within a content model where it permits instances to use the alternative name. Further it may to establish constraints on the relation, indicate key relationships, etc.

Class Hierarchies

ElementTypes can be organized into categories using the *superType* attribute, as in

```
<elementType id="price">
 <string/>
</elementType>
<elementType id="ThingsI'veBoughtRecently">
 <element type="#price"/>
</elementType>
<elementType id="PencilsI'veBoughtRecently">
 <superType type="#ThingsI'veBoughtRecently"/
 >
 <element type="#price"/>
</elementType>
<elementType id="BooksI'veBoughtRecently">
 <superType type="#ThingsI'veBoughtRecently"/
 >
 <element type="#price"/>
</elementType>
```

This simply indicates that, in some fashion, *PencilsI'veBoughtRecently* and *BooksI'veBoughtRecently* are subsets of *ThingsI'veBoughtRecently.* It implies that every valid instance of the subset is a valid instance of the superset. The superset type must have an *open* content model.There are restrictions that should be followed, based on the principle that all instances of the species (subtype) must be instances of the genus (supertype):The genus type must have content="OPEN".It must have either no groups or only groups with groupOrder="AND" (that is, no order constraints).You can add new elements and attributes.Occurs cardinality can be decreased but not increased.Ranges and other constraints are cummulative, that is, all apply (though the exact effect of this depends on the semantics of the constraint type).Default values can be made FIXED defaults.To indicate that the content model of the subset should inherit the content model of a superset, we use a particular kind of superType called "genus" of which only one is allowed per ElementType. This copies the content model of the referenced element type and permits addition of new elements to it. Further, sub-elements occurring in the superset type, if declared again, are replaced by the newer declarations.

```
<elementType id="Book">
 <element type="#title"/>
 <element type="#author" occurs="ONEORMORE"/
 >
</elementType>
<elementType id="BooksI'veBoughtRecently">
 <genus type="#Book"/>
 <superType type="#ThingsI'veBoughtRecently"/
 >
 <element type="#price"/>
</elementType>
```

The above has the same effect as

```
<elementType id="Book">
 <element type="#title"/>
 <element type="#author" occurs="ONEORMORE"/
 >
</elementType>
 <elementType id="BooksI'veBoughtRecently">
 <superType type="#Book"/>
 <superType type="#ThingsI'veBoughtRecently"/
 >
 <element type="#title"/>
 <element type="#author" occurs="ONEORMORE"/
 >
 <element type="#price"/>
</elementType>
```

Elements which are References

ElementTypes and the content model elements defined so far are sufficient to declare a tree structure of elements. However, some elements such as "author" are*not only* usable on their own, they also act as references to other elements. For example, "Henry Ford" is the value of the *author* subelement of a *book*element. "Henry Ford" is also the value of the *name* element in a *person* element, and it can be used to connect these two.

```
<Book>
 <author>Henry Ford</author>
```

```
 <author>Samuel Crowther</author>
 <title>My Life and Work</title>
</Book>
<Person><name>Henry Ford</name></Person>
<Person><name>Samuel Crowther</name></Person>
```

In this capacity, such subelement are often referred to as *relations* when using "knowledge representation" terminology or "keys" when using database terms. (The meaning of "relation" and "key" are slightly different, but the fact which the terms recognize is the same.)

To make such references explicit in the schema, we add declarations for *keys* and *foreign keys.*

```
<elementType id="name">
 <string/>
</elementType>
<elementType id="Person">
 <element id="p1" type="#name"/>
 <key id="k1"><keyPart href="#p1"/></key>
</elementType>
<elementType id="author">
 <string/>
 <foreignKey range="#Person" key="#k1"/>
</elementType>
<elementType id="title">
 <string/>
</elementType>
<elementType id="Book">
 <element type="#title"/>
 <element type="#author" occurs="ONEORMORE"/
 ></elementType>
```

The *key* element within *person* tells us that a person can be uniquely identified by his *name.* The *foreignKey* element within the *author* element definition says that the contents of an author element are a foreign key indentifying a person by *name.*An uninformed user agent can still display the string "Henry Ford" even if it cannot determine that is supposed to be a person. A savvy agent that reads the schema can do more. It can locate the actual person.This is the information needed for a *join* in database terminology.This mechanism not only handles the typical way in which properties are expressed in databases, it also handles all cases in which the contents of an element are to be interpreted as strings from a restricted vocabulary, such as enumerations, XML nmtokens, etc.

```
<Book>
 <author>Henry Ford</author>
 <author>Samuel Crowther</author>
 <title>My Life and Work</title>
 <lccn>HD9710.U54 F58 1973</lccn>
 <dewey>629.2/092/4 B</dewey >
 <isbn>0405050887</isbn>
 <series>Business<series>
</Book>
```

Although not shown here, presumably *lccn, dewey* and *isbn* are declared in the schema to be foreign keys to corrresponding fields of catalog records. *Series* is a foreign key to a categorization of books, of which "Business" is one category.

Keys can contain URIs, as in

```
<Book>
 <author>http://SSA.gov/blab/people/
Henry+Ford</author>
 <author>http://SSA.gov/blab/people/
Samuel+Crowther</author>
 <title>My Life and Work</title>
</Book>
```

This is indicated in the schema by a datatype of "URI":

```
<elementType id="author">
 <string/>
 <datatype dt="uri"/>
</elementType>
```

One-to-Many Relations

Element relations are binary. That is, we never express an n-to-1 relationship directly. We do not, for example, list within *books* a single relation that somehow resolves to all the *authors*. Instead, we always write the relationship on the 1-to-n side, but allow multiple occurrances of the *subelement*, for example, allowing*books* to have multiple occurrences of *author*.

```
<Person><name>Henry Ford</name></Person>
<Person><name>Samuel Crowther</name></Person>
<Person><name>Harvey S. Firestone</name></
Person>
<Book>
 <author>Henry Ford</author>
 <author>Samuel Crowther</author>
 <title>My Life and Work</title>
</Book>
<Book>
 <author>Harvey S. Firestone</author>
 <author>Samuel Crowther</author>
 <title>Men and Rubber</title>
</Book>
```

This example shows a book with several persons as author, and also a person who is author of several books. We discussed such many-to-many relations more under the topic of *correlations*.

Multipart Keys

When the foreignKey element does not have foreignKeyPart sub-elements (as it does not above) then the entirety of the element's contents (*e.g.* "Henry Ford") should be used as the key value. However, for multipart foreign keys, or cases where the element has several sub-elements, foreignKeyPart is used, as shown below.

```
<elementType id="firstName">
 <string/>
</elementType>
<elementType id="lastName">
 <string/>
</elementType>
<elementType id="Person">
 <element id="pp1" type="#firstName"/>
 <element id="pp2" type="#lastName"/>
 <key id="k1">
     <keyPart href="#pp1"/>
     <keyPart href="#pp2"/>
```

```
 </key>
</elementType>
<elementType id="author">
 <element id="ap1" type="#firstName"/>
 <element id="ap2" type="#lastName"/>
 <domain type="#Book"/>
 <range type="#Person"/>
 <foreignKey range="#Person" key="#k1">
 <foreignKeyPart href="#ap1"/>
 <foreignKeyPart href="#ap2"/>
 </foreignKey>
</elementType>
...
<Book>
 <title>My Life and Work</title>
 <author>
 <firstName>Henry</firstName>
 <lastName>Ford</lastName>
 </author>
</Book>
```

Attributes as References

An alternative way to express a reference is with an attribute.

```
<person id="person1"><name>Henry Ford</name></
Person>
<person id="person2"><name>Samuel Crowther</
name></Person>
<Book>
 <author name="Henry Ford"/>
 <author name="Samuel Crowther"/>
 <title>My Life and Work</title>
</Book>
```

This allows us to link a book to a person, through the author relation, using an attribute of the relation. This exactly parallels the construction we saw above under "multipart keys," where a *subelement* of author contained the author's name. Here, an *attribute* of author contains the name. We can express this in our schema as

```
<elementType id="author">
 <attribute name="name" id="authorname"/>
 <foreignKey range="#Person" key="#k1">
 <foreignKeyPart href="#authorname"/>
 </foreignKey>
</elementType>
```

A widely-used variant of this is to use a URI as a foreign key:

```
<Book>
 <author href="http://SSA.gov/blab/people/
Henry+Ford">
 <author href="http://SSA.gov/blab/people/
Samuel+Crowther"/>
 <title>My Life and Work</title>
</Book>
```

In this case, we are using the *href* attribute to contain a URI. This is a particular kind of foreign key, where the *range* is any possible resource, and where that resource is not identified by some combination of its properties but instead by a name-resolution service. We indicate this by using an attribute element, with dt= "URI".

```
<elementType id="author">
 <attribute name="href" id="authorhref"
dt="uri"/>
</elementType>
```

Constraints & Additional Properties

Min and Max Constraints

Elements can be limited to restricted ranges of values. The *min* and *max* elements define the lower and upper bounds.

```
<elementType id="age">
 <string/>
</elementType>
<elementType id="Person">
 <element hef="#age"><min>0</min><max>131</
max></element>
</elementType>
```

Such intervals are *half-open* (that is, the *min* value is in the interval, and the *max* value is the smallest value not in the interval).This rule leads to the simplest calculation in most cases, and is unambiguous with respect to precision. In the above example, it is clear by these rules the 130.9999 is in the interval and 131 is not. However, had we said "all numbers from 0 to 130.99," in practice we would have some ambiguity regarding the status of 130.9999. Or interpretation would depend on the precision that we inferred for the original statement. The issue is particularly ambiguous for dates. (What exactly does "From December 5 to December 8" mean? The use of half-open intervals for representation does not, however, put any requirements on how processors must display intervals.

For example, dates in some contexts display differently than their storage. That is, the interval <min>1997-12-05</min><max>1997-12-09</max> might be displayed as "December 5 through December 8".In certain cases this rule for a half-open interval is impractical (for example, what letter follows "z" in the latin alphabet?) If so, use *maxInclusive*:

```
<elementType id="student">
 <element type ="#grade"><min>
A<min><maxInclusive>Z</maxInclusive></
element>
</elementType>
```

Domain and Range Constraints

We can use the *domain* and *range* elements to add constraints to an element's use or value. The *domain* element, if present, indicates that the element may only be used as a property of certain other elements.

That is, syntactically it may appear only in the content model of those other element types. It constrains the sorts of schemas that can be written with the element.

```
<elementType id="author">
 <string/>
 <domain type="#Book"/>
 <attribute name="href" dt="uri"/>
</elementType>
```

The *domain* property above permits *author* elements to be used only within elements which are either *books* or subsets of *books*. Use of domain is optional. If omitted, there is simply no restriction.The *range* element is used with elements which are references and declares a restriction on the types of elements to which the relation may refer. Graphically, it describes the target end of a directed edge. Each *range* element references one elementType, any of which are valid. In this case, below, we have said that an*author* element must have an *href* attribute which is a URI reference to a *Person* or to an element type which is *Person* or a subset of *Person.*

```
<elementType id="author">
 <string/>
 <domain type="#Book"/>
 <attribute name="href" dt="uri"
range="#Person"/>
</elementType>
```

Other useful propertiesElement and attribute types can have an unlimited amount of further information added to them in the schema due to the open nature of XML with namespaces.

Using Elements from Other Schemas

A schema may use elements and attributes from other schemas in content models. For example, a subelement named "http://books.org/date" could be used within a *book* element as follows:

```
<?XML version='1.0' ?>
<?xml:namespace name="urn:uuid:BDC6E3F0-6DA3-
11d1-A2A3-00AA00C14882/" as="s"/?>
<s:schema>
 <elementType id="author">
 <string/>
 </elementType>
 <elementType id="title">
 <string/>
 </elementType>
 <elementType id="Book">
 <element type="#title" occurs="OPTIONAL"/
>
```

```
        <element type="#author"
occurs="ONEORMORE"/>
        <element href="http://books.org/date"/>
      </elementType>
    </s:schema>
```

This can be abbreviated by adopting the rule that namespace-qualified names may be used within the *href attribute* value of an *element* or *attribute* element.

```
    <?XML version='1.0' ?>
    <?xml:namespace name="urn:uuid:BDC6E3F0-6DA3-
    11d1-A2A3-00AA00C14882/" as="s"/?>
    <?xml:namespace name=" http://books.org/"
as="bk"/?>
    <s:schema>
     <elementType id="author">
     <string/>
     </elementType>
     <elementType id="title">
     <string/>
     </elementType>
     <elementType id="Book">
     <element type="#title" occurs="OPTIONAL"/
    >
        <elementtype="#author" occurs="ONEORMORE"/
        >
     <element href="bk:date"/>
     </elementType>
    </s:schema>
```

XML-Specific Elements

Attributes

XML-Data schemas contain a number of facilities to match features of XML DTDs or to support certain characteristics of XML. The XML syntax allows that certain properties can be expressed in a form called "attributes." To support this, an elementType can contain attribute declarations, which are divided into attributes with enumerated or notation values, and all other kinds.An attribute may be given a default value. Whether it is required or optional is signaled by *presence*. (Presence ordinarily defaults to IMPLIED, but if omitted and there is an explicit default, presence is set to the SPECIFIED.) See the DTD at the end of this document for syntactic details.Attributes with enumerated (and notation) values permit a values attribute, a space-separated list of legal values. The values attribute is required when the atttype is ENUMERATION or NOTATION, else it is forbidden. In these cases, if a default is specified, it must be one of the specified values.

```
<elementType id="Book">
 <element type="#title"/>
 <element type="#author" occurs="ONEORMORE"/
 >
 <attribute name="copyright"/>
 <attribute name="ageGrp" atttype
="ENUMERATION" values="child adult"
default="adult"/>
</elementType>
```

Describes an instance such as

```
<book copyright="1922" ageGrp="adult">
 <title>My Life and Work</title>
 <author>
 <firstName>Henry</firstName>
 <lastName>Ford</lastName>
 </author>
</Book>
```

Attributes may also reference elementTypes, meaning that one may use the element type but with attribute syntax. This allows an attribute to explicitly have the same name and semantics even when used on different element types. There are of course some limits: The attribute can still occur only once in an instance, and it cannot contain other elements. However, this allows the semantics of the element type to be employed in attribute syntax.

```
<elementType id="Book">
 <attribute href="bk:title"/>
```

```
<attribute href="bk:author"/>
<attribute name="copyright"/>
<attribute name="ageGrp" type="ENUMERATION"
values="children adult" default="adult"/>
</elementType>
```

Describes an instance such as

```
<book bk:author="Henry Ford" bk:title="My Life
and Work" ageGrp="adult"/>
```

The Internal and External Entity Declaration Element type: IntEntityDcl and Ext EntityDcl

This and the next two declarations cover entities. Entities are a shorthand mechanism, similar to macros in a programming language.

```
<intEntityDcl name="LTG">
 Language Technology Group
</intEntityDcl>
<extEntityDcl name="dilbert" notation="#gif"
 systemId="http://www.ltg.ed.ac.uk/~ht/
dilb.gif"/>
```

Here as elsewhere, following XML, systemId must be a URI, absolute or relative, and publicId, if present, must be a Public Identifier (as defined in ISO/IEC 9070:1991, Information technology — SGML support facilities — Registration procedures for public text owner identifiers). If a notation is given, it must be declared (see below) and the entity will be treated as binary, *i.e,* not substituted directly in place of references.

```
<notationDcl name="gif" systemId='http://
who.knows.where/'/>
```

The external declarations element type: extDcls

Although we allow an external entity with declarations to be included, we recommend a different declaration for schema modularization. The extDcls declaration gives a clean mechanism for importing (fragments of) other schemas. It replaces the common SGML idiom of declaring an external parameter entity and then immediately referring to it, and has the same import, namely, that the text referred to by the combination of systemId and publicId is included in the schema in place of the extDcls element, and that replacement text is then subject to the same validity constraints and interpretation as the rest of the schema.Note that in many cases the desired effect may be better represented by referencing elements (and attributes) from the other schema or subclassing from them.

Datatypes

A dataype indicates that the contents of an element can be interpreted as both a string and also, more specifically, as an object that can be interpreteted more specifically as a number, date, etc. The datatype indicates that the element's contents can be parsed or interpreted to yeild an object more specific than a string.That is, we distinguish the "type" of an element from its "datatype." The former gives the semantic meaning of an element, such as "birthday" indicating the date on which someone was born.

The "datatype" represents the parser class needed to decode the element's contents into an object type more specific than "string." For example, "19541022" is the 22nd of October, 1954 in ISO 8601 date format. (That is, ISO 8601 parsing rules will decode "19541022" into a date, which can then be stored as a date rather than a string.For example, we would like an XML author to be able to say that the contents of a "size" element is an integer, meaning that it should be parsed according to numeric parsing rules and that it can be stored in integer format. In some contexts an API can expose it as an integer rather than a string.

```
<item>
 <name>shirt</name>
 <size>8</size>
</item>
```

There are two main contexts for datatypes. First, when dealing with database APIs, such as ODBC, all elements with the same name typically contain the same type of contents. For example, all sizes contain integers or all birthdays contain dates. We will return to this case shortly.Second, and by contrast, the type of the content may vary widely from instance to instance. The softer we make our software, the more often these flexible cases occur.

For example, size could contain the integer 8, or the word "small" or even a formula for computing the size.We expose the datatype of an element instance by use of a *dt:dt* attribute, where the value of the attribute is a URI giving the datatype. (The URI might be explicitly in URI format or might rely on the XML namespace facility for resolution.) For example, we might find a document containing something like:

```
<?namespace name="urn:uuid:C2F41010-65B3-11d1-
A29F-00AA00C14882/" as="dt"?>
<?namespace name="http://zoosports.com/dt?"
as="zoo"?>
<purchases>
 <item>
 <name>shirt</name>
 <size dt:dt="int">8</size>
 </item>
 <item>
 <name>shoes</name>
     <size>large</size>
 </item>
 <item>
     <name>suit</name>
     <size dt:dt="zoo:script">
     =(shirtsize*1.05) + 3
 </size>
 </item>
</purchases>
```

Clearly this technique works for the heterogeneous typing in the above example. It also works for the database case where all element's of the same type have the same datatype.

```
<item> <name>shirt</name> <size
dt:dt="int">8</size> </item>
<item> <name>shoes</name> <size
dt:dt="int">6</size> </item>
```

```
<item> <name>suit</name> <size
dt:dt="int">12</size> </item>
```

As written above, this is inefficient. Fortunately, XML allows us in schemasto put attributes with default or fixed values, so we could say once that all *size*elements have a datatype with value "int". Having done so, our our instance just looks like:

```
<item> <name>shirt</name> <size>14</size> </
item>
<item> <name>shoes</name> <size>6</size> </
item>
<item> <name>suit</name> <size>16</size> </
item>
```

In a DTD, we can set a *fixed* attribute value, so that all *size* elements have datatype "int" or we can set it as a *default* attribute value so that it is an integer except where explicitly noted otherwise.

```
<item> <name>shirt</name> <size>14</size> </
item>
<item> <name>shoes</name> <size
dt:dt="string">large</size> </item>
<item> <name>suit</name> <size>16</size> </
item>
```

XML DTDs today allow such attributes. For example, a DTD can say that all shirt elements have integer datatype by the following:

```
<!ELEMENT size PCDATA >
<!ATTLIST size dt:dt "int" #FIXED >
```

XML-Data schemas allow the equivalent, though with specialized syntax:

```
<elementType id="size" >
 <datatype dt="int"/>
</elementType>
```

Elements use *datatype* subelements to give the datatype so that an optional *presence* attribute of the datatype element can indicate whether the datatype is*fixed* or merely a *default*. Attributes can also have datatypes. Because there is no possibility of their being anything other than a fixed type, the datatype of an attribute is signalled by a dt attribute:

```
<attribute id="size" dt="int"/>
```

How Typed Data is Exposed in the API

Different APIs to typed data will use the datatype attribute differently. The basic XML parser API should expose all element contents as strings regardless of any datatype attribute. (It might also contain supplementary methods to read values as more specific types such as "integer," thereby getting more efficiency.) An ODBC interface could use the datatype attribute to expose each type of element as a column, with the column's datatype determined by the element type's datatype.

Complex Data Types

If a datatype requires a complex structure for storage, or an object-based storage, this is also handled by the dt:dt attribute, where the datatype's storage format can be a structure, Java class, COM++ class, etc. For example, if an application needed to have an element stored in a "ScheduleItem" structure and using some private format, it could note this like

```
<whendt:dt="zoo:ScheduleItem">M*D1W4B19971022;
100</  when>
```

The datatype does not require a private format. It could also use subelements and attributes such as

```
<when dt:dt="zoo:ScheduleItem2">
 <month>*</month>
 <day>1</day>
 <week>4</week>
 <begin>19971022</begin>
 <recurs>100</recurs>
</when>
```

In the case of the graph-oriented interfaces (*e.g.* XML/RDF) the mapping from the XML tree to a graph should add a *wrapping node* for each non-string data type. The datatype property gives the type of that node.

For example, the following two are graphically equivalent:

```
<size dt:dt="int">8</size>
```

```
<size><dt:int>8</dt:int></size>
```

Versioning of Instances

Adding an attribute to an element does not change the other attributes or pose any special versioning problems. For example, an application written to expect an instance to contain "<birthday>19541022</birthday>" is not harmed if the schema reveals that this is ISO 8601 format.

Versioning within datatypes should be handled by the author's making sure that that subtypes of datatypes retain all the characteristics of the supertype.If a down-level application is given a datatype it cannot process, it should expose the element contents as a supertype of the indicated datatype.

In practice, this will usually mean that unrecognized datatypes will be the same as "dt:string". However, there are cases in which a type will be promoted, for example exposing a boolean in a byte or word rather than a bit, exposing a floating point number in a language's native format, etc.

The Datatypes Namespace

The datatype attribute "dt" is defined in the namespace named "urn:uuid:C2F41010-65B3-11d1-A29F-00AA00C14882/ ". (See the XML Namespaces Note at the W3C site for details of namespaces.) The full URN of the attribute is "urn:uuid:C2F41010-65B3-11d1-A29F-00AA00C14882/dt".You will have noticed that the value of the attribute, as used in the examples above, is not lexically a full URI. For example, it reads "int" or "string" etc. Datatype attribute values are abbreviated according to the following rule: If it does not contain a colon, it is a datatype defined in the datatypes namespace "urn:uuid:C2F41010-65B3-11d1-A29F-00AA00C14882/". If it contains a colon, it is to be expanded to a full URI according to the same rules used for other names, as defined by the XML Namespaces Note. For example

```
<?namespace name="urn:uuid:C2F41010-65B3-11d1-
A29F-00AA00C14882/" as="dt"?>
<?namespace name="http://zoosports.com/dt?"
```

```
as="zoo"?>
   <item>
    <size dt:dt="int">8</size>
    <name dt:dt="zoo:clothing">shirt</name>
   </item>
```

Has two datatypes whose full names are "urn:uuid:C2F41010-65B3-11d1-A29F-00AA00C14882/integer" and "http://zoosports.com/dt?clothing".

What a datatype's URI Means

Datatypes are identified by URIs. The URI as simply a reference to a section of a document that defines the appropriate parser and storage format of the element. To make this broadly useful, this document defines a set of common data types including all common forms of dates, plus all basic datatypes commonly used in SQL, C, C++, Java and COM (including strings). The best form of such a document is that it should itself be an XML-Data schema where each datatype is an element declaration. For this purpose we define a*<Syntax>* subelement which can be used in lieu of a content model. We also define an *<objecttype>* subelement. Each has a URI as its value. This integrates data types with element types in general.

```
<schema:elementType id="int">
  <syntax href="urn:uuid:C2F41010-65B3-11d1-
A29F-00AA00C14882/num_to_int"/>
  <objectType href="urn:uuid:C2F41010-65B3-
11d1-A29F-00AA00C14882/integer32"/>
</schema:elementType>
<schema:elementType id="date.iso8601">
  <syntax href="urn:uuid:C2F41010-65B3-11d1-
A29F-00AA00C14882/date.iso8601_to_int32"/>
  <objecttype href="urn:uuid:C2F41010-65B3-
11d1-A29F-00AA00C14882/integer32"/>
</schema:elementType>
```

The objecttype sub-element can reference a structure, Java class, COM++ coClass, etc. The syntax subelement identifies a parser which can decode the element's content (and/or attributes) into the object type given the storage type URI.

Input to the parser is the element object exposing all its attributes and content tree (that is, the subtree of the grove beginning with the element containing the dt attribute).

The objectType attribute in particular is assumed available to the parser so that a single parser can support several objecttypes.Having said this, all *basic* data types should be built into the parsers for efficiency and in order to ground the process. For these, the datatype elements serve only to formally document the storage types and parsers, and to give higher-level systems (such as RDF) a more formal basis for datatypes.I do not currently propose that we attempt to write any universal notation for parsing rules. Certain popular kinds of formats, particularly dates, are not easily expressed in anything but natural language or code, and the parsers must be custom written code. In other words, the URIs for the basic syntax and objecttype elements probably resolve only to text descriptions.

Structured Data Type Attributes

Attributes in cannot XML have structure. I will separately propose some techniques to avoid this problem, specifically that the XML API should contain a method that treats attributes and subelements indistinguishably, and also that the content which is an element's value can be syntactically separated from content which is an element's properties.

Specific Datatypes

This includes all highly-popular types and all the built-in types of popular database and programming languages and systems such as SQL, Visual Basic, C, C++ and Java(tm).

Name	Parse type	Storage type	Examples
string	pcdata	string (Unicode)	Ομωνυμα λεγαται ων ον ομα μονον κοινον, ο δε κατα τουνομα λογοσ τη ς ουσιας ετεροσ, οιον ζυ ον ο τε ανθροπος και το γεγραμμενον.
number	A number, with no limit on digits, may potentially have a leading sign, fractional digits, and optionally an exponent. Punctuation as in US English.	string	15, 3.14, -123.456E+10

int	A number, with optional sign, no fractions, no exponent.	32-bit signed binary	1, 58502, -13
float	Same as for "number."	64-bit IEEE 488	.314159265358979E+1
fixed.14.4	Same as "number" but no more than 14 dights to the left of the decimal point, and no more than 4 to the right.	64-bit signed binary	12.0044
boolean	"1" or "0"	bit	0, 1 (1=="true")
dateTime.iso8601	A date in ISO 8601 format, with optional time and no optional zone. Fractional seconds may be as precise as nanoseconds.	Structure or object containing year, month, hour, minute, second, nanosecond.	19941105T08:15:00301
dateTime.iso8601tz	A date in ISO 8601 format, with optional time and optional zone. Fractional seconds may be as precise as nanoseconds.	Structure or object containing year, month, hour, minute, second, nanosecond, zone.	19941105T08:15:5+03
date.iso8601	A date in ISO 8601 format. (no time)	Structure or object containing year, month, day.	19541022
time.iso8601	A time in ISO 8601 format, with no date and no time zone.	Structure or object exposing day, hour, minute	
time.iso8601.tz	A time in ISO 8601 format, with no date but optional time zone.	Structure or object containing day, hour, minute, zonehours, zoneminutes.	08:15-05:00
i1	A number, with optional sign, no fractions, no exponent.	8-bit binary	1, 255
i2	"	16-bit binary	1, 703, -32768
i4	"	32-bit binary	
i8	"	64-bit binary	

ui1	A number, unsigned, no fractions, no exponent.	8-bit unsigned binary	1, 255
ui2	"	16-bit unsigned binary	1, 703, -32768
ui4	"	32-bit unsigned binary	
ui8	"	64-bit unsigned binary	
r4	Same as "number."	IEEE 488 4-byte float	
r8	"	IEEE 488 8-byte float	
float.IEEE.754.32	"	IEEE 754 4-byte float	
float.IEEE.754.64	"	IEEE 754 8-byte float	
uuid	Hexidecimal digits representing octets, optional embedded hyphens which should be ignored.	128-bytes Unix UUID structure	F04DA480-65B9-11d1-A29F-00AA00C14882
uri	Universal Resource Identifier	Per W3C spec	
bin.hex	Hexidecimal digits representing octets	no specified size	
char	string	1 Unicode character (16 bits)	
string.ansi	string containing only ascii characters <= 0xFF.	Unicode or single-byte string.	This does

All of the dates and times above reading "iso8601.." actually use a restricted subset of the formats defined by ISO 8601. Years, if specified, must have four digits. Ordinal dates are not used. Of formats employing week numbers, only those that truncate year and month are allowed (5.2.3.3 d, e and f).

Mapping between Schemas

Certain uses of data emphasize syntax, others "conceptual" relations. Syntactic schemas often have fewer elements compared to explicitly conceptual ones. Further, it is usually easier to design a schema that merely covers syntax rather than designing a well-thought-out conceptual data model. An effect of this is that many practical schemas will not contain all the elements that a conceptual schema would, either for reasons of economy or because the initial schema was simply syntactic. But is it useful to make the implicit explicit over time so that more generic processors can make use of data.

For example, the following schema is essentially syntax:

```
<elementType id="author">
 <string/>
</elementType>
<elementType id="title">
 <string/>
</elementType>
<elementType id="Book">
 <element type="#title"/>
 <element type="#author" occurs="ONEORMORE"/
 >
</elementType>
```

With instances looking like this:

```
<Book>
 <title>Paradise Lost</title>
 <author>Milton</author>
</Book>
```

On the other hand, a conceptual schema could look like this:

```
<elementType id="name">
 <string/>
</elementType>
<elementType id="Person">
 <element type="#name/>
</elementType>
<elementType id="creator">
 <range type="#Person/>
</elementType>
<elementType id="title">
 <string/>
</elementType>
 <elementType id="Book">
 <element type="#title"/>
```

```
<element type="#creator" occurs="ONEORMORE"/
 >
</elementType>
```

If fully explicit, its instances would look something like this:

```
<Person id="thing1">
 <name>Milton</Person>
</Person>
<Book>
 <title>Paradise Lost</title>
 <creator>
 <Person>
 <name>Milton</name>
     </Person>
 </creator>
</Book>
```

In any case, what we want to express is a diagram such as this:

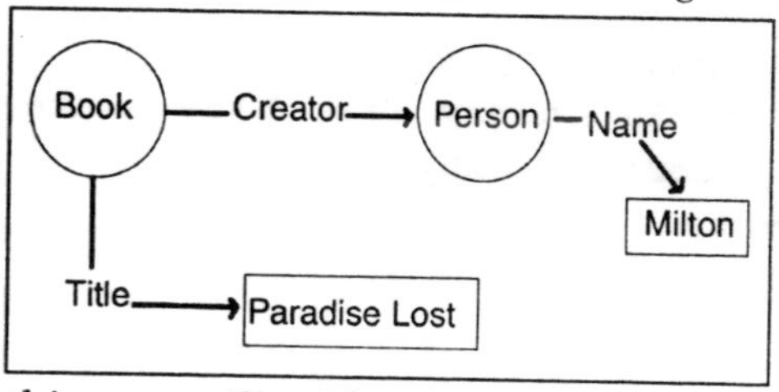

To do this, we will add mapping information into the syntactic schema which tells us how to interpolate the implied elements (and also to map *author* to*creator*) thereby creating a conceptual data model.

```
<?xml:namespace href="uri-to-the-conceptual-
schema" as="c" ?>
<elementType id="author">
 <string/>
</elementType>
<elementType id="title">
 <string/>
</elementType>
<elementType id="Book">
 <mapsTo type="c:book"/>
 <element type="#title"> <mapsTo
```

```
type="c:title"/> </element>
    <element type="#author" occurs
="ONEORMORE">
    <mapsTo type="string">
    <implies type="c:name">
    <implies type="c:person">
    <implies type="c:creator"/>
    </implies>
    </implies>
    </mapsTo>
    </element>
   </elementType>
```

A more complex case could involve needing to map several properties to have a common implied node. For example, suppose we wanted that a *street* element and *city* element should both imply the same *address* node.

```
<Person>
 <name>Mary Poppins</name>
 <street>17 Cherry Tree Lane</street>
 <city>London</city>
</Person>
```

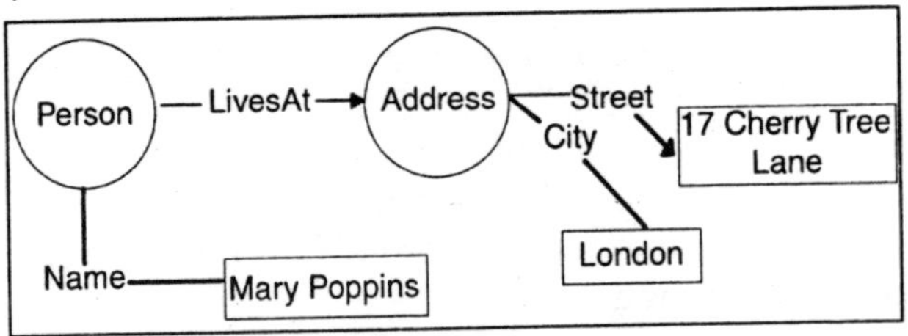

That is, rather than creating two *address* nodes, we want to create only a single onc, and subordinate both the *street* and *city* to it. If the conceptual schema has elements *livesAt, address, street* and *city*, we could write a mapping thus:

```
...definitions of name, street and city...
 <elementType id="Person">
 <mapsTo type="c:person"/>
    <element type="#name"> <string/>
    <mapsTo type="c:name"/> </element>
 <element type="#street">
```

```
    <string/>
    <mapsTo type="c:street">
        <impliestype="c::address" id=
"livesAtAddress">
    <implies type="c:livesAt"/>
    </implies>
    </mapsTo>
    </element>
    <element type="#city">
    <string/>
    <mapsTo type="c:city">
    <implies type="#livesAtAddress"/>
    </mapsTo>
    </element>
   </elementType>
```

Elements may be repeated, so mapping rules need to accommodate repetitions. Suppose that someone has two addresses in the grammatical syntax, this needs to map to two addresses in the graph while still keeping the structure correct.

```
   <Person>
    <name>Mary Poppins</name>
    <street>17 Cherry Tree Lane</street>
    <city>London</city>
    <street>One Park Lane</street>
    <city>London</city>
   </Person>
```

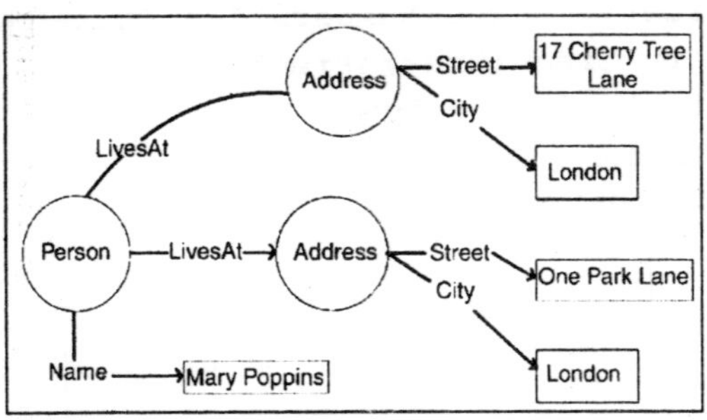


```
   <elementType id="Person">
    <mapsTo type="c:person"/>
    <element type="#name"> <string/> <mapsTo
```

```
type="c:name"/> </element>
    <group occurs="ZEROORMORE"/>
    <element type="#street">
    <string/>
    <mapsTo type="c:street">
    <implies type="c::address" id
   ="livesAtAddress">
          <implies type="c:livesAt"/>
    </implies>
    </mapsTo>
    </element>
    <element type="#city">
    <string/>
    <mapsTo type="c:city">
    <implies type="#livesAtAddress"/>
    </mapsTo>
    </element>
    </group>
   </elementType>
```

Mappings within groups are handled together. Since *street* and *city* are in a single group, each occurrence of such a group results in one *address*.Text markup can also be handled by mapping. Suppose that for some reason we choose to markup the number portion of a street address.

```
<Person>
 <name>Mary Poppins</name>
 <street>< streetNumber>17</ streetNumber >
 Cherry Tree Lane</street>
 <city>London</city>
</Person>
```

If this should be reflected in the graph,

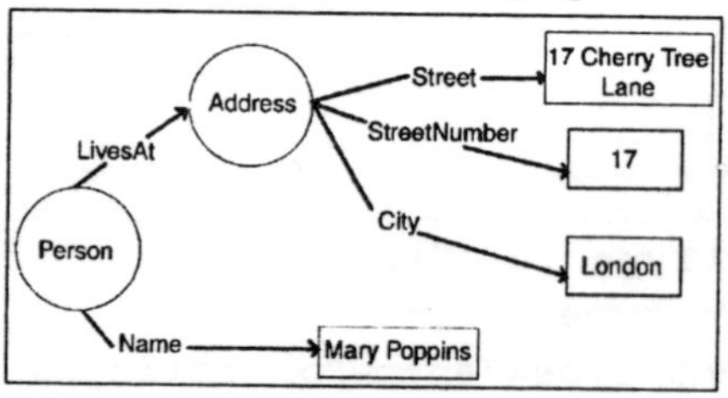

We can do that with mapping such as:

```
<elementType id="streetNumber">
 <string/>
</elementType>
<elementType id="street>
 <mixed>
 <element type="# streetNumber">
     <mapsTo type="c: streetNumber">
     <implies type="#livesAtAddress"/>
 </mapsTo>
 </element>
 </mixed>
</elementType>
...Person defined as before...
```

Appendix A: Examples

Some data:

```
<?xml:namespace name="http://company.com/
schemas/books/" as="bk"/>
<?xml:namespace name="http://www.ecom.org/
schemas/dc/" as="ecom"?>
<bk:booksAndAuthors>
 <Person>
 <name>Henry Ford</name>
 <birthday>1863</birthday>
 </Person>
 <Person>
 <name>Harvey S. Firestone</name>
 </Person>
 <Person>
 <name>Samuel Crowther</name>
 </Person>
 <Book>
 <author>Henry Ford</author>
 <author>Samuel Crowther</author>
 <title>My Life and Work</title>
 </Book>
 <Book>
```

```
<author>Harvey S. Firestone</author>
<author>Samuel Crowther</author>
<title>Men and Rubber</title>
<ecom:price>23.95</ecom:price>
</Book>
</bk:booksAndAuthors>
```

The schema for http://company.com/schemas/books:

```
<?xml:namespace name="urn:uuid:BDC6E3F0-6DA3-
11d1-A2A3-00AA00C14882/" as="s"/?>
<?xml:namespace href="http://www.ecom.org/
schemas/ecom/" as="ecom" ?>
<s:schema>
<elementType id="name">
<string/>
</elementType>
<elementType id="birthday">
<string/>
<dataType dt="date.ISO8601"/>
</elementType>
<elementType id="Person">
<element type="#name" id="p1"/>
<elementtype="#birthday"occurs="OPTIONAL">
<min>1700-01-01</min><max>2100-01-01</
max>
</element>
<key id="k1"><keyPart href="#p1"/></key>
</elementType>
<elementType id="author">
<string/>
<domain type="#Book"/>
<foreignKey range="#Person" key="#k1"/>
</elementType>
<elementType id="writtenWork">
<element type="#author" occurs
="ONEORMORE"/>
</elementType> <elementType id="Book" >
<genus type="#writtenWork"/>
<superType href=" http://www.ecom.org/
```

```
schemas/ecom/commercialItem"/>
       <superType href=" http://www.ecom.org/
   schemas/ecom/inventoryItem"/>
       <group groupOrder="SEQ" occurs="OPTIONAL">
        <element type="#preface"/>
        <element type="#introduction"/>
    </group>
        <element href="http://www.ecom.org/
    schemas/ecom/price"/>
        <element href="ecom:quantityOnHand"/>
    </elementType>
    <elementTypeEquivalent id="livre"
 type="#Book"/>
    <elementTypeEquivalent id="auteur"
 type="#author"/>
   </s:schema>
```

XML DTD for XML-Data schemas

```
   <!ENTITY% nodeattrs 'id ID #IMPLIED'>
   <!— href is as per XML-LINK, but is not
required unless there is no content —>
   <!ENTITY% linkattrs
       'id ID #IMPLIED
       href CDATA #IMPLIED'>
   <!ENTITY% typelinkattrs
       'id ID #IMPLIED
       type CDATA #IMPLIED'>
   <!ENTITY% exattrs
       'name CDATA #IMPLIED
       content (OPEN|CLOSED)"OPEN"' >
   <!ENTITY% elementTypeElements1
       'genus? correlative? superType*'>
   <!ENTITY% elementTypeElements2
       'description,
       (min|minExclusive)?,
       (max | maxInclusive)?,
       domain*,
       key*,
```

```
    foreignKey*,
    (datatype | (syntax?, objecttype+))?
    mapsTo?'>
<!ENTITY% elementConstraints
    'min? max? default?'>
<!ENTITY% elementAttrs
    'occurs (REQUIRED|OPTIONAL|ONEORMORE|
    ZEROORMORE) "REQUIRED" '>
<!ENTITY% rangeAttribute
    'range CDATA #IMPLIED' >
<!— The top-level container —>
<!element schema ((elementType|linkType|
    extendType
    intEntityDcl|extEntityDcl|
    notationDcl|extDcls)*)>
<!attlist schema%nodeattrs;>
<!— Element Type Declarations —>
<!element elementType (%elementTypeElements1;,
    ((element|group)*|empty|any|string|
    mixed)?,
    attribute*
    %elementTypeElements2)>
<!attlist elementType%nodeattrs;
    %exattrs >
<!— Element types allowed in content model —
>
<!— Note this is just short for a model group
with only one element in it —>
<!element element (%elementConstraints;) >
<!— The type is required —>
<!attlist element%typelinkattrs;
    %elementAttrs;
    presence (FIXED) #IMPLIED >
<!— A group in a content model: and, sequential
or disjunctive —>
<!element group ((group|element)+)>
<!attlist group%nodeattrs;%elementattrs;
    presence (FIXED) #IMPLIED
```

```
        groupOrder (AND|SEQ|OR) 'SEQ'>
    <!element any EMPTY>
    <!element empty EMPTY>
    <!element string EMPTY>
    <!— mixed content is just a flat, non-empty
    list of elements —>
    <!— We don't need to say anything about
<string/> (CDATA), it's implied —>
    <!element mixed (element+)>
    <!attlist mixed%nodeattrs;>
    <!element superType EMPTY>
    <!attlist superType%linkattrs;>
    <!element genus EMPTY>
    <!attlist genus%typelinkattrs;>
    <!element description MIXED>
    <!attlist description%nodeattrs;>
    <!element domain EMPTY>
    <!attlist domain%typelinkattrs;>
    <!element default MIXED>
    <!attlist default%nodeattrs;>
    <!element min MIXED>
    <!attlist min%nodeattrs; >
    <!element max MIXED>
    <!attlist max%nodeattrs; >
    <!element maxInclusive MIXED>
    <!attlist maxInclusive%nodeattrs; >
    <!element minExclusive MIXED>
    <!attlist minExclusive%nodeattrs; >
    <!element key (keyPart+)>
    <!attlist key%nodeattrs;>
    <!element keyPart EMPTY>
    <!attlist keyPart%linkattrs;>
    <!element foreignKey foreignKeyPart* >
    <!attlist foreignKey%nodeattrs;
        %rangeAttribute;
        key CDATA #IMPLIED >
    <!element foreignKeyPart EMPTY>
    <!attlist foreignKeyPart%linkattrs;>
```

```
<!— Datatype support —>
<!element datatype (elementType?) >
<!attlist datatype%typelinkattrs;
   presence (IMPLIED|SPECIFIED
|REQUIRED|FIXED) #IMPLIED >
<!element syntax >
<!attlist syntax%linkattrs; >
<!element objecttype >
<!attlist objecttype%linkattrs; >
<!— Mapping support —>
<!element mapsTo (implies?)>
<!attlist mapsTo%typelinkattrs;>
<!element implies (implies?)>
<!attlist implies%typelinkattrs;>
<!— Alias support —>
<!element elementTypeEquivalent EMPTY>
<!attlist elementTypeEquivalent
%typelinkattrs; >
<!element correlative EMPTY>
<!attlist correlative%linkattrs;>
<! Subtype of ElementType that is explicitly
a relation.->
<!element                    relationType
(%elementTypeElements1;,
((element|group)*|empty|any|string|mixed)?,
attribute*
%elementTypeElements2)>
<!attlist relationType%nodeattrs;
%exattrs; >
<!— Attributes —>
<!— default value must be present if presence
is specified or fixed —>
<!— presence defaults to specified if default
is present, else implied —>
<!element attribute (%PropertyElements1,
   %PropertyElements2,
```

```
        %elementConstraints)>
    <!attlist attribute%typelinkattrs;
        name CDATA #IMPLIED
        %elementAttrs
        dt CDATA #IMPLIED
        atttype (URIREF|
           ID|IDREF|IDREFS|ENTITY|ENTITIES|
           NMTOKEN|NMTOKENS|
           ENUMERATION|NOTATION|CDATA) CDATA
        %rangeAttribute;
        default CDATA #IMPLIED
        values NMTOKENS #IMPLIED
        presence (IMPLIED    |SPECIFIED
    |REQUIRED|FIXED)        #IMPLIED >
    <!- Notation and Entity Declarations ->
    <!- Note: as this is written, only external
    entities can have structure without
escaping it ->
    <!- 'par' is TRUE iff parameter entity. ->
    <!- systemID and publicId (if present) must
    have the  required syntax ->
    <!ENTITY% notationattrs '%nodeattrs
        systemID CDATA #IMPLIED
        publicID CDATA #IMPLIED'>
    <!ENTITY% entityattrs '%notationattrs
        name CDATA #IMPLIED
        par (TRUE | FALSE) "FALSE">
    <!- Notation Declarations ->
    <!element notationDcl EMPTY>
    <!attlist notationDcl%notationattrs>
    <!element intEntityDcl PCDATA>
    <!attlist intEntityDcl%entityattrs; >
    <!- The entity will be treated as binary if a
    notation is present ->
    <!element extEntityDcl EMPTY>
    <!attlist extEntityDcl%entityattrs;
```

```
    notation CDATA #IMPLIED>
<!- External entity with declarations to be
included ->
<!element extDcls EMPTY>
<!attlist extDcls%entityattrs;>
```

DTD

DEFINITION

Recall from earlier that XML 1.0 contains a built-in schema language:

Document Type Definition

```
<!DOCTYPE root-element [doctype-declaration...
]>
```

Determines the name of the root element and contains the document type declarations

```
<!ELEMENT element-name content-model>
```

Associates a *content model* to all elements of the given namecontent models:

EMPTY: no content is allowed

ANY: any content is allowed

(#PCDATA|*element-name*|...)*: "mixed content", arbitrary sequence of character data and listed elements*deterministic regular expression over element names*: sequence of elements matching the expression

choice: (...|...|...)

sequence: (.........)

optional:...?

zero or more:...*

one or more:...+

<!ATTLIST *element-name attr-name attr-type attr-default...*>

Declares which attributes are allowed or required in which elementsattribute types:

CDATA: any value is allowed (the default)(*value*|...): enumeration of allowed valuesID, IDREF, IDREFS: ID attribute values must be unique (contain "element identity"), IDREF attribute values must match some ID (reference to an element)ENTITY, ENTITIES, NMTOKEN, NMTOKENS,

NOTATION: just forget these... (consider them deprecated) attribute defaults:

- #REQUIRED: the attribute must be explicitly provided
- #IMPLIED: attribute is optional, no default provided
- *"value"*: if not explicitly provided, this value inserted by default
- #FIXED *"value"*: as above, but only this value is allowed

EXAMPLE DTD

A DTD for our recipe collections, recipes.dtd:

```
<!ELEMENT collection (description,recipe*)>
<!ELEMENT description ANY>
<!ELEMENT recipe (title,ingredient*,preparation,comment?,
nutrition)>
<!ELEMENT title (#PCDATA)>
<!ELEMENT ingredient    (ingredient*,
preparation)?>
<!ATTLIST ingredient name CDATA #REQUIRED
amount CDATA #IMPLIED
    unit CDATA #IMPLIED>
<!ELEMENT preparation (step*)>
<!ELEMENT step (#PCDATA)>
<!ELEMENT comment (#PCDATA)>
<!ELEMENT nutrition EMPTY>
<!ATTLIST nutrition protein CDATA #REQUIRED
    carbohydrates CDATA #REQUIRED
    fat CDATA #REQUIRED
    calories CDATA #REQUIRED
    alcohol CDATA #IMPLIED>
```

By inserting:

```
<!DOCTYPE collection SYSTEM "recipes.dtd">
```

In the headers of recipe collection documents, we state that they are intended to conform to recipes.dtd.Alternatively, the DTD can be given locally with <!DOCTYPE collection [...]>.This grammatical description has some obvious shortcomings:we cannot express that, *e.g.* protein, must contain a non-negative numberunit should only be allowed when amount is presentthe comment element should be allowed to appear anywherenested ingredient elements should only be allowed when amount is absent

PROBLEMS WITH DTD

Mixed into the XML 1.0 spec (would be much less confusing if specified separately + even non-validating processors must look at the DTD) No constraints on character data (if character data is allowed, *any* character data is allowed) Too simple attribute value models (enumerations are clearly insufficient) Cannot mix character data and regexp content models (and the content models are generally hard to use for complex requirements)no support for Namespaces (of course, XML 1.0 was defined before Namespaces)very limited support for modularity and reuse (the entity mechanism is too low-level)

No support for schema evolution, extension, or inheritance of declarations (difficult to write, maintain, and read large DTDs, and to define families of related schemas)

Limited white-space control (xml:space is rarely used)

No embedded, structured self-documentation (<!— comments —> are not enough)

Content and attribute declarations cannot depend on attributes or element context (*many* XML languages use that, but their DTDs have to "allow too much")too simple ID attribute mechanism (no points-to requirements, uniqueness scope, etc.)only defaults for attributes, not for elements (but that would often be convenient)cannot specify "any element" or "any attribute" (useful for partial specifications and during schema development)defaults cannot be specified separate from the declarations (would be convenient to have defaults in separate modules)

XML SCHEMA

OVERVIEW

The XML 1.0 specification defines the concepts of well-formedness and validity; it is very simple to check a document for well-formedness, while validation requires more work but allows the user to define more powerful constraints on document structure. XML validity requires that a document follow the constraints expressed in its document type definition, which provides the rough equivalent of a context-free grammar for a document type.

For some uses, applications may need definitions of markup constructs more informative, or constraints on document structure tighter than, looser than, or simply different from those which can be expressed using document type definitions as defined in XML 1.0. There is also a widespread desire to allow markup constructs and constraints to be specified in an XML-based syntax, in order to allow tools for XML documents to be used on the specifications.

By charter, the XML Schema Working Group is assigned to address the following issues:

Structural schemas

Amechanism somewhat analogous to DTDs for constraining document structure (order, occurrence of elements, attributes). Specific goals beyond DTD functionality areintegration with namespacesdefinition of incomplete constraints on the content of an element typeintegration of structural schemas with primitive data typesin

Heritance: Existing mechanisms use content models to specify part-of relations. But they only specify kind-of relations implicitly or informally. Making kind-of relations explicit would make both understanding and maintenance easier

Primitive data typing

Integers, dates, and the like, based on experience with SQL, Java primitives, etc.; byte sequences ("binary data") also need to be considered

Conformance

The relation of schemata to XML document instances, and obligations on schema-aware processors, must be defined. The Working Group will define a process for checking to see that the constraints expressed in a schema are obeyed in a document (schema-validation); the relationship between schema-validity and validity as defined in XML 1.0 will be defined.The XML Schema work is interdependent with several other areas of W3C activity. These are listed below under Design Principles.

PURPOSE

The purpose of the XML schema language is to provide an inventory of XML markup constructs with which to write schemas.The purpose of a schema is to define and describe a class of XML documents by using these constructs to constrain and document the meaning, usage and relationships of their constituent parts: datatypes, elements and their content, attributes and their values, entities and their contents and notations. Schema constructs may also provide for the specification of implicit information such as default values.

Schemas document their own meaning, usage, and function.Thus, the XML schema language can be used to define, describe and catalogue XML vocabularies for classes of XML documents.

Any application of XML can use the Schema formalism to express syntactic, structural and value constraints applicable to its document instances. The Schema formalism will allow a useful level of constraint checking to be described and validated for a wide spectrum of XML applications. For applications which require other, arbitrary or complicated constraints, the application must perform its own additional validations.

USAGE SCENARIOS

The following usage scenarios describe XML applications that should benefit from XML schemas. They represent a wide range of activities and needs that are representative of the problem space to be addressed. They are intended to be used during the development of XML schemas as design cases that should be reviewed when critical decisions are made. These usage scenarios should also prove useful in helping non-members of the XML Schema Working Group understand the intent and goals of the project.

- *Publishing and syndication*: Distribution of information through publishing and syndication services. Involves collections of XML documents with complex relations among them. Structural schemas describe the properties of headlines, news stories, thumbnail images, cross-references, etc. Document views under control of different versions of a schema.
- *Electronic commerce transaction processing*: Libraries of schemas define business transactions within markets and between parties. A schema-aware processor is used to validate a business document, and to provide access to its information set.
- *Supervisory control and data acquisition*: The management and use of network devices involves the exchange of data and control messages. Schemas can be used by a server to ensure outgoing message validity, or by the client to allow it to determine what part of a message it understands. In multi-vendor environment, discriminates data governed by different schemas (industry-standard, vendor-specific) and know when it is safe to ignore information not understood and when an error should be raised instead; provide transparency control. Applications include media devices, security systems, plant automation, process control.
- *Traditional document authoring/editing governed by schema constraints*: One important class of application uses a schema definition to guide an author in the development of documents. A simple example might be a memo, whereas a more sophisticated example is the technical service manuals for a wide-body intercontinental aircraft. The application can ensure that the author always knows whether to enter a date or a part-number, and might even ensure that the data entered is valid.
- *Use schema to help query formulation and optimization*:

A query interface inspect XML schemas to guide a user in the formulation of queries. Any given database can emit a schema of itself to inform other systems what counts as legitimate and useful queries.

- *Open and uniform transfer of data between applications, including databases*: XML has become a widely used format for encoding data (including metadata and control data) for exchange between loosely coupled applications. Such exchange is currently hampered by the difficulty of fully describing the exchange data model in terms of XML DTDs; exchange data model versioning issues further complicate such interactions. When the exchange data model is represented by the more expressive XML Schema definitions, the task of mapping the exchange data model to and from application internal data models will be simplified.
- Metadata Interchange: There is growing interest in the interchange of metadata (especially for databases) and in the use of metadata registries to facilitate interoperability of database design, DBMS, query, user interface, data warehousing, and report generation tools. Examples include ISO 11179 and ANSI X3.285 data registry standards, and OMG's proposed XMI standard.

DESIGN PRINCIPLES

In the design of any language, trade-offs in the solution space are necessary. The following design principles should guide the working group in making these trade-offs. Design principles are desirable, but not fully measurable, characteristics.

The XML schema language shall be:

- More expressive than XML DTDs;
- Expressed in XML;
- Self-describing;
- Usable by a wide variety of applications that employ XML;

- Straightforwardly usable on the Internet;
- optimized for interoperability;
- Simple enough to implement with modest design and runtime resources;
- Coordinated with relevant W3C specs (XML Information Set, Links, Namespaces, Pointers, Style and Syntax, as well as DOM, HTML, and RDF Schema).

The XML schema language specification shall:

- Be prepared quickly;
- Be precise, concise, human-readable, and illustrated with examples.

REQUIREMENTS

Structural Requirements

The XML schema language must define:

- Mechanisms for constraining document structure (namespaces, elements, attributes) and content (datatypes, entities, notations);
- Mechanisms to enable inheritance for element, attribute, and datatype definitions;
- Mechanism for URI reference to standard semantic understanding of a construct;
- Mechanism for embedded documentation;
- Mechanism for application-specific constraints and descriptions;
- Mechanisms for addressing the evolution of schemata;
- Mechanisms to enable integration of structural schemas with primitive data types.

Datatype Requirements

The XML schema language must:

- Provide for primitive data typing, including byte, date, integer, sequence, SQL & Java primitive data types, etc.;
- Define a type system that is adequate for import/

export from database systems (e.g., relational, object, OLAP);
- Distinguish requirements relating to lexical data representation vs. those governing an underlying information set;
- Allow creation of user-defined datatypes, such as datatypes that are derived from existing datatypes and which may constrain certain of its properties (e.g., range, precision, length, mask).

Conformance

The XML schema language must:
- Describe the responsibilities of conforming processors;
- Define the relationship between schemas and XML documents;
- Define the relationship between schema validity and XML validity;
- Define the relationship between schemas and XML DTDs, and their information sets;
- Define the relationship among schemas, namespaces, and validity;
- Define a useful XML schema for XML schemas;XML Schema

STRUCTURES

- A Schema for Schemas (normative)
- B References (normative)
- C Outcome Tabulations (normative)
- C.1 Validation Rules
- C.2 Contributions to the post-schema-validation infoset
- C.3 Schema Representation Constraints
- C.4 Schema Component Constraints
- D Required Information Set Items and Properties (normative)
- E Schema Components Diagram (non-normative)
- F Glossary (non-normative)

- G DTD for Schemas (non-normative)
- H Analysis of the Unique Particle Attribution Constraint (non-normative)
- I References (non-normative)
- J Acknowledgements (non-normative)

Introduction

This document sets out the structural part (XML Schema: Structures) of the XML Schema definition language.This document is primarily intended as a language definition reference. As such, although it contains a few examples, it is notprimarily designed to serve as a motivating introduction to the design and its features, or as a tutorial for new users. Rather it presents a careful and fully explicit definition of that design, suitable for guiding implementations. For those in search of a step-by-step introduction to the design, the non-normative [XML Schema: Primer] is a much better starting point than this document.

Purpose

The purpose of XML Schema: Structures is to define the nature of XML schemas and their component parts, provide an inventory of XML markup constructs with which to represent schemas, and define the application of schemas to XML documents.The purpose of an XML Schema: Structures schema is to define and describe a class of XML documents by using schema components to constrain and document the meaning, usage and relationships of their constituent parts: datatypes, elements and their content and attributes and their values. Schemas may also provide for the specification of additional document information, such as normalization and defaulting of attribute and element values.

Schemas have facilities for self-documentation. Thus, XML Schema: Structures can be used to define, describe and catalogue XML vocabularies for classes of XML documents.Any application that consumes well-formed XML can use the XML Schema: Structures formalism to express syntactic, structural and value constraints applicable to its document instances. The XML Schema: Structures formalism allows a useful level of constraint checking to be described and implemented for a wide spectrum of XML applications. However, the language defined by this specification does not attempt to provide all the facilities that might be needed by any application. Some applications may require constraint capabilities not expressible in this language, and so may need to perform their own additional validations.

Dependencies on Other Specifications

The definition of XML Schema: Structures depends on the following specifications:

[XML-Infoset], [XML-Namespaces], [XPath], and [XML Schemas: Datatypes].See Required Information Set Items and Properties (normative) (§D) for a tabulation of the information items and properties specified in [XML-Infoset] which this specification requires as a precondition to schema-aware processing.

Documentation Conventions and Terminology

The section introduces the highlighting and typography as used in this document to present technical material.Special terms are defined at their point of introduction in the text. For example [Definition:] a term is something used with a special meaning.

The definition is labeled as such and the term it defines is displayed in boldface. The end of the definition is not specially marked in the displayed or printed text. Uses of defined terms are links to their definitions, set off with middle dots, for instance ·term·.Non-normative examples are set off in boxes and accompanied by a brief explanation:

Example:

```
<schema targetNamespace="http://www.
example.com/XMLSchema/1.0/mySchema">
```

And an explanation of the example.The definition of each kind of schema component consists of a list of its properties and their contents, followed by descriptions of the semantics of the properties:

Schema Component: Example

{example property}

Definition of the property.References to properties of schema components are links to the relevant definition as exemplified above, set off with curly braces, for instance {example property}.

The correspondence between an element information item which is part of the XML representation of a schema and one or more schema components is presented in a tableau which illustrates the element information item(s) involved. This is followed by a tabulation of the correspondence between properties of the component and properties of the information item. Where context may determine which of several different components may arise, several tabulations, one per context, are given.

The property correspondences are normative, as are the illustrations of the XML representation element information items.In the XML representation, bold-face attribute names (*e.g.* count below) indicate a required attribute information item, and the rest are optional. Where an attribute information item has an enumerated type definition, the values are shown separated by vertical bars, as for size below; if there is a default value, it is shown following a colon.

Where an attribute information item has a built-in simple type definition defined in [XML Schemas: Datatypes], a hyperlink to its definition therein is given.The allowed content of the information item is shown as a grammar fragment, using the Kleene operators ?, * and +. Each element name therein is a hyperlink to its own illustration.Note: The illustrations are derived automatically from the Schema for Schemas (normative) (§A). In the case of apparent conflict, the Schema for Schemas (normative) (§A) takes precedence, as it, together with the ·Schema Representation Constraints·, provide the normative statement of the form of XML representations.

XML Representation Summary: example Element Information Item

```
<example
count = integer
```

```
size = (large | medium | small): medium>
Content: (all | any*)
</example>
```

Example Schema Component

Property	Representation
{example property}	Description of what the property corresponds to, *e.g.* the value of the size [attribute]

References to elements in the text are links to the relevant illustration as exemplified above, set off with angle brackets, for instance <example>.

References to properties of information items as defined in [XML-Infoset] are notated as links to the relevant section thereof, set off with square brackets, for example [children]. Properties which this specification defines for information items are introduced as follows:

PSVI Contributions for example information items

[***new property***]

The value the property gets.References to properties of information items defined in this specification are notated as links to their introduction as exemplified above, set off with square brackets, for example [new property].

The following highlighting is used for non-normative commentary in this document:

Note: General comments directed to all readers.Following [XML 1.0 (Second Edition)], within normative prose in this specification, the words may and must are defined as follows:

- *May*: Conforming documents and XML Schema-aware processors are permitted to but need not behave as described.
- *Must*: Conforming documents and XML Schema-aware processors are required to behave as described; otherwise they are in error.Note however that this specification provides a definition of error and of conformant processors' responsibilities with respect to errors (Schemas and Schema-validity Assessment (§5)) which is considerably more complex than that of [XML 1.0 (Second Edition)].

Conceptual Framework

This chapter gives an overview of XML Schema: Structures at the level of its abstract data model. Schema Component Details (§3) provides details on this model, including a normative representation in XML for the components of the model.

Readers interested primarily in learning to write schema documents may wish to first read [XML Schema: Primer] for a tutorial introduction, and only then consult the sub-sections of Schema Component Details (§3) named XML Representation of... for the details.

Overview of XML Schema

An XML Schema consists of components such as type definitions and element declarations. These can be used to assess the validity of well-formed element and attribute information items (as defined in [XML-Infoset]), and furthermore may specify augmentations to those items and their descendants.

This augmentation makes explicit information which may have been implicit in the original document, such as normalized and/or default values for attributes and elements and the types of element and attribute information items. [Definition:] We refer to the augmented infoset which results from conformant processing as defined in this specification as the post-schema-validation infoset, or PSVI.

Schema-validity assessment has two aspects:

1. Determining local schema-validity, that is whether an element or attribute information item satisfies the constraints embodied in the relevant components of an XML Schema;
2. Synthesizing an overall validation outcome for the item, combining local schema-validity with the results of schema-validity assessments of its descendants, if any, and adding appropriate augmentations to the infoset to record this outcome.

Throughout this specification, [Definition:] the word valid and its derivatives are used to refer to clause 1 above, the determination of local schema-validity.Throughout this specification, [Definition:] the word assessment is used to refer to the overall process of local validation, schema-validity assessment and infoset augmentation.

ML Schema Abstract Data Model: Type Definition Components Declaration Components Model Group Components Identity-constraint Definition Components Group Definition Components Annotation ComponentsThis specification builds on [XML 1.0 (Second Edition)] and [XML-Namespaces].

The concepts and definitions used herein regarding XML are framed at the abstract level of information items as defined in [XML-Infoset].

By definition, this use of the infoset provides a priori guarantees of well-formedness (as defined in [XML 1.0 (Second Edition)]) and namespace conformance(as defined in [XML-Namespaces]) for all candidates for ·assessment· and for all ·schema documents·.Just as [XML 1.0 (Second Edition)] and [XML-Namespaces] can be described in terms of information items, XML Schemas can be described in terms of an abstract data model.

In defining XML Schemas in terms of an abstract data model, this specification rigorously specifies the information which must be available to a conforming XML Schema processor. The abstract model for schemas is conceptual only, and does not mandate any particular implementation or representation of this information.

To facilitate interoperation and sharing of schema information, a normative XML interchange format for schemas is provided.[Definition:] Schema component is the generic term for the building blocks that comprise the abstract data model of the schema. [Definition:] An XML Schema is a set of ·schema components·. There are 13 kinds of component in all, falling into three groups.

The primary components, which may (type definitions) or must (element and attribute declarations) have names are as follows:

1. Simple type definitions
2. Complex type definitions

3. Attribute declarations
4. Element declarations

The secondary components, which must have names, are as follows:

- Attribute group definitions
- Identity-constraint definitions
- Model group definitions
- Notation declarations

Finally, the "helper" components provide small parts of other components; they are not independent of their context:

- Annotations
- Model groups
- Particles
- Wildcards
- Attribute Uses

During ·validation·, [Definition:] declaration components are associated by (qualified) name to information items being·validated·.On the other hand, [Definition:] definition components define internal schema components that can be used in other schema components.[Definition:] Declarations and definitions may have and be identified by names, which are NCNames as defined by [XML-Namespaces].[Definition:] Several kinds of component have a target namespace, which is either ·absent· or a namespace name, also as defined by [XML-Namespaces].

The ·target namespace· serves to identify the namespace within which the association between the component and its name exists. In the case of declarations, this in turn determines the namespace name of, for example, the element information items it may ·validate·.

Note: At the abstract level, there is no requirement that the components of a schema share a ·target namespace·. Any schema for use in ·assessment· of documents containing names from more than one namespace will of necessity include components with different ·target namespaces·. This contrasts with the situation at the level of the XML representation of components, in which each schema document contributes definitions and declarations to a single target namespace.Validation·, defined in detail in Schema Component Details (§3), is a relation between information items and schema components. For example, an attribute information item may ·validate· with respect to an attribute declaration, a list of element information items may ·validate· with respect to a content model, and so on. The following sections briefly introduce the kinds of components in the schema abstract data model, other major features of the abstract model, and how they contribute to ·validation·.

Type Definition Components

The abstract model provides two kinds of type definition component: simple and complex.[Definition:] This specification uses the phrase type definition in cases where no distinction need be made between simple and complex types.Type definitions form a hierarchy with a single root. The subsections below first describe characteristics of that hierarchy, then provide an introduction to simple and complex type definitions themselves.

Type Definition Hierarchy

[Definition:] Except for a distinguished ·ur-type definition·, every ·type definition· is, by construction, either a ·restriction· or an·extension· of some other type definition. The graph of these relationships forms a tree known as the Type Definition Hierarchy.[Definition:] A type definition whose declarations or facets are in a one-to-one relation with those of another specified type definition, with each in turn restricting the possibilities of the one it corresponds to, is said to be a restriction.

The specific restrictions might include narrowed ranges or reduced alternatives. Members of a type, A, whose definition is a ·restriction· of the definition of another type, B, are always members of type B as well.[Definition:] A complex type definition which allows element or attribute content in addition to that allowed by another specified type definition is said to be an extension.[Definition:] A distinguished complex type definition, the ur-type definition, whose name is *anyType* in the XML Schema namespace, is present in each ·XML Schema·, serving as the root of the type definition hierarchy for that schema.[Definition:] A type definition used as the basis for an ·extension· or ·restriction· is known as the base type definition of that definition.

Simple Type Definition

A simple type definition is a set of constraints on strings and information about the values they encode, applicable to the·normalized value· of an attribute information item or of an element information item with no element children. Informally, it applies to the values of attributes and the text-only content of elements.

Each simple type definition, whether built-in (that is, defined in [XML Schemas: Datatypes]) or user-defined, is a ·restriction· of some particular simple ·base type definition·. For the built-in primitive type definitions, this is [Definition:] the simple ur-type definition, a special restriction of the ·ur-type definition·, whose name is anySimpleType in the XML Schema namespace.

The·simple ur-type definition· is considered to have an unconstrained lexical space, and a value space consisting of the union of the value spaces of all the built-in primitive datatypes and the set of all lists of all members of the value spaces of all the built-in primitive datatypes.The mapping from lexical space to value space is unspecified for items whose type definition is the ·simple ur-type definition·.

Accordingly this specification does not constrain processors' behaviour in areas where this mapping is implicated, for example checking such items against enumerations, constructing default attributes or elements whose declared type definition is the·simple ur-type definition·, checking identity constraints involving such items.Note: The Working Group expects to return to this area in a future version of this specification.Simple types may also be defined whose members are lists of items themselves constrained by some other simple type definition, or whose membership is the union of the memberships of some other simple type definitions. Such list and union simple type definitions are also restrictions of the ·simple ur-type definition·.For detailed information on simple type definitions, see Simple Type Definitions (§3.14) and [XML Schemas: Datatypes]. The latter also defines an extensive inventory of pre-defined simple types.

Complex Type Definition

A complex type definition is a set of attribute declarations and a content type, applicable to the [attributes] and [children] of an element information item respectively. The content type may require the [children] to contain neither element nor character information items (that is, to be empty), to be a string which belongs to a particular simple type or to contain a sequence of element information items which conforms to a particular model group, with or without character information items as well.

Each complex type definition other than the ·ur-type definition· is either:

- A restriction of a complex ·base type definition·or
- An ·extension· of a simple or complex ·base type definition·

A complex type which extends another does so by having additional content model particles at the end of the other definition's content model, or by having additional attribute declarations, or both.

Note: This specification allows only appending, and not other kinds of extensions. This decision simplifies application processing required to cast instances from derived to base type. Future versions may allow more kinds of extension, requiring more complex transformations to effect casting.For detailed information on complex type definitions, see Complex Type Definitions (§3.4).

Declaration Components

There are three kinds of declaration component: element, attribute, and notation. Each is described in a section below.

Also included is a discussion of element substitution groups, which is a feature provided in conjunction with element declarations.

Element Declaration

An element declaration is an association of a name with a type definition, either simple or complex, an (optional) default value and a (possibly empty) set of identity-constraint definitions.

The association is either global or scoped to a containing complex type definition. A top-level element declaration with name 'A' is broadly comparable to a pair of DTD declarations as follows, where the associated type definition fills in the ellipses:

```
<!ELEMENT A...>
<!ATTLIST A...>
```

Element declarations contribute to ·validation· as part of model group ·validation·, when their defaults and type components are checked against an element information item with a matching name and namespace, and by triggering identity-constraint definition ·validation·.For detailed information on element declarations, see Element Declarations (§3.3).

Element Substitution Group

In XML 1.0, the name and content of an element must correspond exactly to the element type referenced in the corresponding content model.[Definition:] Through the new mechanism of element substitution groups, XML Schemas provides a more powerful model supporting substitution of one named element for another. Any top-level element declaration can serve as the defining member, or head, for an element substitution group. Other top-level element declarations, regardless of target namespace, can be designated as members of the substitution group headed by this element.

In a suitably enabled content model, a reference to the head·validates· not just the head itself, but elements corresponding to any other member of the substitution group as well.All such members must have type definitions which are either the same as the head's type definition or restrictions or extensions of it. Therefore, although the names of elements can vary widely as new namespaces and members of the substitution group are defined, the content of member elements is strictly limited according to the type definition of the substitution group head.Note that element substitution groups are not represented as separate components. They are specified in the property values for element declarations (Element Declarations (§3.3)).

Attribute Declaration

An attribute declaration is an association between a name and a simple type definition, together with occurrence information and (optionally) a default value. The association is either global, or local to its containing complex type definition. Attribute declarations contribute to ·validation· as part of complex type definition ·validation·, when their occurrence, defaults and type components are checked against an attribute information item with a matching name and namespace.For detailed information on attribute declarations, see Attribute Declarations (§3.2).

Notation Declaration

A notation declaration is an association between a name and an identifier for a notation. For an attribute information item to be·valid· with respect to a NOTATION simple type definition, its value must have been declared with a notation declaration.For detailed information on notation declarations, Notation Declarations (§3.12).

Model Group Components

The model group, particle, and wildcard components contribute to the portion of a complex type definition that controls an element information item's content.

Model Group

A model group is a constraint in the form of a grammar

fragment that applies to lists of element information items. It consists of a list of particles, *i.e* element declarations, wildcards and model groups. There are three varieties of model group:

- Sequence (the element information items match the particles in sequential order);
- Conjunction (the element information items match the particles, in any order);
- Disjunction (the element information items match one of the particles).

For detailed information on model groups, Model Groups (§3.8).

Particle

A particle is a term in the grammar for element content, consisting of either an element declaration, a wildcard or a model group, together with occurrence constraints. Particles contribute to ·validation· as part of complex type definition ·validation·, when they allow anywhere from zero to many element information items or sequences thereof, depending on their contents and occurrence constraints.[Definition:] A particle can be used in a complex type definition to constrain the ·validation· of the [children] of an element information item; such a particle is called a content model.

Note: XML Schema: Structures ·content models· are similar to but more expressive than [XML 1.0 (Second Edition)] content models; unlike [XML 1.0 (Second Edition)], XML Schema: Structures applies ·content models· to the ·validation· of both mixed and element-only content.For detailed information on particles, Particles (§3.9).

- *Attribute Use:* An attribute use plays a role similar to that of a particle, but for attribute declarations: an attribute declaration within a complex type definition is embedded within an attribute use, which specifies whether the declaration requires or merely allows its attribute, and whether it has a default or fixed value.
- *Wildcard:* A wildcard is a special kind of particle which matches element and attribute information items dependent on their namespace name,

independently of their local names.For detailed information on wildcards, Wildcards (§3.10).

Identity-constraint Definition Components

An identity-constraint definition is an association between a name and one of several varieties of identity-constraint related to uniqueness and reference. All the varieties use [XPath] expressions to pick out sets of information items relative to particular target element information items which are unique, or a key, or a ·valid· reference, within a specified scope. An element information item is only ·valid· with respect to an element declaration with identity-constraint definitions if those definitions are all satisfied for all the descendants of that element information item which they pick out.For detailed information on identity-constraint definitions, Identity-constraint Definitions (§3.11).

Group Definition Components

There are two kinds of convenience definitions provided to enable the re-use of pieces of complex type definitions: model group definitions and attribute group definitions.

- *Model Group Definition*: A model group definition is an association between a name and a model group, enabling re-use of the same model group in several complex type definitions.For detailed information on model group definitions, Model Group Definitions (§3.7).
- *Attribute Group Definition*: An attribute group definition is an association between a name and a set of attribute declarations, enabling re-use of the same set in several complex type definitions.

Annotation Components

An annotation is information for human and/or mechanical consumers. The interpretation of such information is not defined in this specification.For detailed information on annotations.

Constraints and Validation Rules

The [XML 1.0 (Second Edition)] specification describes two kinds of constraints on XML documents: well-formedness andvalidity constraints. Informally, the well-formedness constraints are those imposed by the definition of XML itself (such as the rules for the use of the < and > characters and the rules for proper nesting of elements), while validity constraints are the further constraints on document structure provided by a particular DTD.The preceding section focused on ·validation·, that is the constraints on information items which schema components supply. In fact however this specification provides four different kinds of normative statements about schema components, their representations in XML and their contribution to the ·validation· of information items:

- *Schema Component Constraint*: Constraints on the schema components themselves, *i.e* conditions components must satisfy to be components at all. Located in the sixth sub-section of the per-component sections of Schema Component Details (§3) and tabulated in Schema Component Constraints (§C.4).
- *Schema Representation Constraint*: Constraints on the representation of schema components in XML beyond those which are expressed inSchema for Schemas (normative) (§A). Located in the third sub-section of the per-component sections of Schema Component Details (§3) and tabulated in Schema Representation Constraints (§C.3).
- *Validation Rules*: Contributions to ·validation· associated with schema components. Located in the fourth sub-section of the per-component sections of Schema Component Details (§3) and tabulated in Validation Rules (§C.1).
- Schema Information Set Contribution: Augmentations to ·post-schema-validation infoset·s expressed by schema components, which follow as a consequence of ·validation· and/or ·assessment·. Located in the fifth sub-section of the per-component sections of Schema

Component Details (§3) and tabulated in Contributions to the post-schema-validation infoset (§C.2).The last of these, schema information set contributions, are not as new as they might at first seem. XML 1.0 validation augments the XML 1.0 information set in similar ways, for example by providing values for attributes not present in instances, and by implicitly exploiting type information for normalization or access. (As an example of the latter case, consider the effect of NMTOKENSon attribute white space, and the semantics of ID and IDREF.) By including schema information set contributions, this specification makes explicit some features that XML 1.0 left implicit.

Conformance

This specification describes three levels of conformance for schema aware processors. The first is required of all processors. Support for the other two will depend on the application environments for which the processor is intended.[Definition:] Minimally conforming processors must completely and correctly implement the ·Schema Component Constraints·,·Validation Rules·, and ·Schema Information Set Contributions· contained in this specification.[Definition:] ·Minimally conforming· processors which accept schemas represented in the form of XML documents as described inLayer 2: Schema Documents, Namespaces and Composition (§4.2) are additionally said to provide conformance to the XML Representation of Schemas.

Such processors must, when processing schema documents, completely and correctly implement all ·Schema Representation Constraints· in this specification, and must adhere exactly to the specifications in Schema Component Details (§3) for mapping the contents of such documents to ·schema components· for use in ·validation· and·assessment.

Note: By separating the conformance requirements relating to the concrete syntax of XML schema documents, this specification admits processors which use schemas stored in optimized binary representations, dynamically created schemas represented as programming language data structures, or implementations in which particular schemas are compiled into executable code such as C or Java.

Such processors can be said to be ·minimally conforming· but not necessarily in ·conformance to the XML Representation of Schemas·.[Definition:] Fully conforming processors are network-enabled processors which are not only both ·minimally conforming· and·in conformance to the XML Representation of Schemas·, but which additionally must be capable of accessing schema documents from the World Wide Web according to Representation of Schemas on the World Wide Web (§2.7) and How schema definitions are located on the Web (§4.3.2).

Note: Although this specification provides just these three standard levels of conformance, it is anticipated that other conventions can be established in the future. For example, the World Wide Web Consortium is considering conventions for packaging on the Web a variety of resources relating to individual documents and namespaces. Should such developments lead to new conventions for representing schemas, or for accessing them on the Web, new levels of conformance can be established and named at that time. There is no need to modify or republish this specification to define such additional levels of conformance.

Names and Symbol Spaces

As discussed in XML Schema Abstract Data Model (§2.2), most schema components (may) have ·names·. If all such names were assigned from the same "pool", then it would be impossible to have, for example, a simple type definition and an element declaration both with the name "title" in a given ·target namespace·

Therefore [Definition:] this specification introduces the term symbol space to denote a collection of names, each of which is unique with respect to the others. A symbol space is similar to the non-normative concept of namespace partition introduced in[XML-Namespaces].

There is a single distinct symbol space within a given ·target namespace· for each kind of definition and declaration component identified in XML Schema Abstract Data Model (§2.2), except that within a target namespace, simple type definitions and complex type definitions share a symbol space. Within a given symbol space, names are unique, but the same name may appear in more than one symbol space without conflict.

For example, the same name can appear in both a type definition and an element declaration, without conflict or necessary relation between the two.Locally scoped attribute and element declarations are special with regard to symbol spaces. Every complex type definition defines its own local attribute and element declaration symbol spaces, where these symbol spaces are distinct from each other and from any of the other symbol spaces.

So, for example, two complex type definitions having the same target namespace can contain a local attribute declaration for the unqualified name "priority", or contain a local element declaration for the name "address", without conflict or necessary relation between the two.

Schema-Related Markup in Documents Being Validated

2.6.1 xsi:type
2.6.2 xsi:nil
2.6.3 xsi:schemaLocation,xsi:noNamespaceSchema Location

The XML representation of schema components uses a vocabulary identified by the namespace. For brevity, the text and examples in this specification use the prefix xs: to stand for this namespace; in practice, any prefix can be used.XML Schema: Structures also defines several attributes for direct use in any XML documents.

These attributes are in a different namespace, which has the namespace name http://www.w3.org/2001/XMLSchema-instance. For brevity, the text and examples in this specification use the prefix xsi: to stand for this latter namespace; in practice, any prefix can be used.

Xsi:type

The Simple Type Definition (§2.2.1.2) or Complex Type Definition (§2.2.1.3) used in ·validation· of an element is usually determined by reference to the appropriate schema components. An element information item in an instance may, however, explicitly assert its type using the attribute xsi:type. The value of this attribute is a ·QName·; see QName Interpretation (§3.15.3)for the means by which the ·QName· is associated with a type definition.

Xsi:nil

XML Schema: Structures introduces a mechanism for signaling that an element should be accepted as ·valid· when it has no content despite a content type which does not require or even necessarily allow empty content. An element may be ·valid· without content if it has the attribute xsi:nil with the value true. An element so labeled must be empty, but can carry attributes if permitted by the corresponding complex type.

Xsi:schemaLocation, xsi:noNamespaceSchemaLocation

The xsi:schemaLocationandxsi:noNamespaceSchema. Location attributes can be used in a document to provide hints as to the physical location of schema documents which may be used for ·assessment·. See How schema definitions are located on the Web (§4.3.2) for details on the use of these attributes.

Representation of Schemas on the World Wide Web

On the World Wide Web, schemas are conventionally represented as XML documents (preferably of MIME type application/xmlor text/xml, but clause 1.1 of Inclusion Constraints and Semantics (§4.2.1)), conforming to the specifications in Layer 2: Schema Documents, Namespaces and Composition (§4.2).

Schema Component Details

Introduction

The following sections provide full details on the

composition of all schema components, together with their XML representations and their contributions to ·assessment·. Each section is devoted to a single component, with separate subsections for,

- *Properties*: Their values and significance
- XML representation and the mapping to properties
- Constraints on representation
- Validation rules
- Post-schema-validation infoset· contributions
- Constraints on the components themselves

The sub-sections immediately below introduce conventions and terminology used throughout the component sections.

Components and Properties

Components are defined in terms of their properties, and each property in turn is defined by giving its range, that is the values it may have. This can be understood as defining a schema as a labeled directed graph, where the root is a schema, every other vertex is a schema component or a literal (string, boolean, number) and every labeled edge is a property. The graph is not acyclic: multiple copies of components with the same name in the same ·symbol space· may not exist, so in some cases re-entrant chains of properties must exist. Equality of components for the purposes of this specification is always defined as equality of names (including target namespaces) within symbol spaces.

Note: A schema and its components as defined in this chapter are an idealization of the information a schema-aware processor requires: implementations are not constrained in how they provide it. In particular, no implications about literal embedding versus indirection follow from the use below of language such as "properties... having... components as values".[Definition:] Throughout this specification, the term absent is used as a distinguished property value denoting absence.Any property not identified as optional is required to be present; optional properties which are not present are taken to have·absent· as their value.

Any property identified as a having a set, subset or list value may have an empty value unless this is explicitly ruled out: this is not the same as ·absent·. Any property value identified as a superset or subset of some set may be equal to that set, unless a proper superset or subset is explicitly called for. By 'string' in Part 1 of this specification is meant a sequence of ISO 10646 characters identified as legal XML characters in [XML 1.0 (Second Edition)].

XML Representations of Components

The principal purpose of XML Schema: Structures is to define a set of schema components that constrain the contents of instances and augment the information sets thereof. Although no external representation of schemas is required for this purpose, such representations will obviously be widely used. To provide for this in an appropriate and interoperable way, this specification provides a normative XML representation for schemas which makes provision for every kind of schema component.[Definition:] A document in this form (*i.e* a <schema> element information item) is a schema document. For the schema document as a whole, and its constituents, the sections below define correspondences between element information items (with declarations in Schema for Schemas (normative) (§A) and DTD for Schemas (non-normative) (§G)) and schema components.

All the element information items in the XML representation of a schema must be in the XML Schema namespace, that is their[namespace name] must be. Although a common way of creating the XML Infosets which are or contain ·schema documents· will be using an XML parser, this is not required: any mechanism which constructs conformant infosets as defined in [XML-Infoset] is a possible starting point.

Two aspects of the XML representations of components presented in the following sections are constant across them all:

1. All of them allow attributes qualified with namespace names other than the XML Schema namespace itself: these appear as annotations in the corresponding schema component;

2. All of them allow an <annotation> as their first child, for human-readable documentation and/or machine-targeted information.

The Mapping between XML Representations and Components. For each kind of schema component there is a corresponding normative XML representation.

The sections below describe the correspondences between the properties of each kind of schema component on the one hand and the properties of information items in that XML representation on the other, together with constraints on that representation above and beyond those implicit in the Schema for Schemas (normative) (§A).

The language used is as if the correspondences were mappings from XML representation to schema component, but the mapping in the other direction, and therefore the correspondence in the abstract, can always be constructed therefrom.In discussing the mapping from XML representations to schema components below, the value of a component property is often determined by the value of an attribute information item, one of the [attributes] of an element information item.

Since schema documents are constrained by the Schema for Schemas (normative) (§A), there is always a simple type definition associated with any such attribute information item. [Definition:] The phrase actual value is used to refer to the member of the value space of the simple type definition associated with an attribute information item which corresponds to its ·normalized value·. This will often be a string, but may also be an integer, a boolean, a URI reference, etc.

This term is also occasionally used with respect to element or attribute information items in a document being ·validated·.Many properties are identified below as having other schema components or sets of components as values. For the purposes of exposition, the definitions in this section assume that (unless the property is explicitly identified as optional) all such values are in fact present. When schema components are constructed from XML representations involving reference by name to other components, this assumption may be violated if one or more references cannot be resolved.

This specification addresses the matter of missing components in a uniform manner, described in Missing Sub-components (§5.3): no mention of handling missing components will be found in the individual component descriptions below.

Forward reference to named definitions and declarations is allowed, both within and between ·schema documents·. By the time the component corresponding to an XML representation which contains a forward reference is actually needed for ·validation· an appropriately-named component may have become available to discharge the reference.

White Space Normalization during Validation: Throughout this specification, [Definition:] the initial value of some attribute information item is the value of the [normalized value]property of that item.

Similarly, the initial value of an element information item is the string composed of, in order, the [character code] of each character information item in the [children] of that element information item.

The above definition means that comments and processing instructions, even in the midst of text, are ignored for all ·validation·purposes.[Definition:] The normalized value of an element or attribute information item is an ·initial value· whose white space, if any, has been normalized according to the value of the whiteSpace facet of the simple type definition used in its ·validation·:

- *Preserve*: No normalization is done, the value is the ·normalized value·
- *Replace*: All occurrences of #x9 (tab), #xA (line feed) and #xD (carriage return) are replaced with #x20 (space).
- *Collapse*: Subsequent to the replacements specified above under replace, contiguous sequences of #x20s are collapsed to a single#x20, and initial and/or final #x20s are deleted.

If the simple type definition used in an item's ·validation· is the ·simple ur-type definition·, the ·normalized value· must be determined as in the preserve case above.

There are three alternative validation rules which may supply the necessary background for the above: Attribute Locally Valid These three levels of normalization correspond to the processing mandated in XML 1.0 for element content, CDATA attribute content and tokenized attributed content, respectively.

Attribute Value Normalization in [XML 1.0 (Second Edition)] for the precedent for replace and collapse for attributes. Extending this processing to element content is necessary to ensure a consistent ·validation· semantics for simple types, regardless of whether they are applied to attributes or elements.

Performing it twice in the case of attributes whose [normalized value] has already been subject to replacement or collapse on the basis of information in a DTD is necessary to ensure consistent treatment of attributes regardless of the extent to which DTD-based information has been made use of during infoset construction.

Note: Even when DTD-based information has been appealed to, and Attribute Value Normalization has taken place, the above definition of ·normalized value· may mean further normalization takes place, as for instance when character entity references in attribute values result in white space characters other than spaces in their ·initial value·s.

Attribute Declarations

Attribute declarations provide for:

- Local ·validation· of attribute information item values using a simple type definition;
- Specifying default or fixed values for attribute information items.

Example:

```
<xs:attributename="age" type="xs
:positiveInteger" use="required"/>
```

The XML representation of an attribute declaration.

The Attribute Declaration Schema Component

The attribute declaration schema component has the following properties:

Schema Component: Attribute Declaration;

{Name}

An NCName as defined by [XML-Namespaces].

{Target namespace}

Either ·absent· or a namespace name, as defined in [XML-Namespaces].

{Type definition}

A simple type definition.

{Scope}

Optional. Either *global* or a complex type definition.

{Value constraint}

Optional. A pair consisting of a value and one of *default, fixed.*

{Annotation}

Optional. An annotation.

The {name} property must match the local part of the names of attributes being ·validated·.The value of the attribute must conform to the supplied {type definition}.A non-·absent· value of the {target namespace} property provides for ·validation· of namespace-qualified attribute information items (which must be explicitly prefixed in the character-level form of XML documents). ·Absent· values of {target namespace}·validate· unqualified (unprefixed) items.A {scope} of *global* identifies attribute declarations available for use in complex type definitions throughout the schema. Locally scoped declarations are available for use only within the complex type definition identified by the {scope} property.

This property is·absent· in the case of declarations within attribute group definitions: their scope will be determined when they are used in the construction of complex type definitions.{value constraint} reproduces the functions of XML 1.0 default and #FIXED attribute values. *default* specifies that the attribute is to appear unconditionally in the ·post-schema-validation infoset·, with the supplied value used whenever the attribute is not actually present; *fixed* indicates that the attribute value if present must equal the supplied constraint value, and if absent receives the supplied value as for *default*. Note that it is values that are supplied and/or checked, not strings.

Note: A more complete and formal presentation of the semantics of {name}, {target namespace} and {value constraint} is provided in conjunction with other aspects of complex type ·validation· [XML-Infoset] distinguishes attributes with names such as xmlns or xmlns:xsl from ordinary attributes, identifying them as[namespace attributes].

Accordingly, it is unnecessary and in fact not possible for schemas to contain attribute declarations corresponding to such namespace declarations, see xmlns Not Allowed (§3.2.6). No means is provided in this specification to supply a default value for a namespace declaration.

XML Representation of Attribute Declaration Schema Components: The XML representation for an attribute declaration schema component is an <attribute> element information item. It specifies a simple type definition for an attribute either by reference or explicitly, and may provide default information. The correspondences between the properties of the information item and properties of the component are as follows:

XML Representation Summary: attribute Element Information Item

```
<attribute
default = string
fixed = string
form = (qualified | unqualified)
id = ID
name = NCName
ref = QName
type = QName
use = (optional | prohibited | required): optional
{any attributes with non-schema namespace...}>
Content: (annotation?, simpleType?)
</attribute>
```

If the <attribute> element information item has <schema> as its parent, the corresponding schema component is as follows:

Table. Attribute Declaration Schema Component

Property	Representation
{name}	The ·actual value· of the name [attribute]
{target namespace}	The ·actual value· of the targetNamespace [attribute] of the parent <schema> element information item, or·absent· if there is none.
{type definition}	The simple type definition corresponding to the <simpleType> element information item in the [children], if present, otherwise the simple type definition ·resolved· to by the ·actual value of the type [attribute], if present, otherwise the ·simple ur-type definition·
{scope}	*global.*
{value constraint}	If there is a default or a fixed [attribute], then a pair consisting of the ·actual value· (with respect to the{type definition}) of that [attribute] and either *default* or *fixed*, as appropriate, otherwise ·absent·.
{annotation}	The annotation corresponding to the <annotation> element information item in the [children], if present, otherwise ·absent.

Otherwise if the <attribute> element information item has <complexType> or <attributeGroup> as an ancestor and the ref[attribute] is absent, it corresponds to an attribute use with properties as follows (unless use='prohibited', in which case the item corresponds to nothing at all):

Table. Attribute Use Schema Component

Property	Representation
{required}	*true* if the use [attribute] is present with ·actual value· required, otherwise *false*.
{attribute declaration}	See the Attribute Declaration mapping immediately below.
{value constraint}	If there is a default or a fixed [attribute], then a pair consisting of the ·actual value· (with respect to the{type definition} of the {attribute declaration}) of that [attribute] and either *default* or *fixed*, as appropriate, otherwise ·absent·.

Table. Attribute Declaration Schema Component

Property	Representation
{name}	The ·actual value· of the name [attribute]
{target namespace}	If form is present and its ·actual value· is qualified, or if form is absent and the ·actual value· ofattributeFormDefault on the <schema> ancestor is qualified, then the ·actual value· of thetargetNamespace [attribute] of the parent <schema> element information item, or ·absent· if there is none, otherwise ·absent·.
{type definition}	The simple type definition corresponding to the <simpleType> element information item in the [children], if present, otherwise the simple type definition ·resolved· to by the ·actual value· of the type [attribute], if present, otherwise the ·simple ur-type definition·.
{scope}	If the <attribute> element information item has <complexType> as an ancestor, the complex definition corresponding to that item, otherwise (the <attribute> element information item is within an <attribute Group>definition), ·absent·.
{value constraint}	·absent·.
{annotation}	The annotation corresponding to the <annotation> element information item in the [children], if present, otherwise ·absent.

Otherwise (the <attribute> element information item has <complexType> or <attributeGroup> as an ancestor and the ref[attribute] is present), it corresponds to an attribute use with properties as follows (unless use='prohibited', in which case the item corresponds to nothing at all): Attribute declarations can appear at the top level of a schema document, or within complex type definitions, either as complete (local) declarations, or by reference to top-level declarations, or within attribute group definitions. For complete declarations, top-level or local, the type attribute is used when the declaration can use a built-in or pre-declared simple type definition.

Bibliography

Alison B.: *New Perspectives on HTML and XHTML*, Austin: Rinehart and Winston Publication, 2003.

Andrea S.: *HTML & XHTML: the Complete Reference*, New York: Microsoft Office Press, 2003.

David F.: *HTML & XHTML: the Definitive Guide*, Oxford: Basil Blackwell Publication, 2005.

Gavin P.:*New Perspectives on HTML, XHTML, and XML: Comprehensive*, New York: Chapman and Hall, 2001.

Hart-Davis: *HTML,XHTML & CSS*, St Louis: Times Mirror/Mosby Collage Publishing, 2001.

Henderson: *Beginning Web Programming with HTML, XHTML, and CSS*, London: Longman Publication, 2003.

Lucinda D.: *HTML, XHTML, and CSS Bible*, Boston: Brown and Company, 2001.

McFarlane: *Mastering HTML and XHTML*, London: Bski International Press, 2002.

Michael: *New Perspectives on Blended HTML, XHTML, and CSS: Introductory*, New Work: Microsoft Office Press, 2000.

Oliver: *HTML, XHTML, and CSS All-in-One Desk Reference For Dummies*, San Diego: Harcourt Brace JOvanovich Press, 2002.

Patrick C.: *New Perspectives on HTML, XHTML and XML: Comprehensive*, London: Bski International Press, 2002.

Powell: *HTML, XHTML and CSS All-In-One For Dummies*, London: Cold Spring Harbor Laboratory, 2004.

Sas Jacobs: *New Perspectives on HTML and XHTML: Brief*, Boston: Brown and Company, 2001.

Teodoru G.: *HTML, XHTML, CSS and XML*, New York: Journal of Experimental Botany, 2003.

Weisfeld M.: *New Perspectives on HTML and XHTML: Introductory*, Cambridge: Massachusetts Publication, 2003.

William J.: *New Perspectives on HTML, XHTML, and Dynamic HTML*, New York: Oxford Press, 2001.

Zicari, R.: *New Perspectives on Creating Web Pages with HTML, XHTML, and XML: Comprehensive*, Cambridge: Massachusetts Publication, 2004.

Index

A

Abbreviated 206, 224, 251
Accentuation 11
Accessibility 4
Ambiguous 222
Annotation 146, 262, 266, 274, 284
Annotation 274, 281, 284
Augmentations 271
Auspices 93

B

Bananas 18, 33, 37, 41, 47, 48, 54, 63, 64, 74, 75, 76, 77, 78, 79, 90, 91, 125, 126, 127
Binds 138
Burlesque 113, 121

C

Canonical 150
Cardinality 207, 212, 215
Catalogue 252, 257
Cedilla 36
Complexity 93, 97, 178
Compositea 149
Conceived 93
Concentrate 97
Conceptual 145, 229, 230, 231, 261, 262, 280
Conflict 124, 125
Consequence 157, 271
Consortium 3, 6, 93, 167, 168, 273
Constraint 156, 159, 161, 166, 206, 221, 222, 244, 247, 256, 257, 259, 271, 272, 275, 276
Contextual 2, 170
Convenience 171, 270
Critical 252

D

Debugger 144
Denied 111
Discriminates 253

E

Enumerations 218, 250, 265
Erroneous 112
Explicit 197, 212, 217, 225, 228, 229, 235, 236, 237, 246, 249, 251, 257, 261, 272, 275, 277, 278, 281, 282
Explosive 3
Extension 151, 172, 184, 189, 197, 250, 264, 265, 266, 268

G

Granularity 201

H

Hierarchy 264

I

Illustrations 1, 259
Implementation 173, 178, 179, 187, 189, 204, 206, 257, 262, 273, 276
Inclusion 171, 177, 182, 190, 191, 192, 193, 194, 275

L

Legacy 198, 200, 201, 203

M

Modularityas 196
Mosaic 3

P

Parser 102, 115, 116, 117, 118, 119, 121, 125, 127, 128, 129, 130, 134, 170, 203, 227, 230, 232, 233, 277
Priority 174, 200, 274
Protocol 7, 40, 43, 44
Punctuation 4, 104

R

Recognize 27, 28, 155, 156, 217, 231
Recommendation 93, 94, 96, 150
Redundancy 171
Relevant 108, 195, 255, 259, 260, 261
Retrieve 115, 135, 200, 201

S

Scenarios 252
scenarios 252
Script 8, 15, 20, 21, 82, 137, 138, 139, 147, 156, 157, 248
Specificationa 151
Syndication 253
Syntactic 147, 173, 205, 206, 208, 213, 222, 225, 233, 236, 237, 252, 257

T

Tableau 259
Toggle 84, 86
Typography 4, 258

U

Umlauts 34

V

Validation 144, 162, 170, 179, 251, 252, 256, 258, 261, 262, 263, 264, 267, 268, 269, 271, 272, 275, 276, 279, 280, 281, 282
Visual 2, 5, 15, 22, 25

W

Wrapped 84, 95